BLACK
SEA

BLACK SEA

NEAL ASCHERSON

🕮 HILL AND WANG

A DIVISION OF FARRAR, STRAUS AND GIROUX
NEW YORK

LIBRARY OF CONGRESS CATALOGING-IN-PUBLICATION DATA
Ascherson, Neal.
Black Sea / Neal Ascherson. — 1st American ed.
p.   cm.
Includes bibliographical references and index.
1. Black Sea Region—History. I. Title.
DJK66.A83   1995   909'.096389—dc20   95-19722   CIP

to my Father

Acknowledgments

MANY PEOPLE, LIVING and dead, have helped me to write this book. The germ of the idea, as I now realise, came to me when I was sixteen years old, as I read Mikhail Rostovtzeff's classic work about the Black Sea past, *Iranians and Greeks in South Russia*. At the time, I was being taught Latin and Greek literature, and I felt it was important not to be stereotyped as a 'classicist'. I tried to find some private niche from which I could understand the classical world not as a Graeco-Roman — or as a schoolboy forced into some post-Victorian version of a Graeco-Roman mind-set — but as a knowing outsider. I wanted to be a monk who wrote Latin in rhyme, or a dangerous Scythian who travelled light and put down no roots. In any case, the result of opening Rostovtzeff was an imaginative invasion and occupation which I have never since thrown off. Most of a lifetime passed before I could carry out the invader's command, before I could stand on the burial mound of a nomad king above the outfall of the Dnieper or the Don. But it was Rostovtzeff who issued the original order.

I would like to honour the authors of several other books on which I drew heavily in certain sections, especially Alan Fisher (*The Crimean Tatars*) and Patricia Herlihy, whose excellent *Odessa: A History* was my main source for that city's nineteenth-century past. François Hartog's *The Mirror of Herodotus*, in a marvellously lucid translation from the French by Janet Lloyd, is at the centre of several of my arguments, and so is Edith Hall's *Inventing the Barbarians*. Anthony Pagden's dark and prophetic book, *European Encounters with the New World*, helped me to understand the meaning of journeys between cultures. For the Black Sea's ecology, most of my data and many ideas are drawn from the work of Laurence Mee and J. F. Caddy, both of whom were patient and

helpful with my enquiries. Tom Nairn's thinking about nationalism has guided all that I have written on that theme.

Two people above all deserve my thanks for their assistance and
support. Marzena Pogorzały carried out elaborate and impeccably
presented research into the sources for the sojourn of Adam
Mickiewicz in Odessa and Crimea, and for the strange ideology of
'Sarmatism' which possessed the old Polish aristocracy. The
volumes of extracts which she left with me remain absorbing
reading in themselves, and I will always be grateful to her.
Professor Anthony Bryer of Birmingham University took me to the
18th World Congress of Byzantinology at Moscow in August
1991, and thereby allowed me to be a witness to the unsuccessful
putsch which exploded a few days after the Congress ended and
ultimately destroyed the Soviet Union. He opened to me his
enormous knowledge of Byzantine history and above all of the
Grand Comnenian Empire of Trebizond, and he tirelessly provided me with ideas and contacts; my mistakes and perverse
reflections on those matters are my own, and I hope that he will
forgive them. I am also deeply grateful to Igor Volkov, of the
department of archaeology at the University of Rostov-on-Don,
who showed me round the city and museum at Azov, furnished me
with specialist literature on the history of the lower Don, and
answered later enquiries with long and helpful letters about the
history of archaeology in southern Russia.

I would like to thank Anatoly Ilyich Kudrenko, director of the
museum at Olbia, and especially Valeriy Fedorovich Chesnok,
director of the Tanais museum, who allowed me to stay on the
site, helped to organise a programme for me and offered me much
friendship and advice. Salutes, too, to Irina Tolochko and Zhenya
Malchenko, to Yura and Volodya Guguev; and to Inna Soltys,
who translated for me in Odessa and showed me her city. I am also
grateful to Dr George Hewitt of the School of Oriental and
African Studies in London, whose introductions and contacts
helped me to enter and study Abkhazia, to the staff of the
Ukrainian Institute for Marine Ecology in Odessa, and to Timothy
Taylor of the University of Bradford, for giving up so much of his
time to conversations with me about Sarmatians and Thracians
and for supplying me with copies of his own work and that of the
late Tadeusz Sulimirski. Finally, I would like to thank Wolfgang
Feurstein for welcoming me at his home in the Black Forest and

for talking so openly and passionately about his work on Lazi culture.

From time to time, I would arrive exhausted, dirty and hungry at the door of successive Moscow correspondents of the *Independent*, sometimes at moments of frantic crisis. I was always made welcome. Nothing can repay the kindness of Peter Pringle and Eleanor Randolph, or of Andrew and Martha Higgins. I will always remember my days and nights with them.

Contents

BLACK
SEA

Introduction

I must admit, I can be perfectly happy reading . . . and equally happy pouring the sands through my fingers and resting with the whole of my being, while the wind pats my cheeks with its cool, damp hands. It seems to be pleased that there is not another soul on the beach, all the way to the horizon where the bluish promontories look like a company of bears lapping the sea-water.

All day long, the stiff grass rustles on the cliffs. Infinitely old, this gentle sound, heard on this shore for century after century, imparts the love of wisdom and simplicity.

Konstantin Paustovsky, *Years of Hope*

At this [Homeric] time, the Sea was not navigable and was called 'Axenos' [inhospitable] because of its wintry storms and the ferocity of the tribes that lived around it, and particularly the Scythians in that they sacrificed strangers . . . but later it was called 'Euxeinos' [friendly to strangers] when the Ionians founded cities on the seaboard.

Strabo, *Geography*

ONE DAY EARLY in 1680, a young Italian named Luigi Ferdinando Marsigli stood on a boat anchored in the middle of the Bosporus, off Istanbul, and lowered a weighted line over the side.

All navigators knew and had always known that the Black Sea ran out in a torrent through the Bosporus to the west, flowing on through the Sea of Marmara and the straits of the Dardanelles to reach the Mediterranean. In the third century BC, Apollonius Rhodius had told how Jason and the Argonauts had fought their way eastwards against the torrent, rowing their vessel upstream through the Bosporus to reach the Black Sea along 'the narrow strait of the winding passage, hemmed in on both sides by rugged cliffs, while an eddying current from below was washing against the ship as she moved on . . . ' The same current now tugged Marsigli's boat towards the distant Mediterranean as she strained at her anchor.

Marsigli had tied white-painted cork markers to the line, at regular intervals. At first, as he payed out the line, he watched the markers moving aft, slowly born westwards by the current flowing from the Black Sea. But then, peering intently over the side, Marsigli saw what he had hoped to see.

The deeper markers, glimmering below him, were beginning to move in the opposite direction. Very slowly, they shifted along until they were under the bows of his boat and the weighted line took the shape of an arc, streaming out west near the surface and then, at a greater depth, curving round to point east. Now he knew. There were two currents in the Bosporus Narrows, and not one. There was an upper flow, but there was also a deeper counterflow, running below it from the Mediterranean into the Black Sea.

Marsigli was only twenty-one. He was to have a long, adventurous and useful life. He was briefly captured by Tatars near Vienna, became an officer in the Habsburg armies on the Danube, and later established Europe's first research centre for oceanography at Cassis, in the south of France. But nothing he did later was more important than his discovery of the Bosporus undercurrent. In methodology and implications, it was a landmark in the new science of the sea. It was also the first step towards the study of the Black Sea for its own sake: not as a ring of shore inhabited by strange people, but as a body of water.

Almost all discoveries have an element of successful presentation about them. The undercurrent (Marsigli's *Corrente Sottano*) was known to those who worked in the waters of the Bosporus for a living, as Marsigli handsomely admitted. In his first account of his achievement, he wrote that 'my speculations had been stimulated not only by ideas formulated in my own inner cogitations but also by reports from many Turkish fishermen and above all by the urgings of Signor Cavalier Finch [Sir John Finch], Ambassador to the Porte of His Majesty the King of England and a great savant in the study of nature: to whom this notion was first disclosed by one of his ships' captains who was not able to reach any clear conclusions by experiment, perhaps for want of time . . .'

Marsigli's true glory is the way in which he followed through and consolidated his initial experiment. After the sounding, he took water samples at varying depths and was able to show that the water of the undercurrent was denser and more saline than the overcurrent running out of the Black Sea. He then constructed a demonstration apparatus: a vertically divided tank filled on one side with dyed sea-water of higher salt content and on the other with less saline water. Opening a hatch in the tank's partition, he allowed the two samples to mingle until the coloured sea-water had found its place as a visible layer at the bottom of the tank. And, without fully understanding what he had done, Marsigli had also discovered one of the basic facts of oceanography: that currents are generated not by gravity, like the flow of rivers, but by other forces which include the principles of fluid mechanics – in this case, a pressure gradient. The movement of heavier Mediterranean water into the Black Sea was impelling the lighter water in the opposite direction.

After Marsigli, other scientists, most of them Russians, began to explore the strange and stubborn nature of the Black Sea. Marsigli had shown that the Sea's water was less salty and dense than that of the Mediterranean, and he had explained a mystery: why its shore-level did not fall in spite of its outflow through the Bosporus. But it was left to others, much later, to uncover the basic fact about the Black Sea which makes it unlike all other seas: that almost all of it is dead.

On the atlas, the Black Sea appears as a kidney-shaped pond, connected to the outer oceans by the thread-like channel of the Bosporus and the Dardanelles. And yet it is a sea, not a fresh-water lake: a salt-water mass some 630 miles across from east to west and 330 miles from north to south – except at its 'waist', where the projecting peninsula of Crimea reduces the north-south distance between the Crimean shore and Turkey to only 144 miles. The Black Sea is deep, reaching down to more than 700 metres in places. But there is a large, shallow shelf in its north-western corner, off the stretch of coast which reaches round from the Danube delta in Romania in the west to Crimea in the north. This shelf, less than a hundred metres deep, has been the breeding-ground for many of the Black Sea's fish species.

As one travels clockwise round the Sea from the Bosporus, the Bulgarian and Romanian shores are seen to be low-lying, like most of the Ukrainian coastline. Then come the towering sea-cliffs of the Crimean mountains. The eastern and southern coasts (Abkhazia, Georgia and Turkey) are mostly mountainous, sometimes fringed with a narrow coastal plain and sometimes – as in north-eastern Turkey – plunging steeply down to the Black Sea in forested ridges and gorges.

But it is the rivers which dominate the Black Sea. Only three major rivers – Rhône, Nile and Po – run into the far bigger Mediterranean. But the Black Sea receives five: the Kuban, the Don, the Dnieper, the Dniester and, above all, the Danube whose drainage basin extends across the whole of eastern and central Europe and almost to the borders of France. The Danube alone carries 203 cubic kilometres of fresh water into the Black Sea every year, more than the entire flow of river water into the North Sea.

It is these rivers, source of so much life, which over tens of thousands of years extinguished life in the Black Sea depths. The inrush of organic matter from the rivers was too much for the bacteria in sea-water which would normally decompose it. They feed by oxidising their nutrients, using the dissolved oxygen normally present in sea-water. But when the organic inflow is so great that the supply of dissolved oxygen is used up, then the bacteria turn to another biochemical process: they strip the oxygen from the sulphate ions which are a component of sea-water, creating in this process a residual gas: hydrogen sulphide, or H_2S.

This is one of the deadliest substances in the natural world. A full breath of it is usually enough to kill a human being. Oil workers know and dread it; they watch for its rotten-eggs reek and at the first whiff they run. They are right to do so. Hydrogen sulphide almost instantly destroys the sense of smell, so that after the first sniff it is impossible to tell whether one is inhaling more.

The Black Sea is the world's biggest single reservoir of hydrogen sulphide. Below a fluctuating depth of between 150 and 200 metres, there is no life. The water is anoxic, without dissolved oxygen, and impregnated with H_2S; because much of the Black Sea is deep, this

4

means that some 90 per cent of the Sea's volume is sterile. It is not the only place in the oceans where H_2S has accumulated. There are anoxic areas on the floor of the Baltic Sea, and under some Norwegian fjords where water circulation is slight. Off the Peruvian coast, hydrogen sulphide is sometimes brought welling up from the depths to the surface in the periodic catastrophes known as 'el Niño', where it kills the entire ecosystem, destroying the coastal fisheries and reacting with paint on ships' bottoms to turn them black (the 'Callao Painter' effect). But the Black Sea deeps remain the largest mass of lifeless water in the world.

And yet, until the last hundred years, the Black Sea has seemed to human beings a place of almost monstrous abundance. The poisonous darkness lay far below, unknown to anyone. Above the hundred-fathom line, the 'haloclyne' or 'oxyclyne' which marks the upper limit of anoxia, the Sea boiled with life. Salmon and huge sturgeon – the beluga can reach the length and weight of a small whale – crowded up the big rivers to spawn (caviar was so plentiful that in fourteenth-century Byzantium it was the food of the poor).* Along the shores and on the shallow north-western shelf of the Black Sea, there lived spiny turbot, sprat, goby, ray, grey mullet and whiting, most of them feeding off underwater prairies of Zostera sea-grass.

On the other side of the Crimean peninsula, in the far north-eastern corner of the Black Sea, is the Sea of Azov, resembling a miniature version of the Black Sea itself with its narrow channel – the Kerch Straits – connecting it to the larger ocean. This small sea, shallow and landlocked, used to be the home of more than a hundred breeds of fish in the 130 miles between the Kerch Straits and the marshy delta of the river Don. At every spate, the Don delta would flood up over miles of reeds and brackish mud, providing spawning-grounds for fat river fish which could be caught by the cart-load. Millions of marine fish on their migrations to breeding areas pushed through the Bosporus at Istanbul, or through the Kerch Straits into the Sea of Azov. Catching them required little more effort than sticking a hand-net out of a sea-side window, and

---

* According to Professor Peter Schreiner of Cologne, an expert on Byzantine diet, an agricultural labourer on average wages needed to work for only fifteen days to earn the price of a 45-kilogram barrel of caviar. Professor Schreiner remarks that a German farm worker today would have to spend all his earnings for eighteen months in order to buy the same barrel.

Strabo wrote that in the Golden Horn, the creek of the Bosporus which runs up under the walls of Istanbul, bonito could be pulled from the water with bare hands.

Out in the open waters, among the schools of dolphin and porpoise, two fish species performed a slow, gyratory migration around the Black Sea, their progress almost as punctual as a shipping schedule. One was the bonito (*palamud*), a member of the mackerel family so important to food and trade that its image appears on some Byzantine coins. The other was the *hamsi*, or Black Sea anchovy.

To this day, the shrunken remnant of the anchovy hordes spawn off the Bay of Odessa in July and most of August, setting off on their anti-clockwise journey round the Sea between the last week of August and the first days of September. Travelling about twelve miles a day, in groups whose biomass even now weighs up to 20,000 tons each, they pass the delta of the Danube, skirt the shores of Romania and Bulgaria, and then turn east along the coast of Anatolian Turkey. By early November, the shoals are midway between Istanbul and Sinop, several hundred miles to the east. The fish have grown heavier and are travelling more slowly in tighter groups as they enter the main fishing areas off Trabzon (Trebizond). Finally, in the New Year, the anchovies reach the south-eastern corner of the Black Sea, somewhere off Batumi, and then divide: some heading north along the Georgian and Abkhazian coasts and round to their point of departure, others returning to Sinop and then cutting straight across the central Black Sea to the Bay of Odessa. One estimate of the *hamsi* biomass, done before genocidal overfishing collapsed the species in the 1980s, suggested that something approaching a million tons of anchovies swam in this circular pilgrimage every year.

Fish brought the Black Sea into history. There were, of course, other factors too: other prodigious sources of food and wealth. The south Russian plains for example, the so-called Pontic Steppe, formed a level expanse of prairie stretching for almost 800 miles from the Volga River to the foothills of the Carpathian Mountains in the west, a band of open country some 200 miles deep between the sea-coast and the forest country to the north. The grasslands of the Pontic Steppe could feed the horses and cattle of a whole nomad nation; later, its best soil was ploughed up and grew the finest wheat in the world before the cultivation of North America. In the mountains of the Caucasus, whose snowy summits were visible from far out at sea, there were both timber and gold. Across the river deltas wandered flocks of edible birds which darkened the sky with their migrations. But in all that apparently infinite plenty of natural life, the fish mattered most.

The voyage of the *Argo* is a Bronze Age legend. When Jason crossed the Black Sea, ran his boat up the river Phasis in Colchis (part of modern Georgia) and tied her fast to the trees overhanging the bank, he was after magical treasure – the Golden Fleece of Colchis. But gold is for heroes. All along the Black Sea coasts, inshore dredgers bring up from the sea-bed big stones pierced with a hole: the anchors of Mycenaean ships. These carried the real Bronze Age venturers. They brought with them from the Aegean luxurious trade goods like ornamental pottery and decorated rapiers, but they were looking for food to bring home, and what they took away seems to have been mostly fish: sun-dried, or cured with salt from the Dnieper and Danube estuaries. When the Mycenaean kingdoms passed away and were replaced by small, hungry city-states perched on Greek and Ionian headlands, the ships returned to the Black Sea on the same errand, which became steadily more desperate as the city-states grew more populous and their small arable hinterlands grew less fertile through over-cultivation. By the seventh century BC, the Ionian Greeks were establishing coastal colonies all round the Black Sea, settling into communities whose first business was the curing, packing and exporting of fish.

Satisfying this need, a very simple one, led unexpectedly into one of the formative moments of human history. The significance lay not just in the meeting of settled, literate people with pastoral nomads. That had happened before, and would happen again. It was important because the literate people brooded on this meeting, and constructed from it – the first 'colonial' encounter in European experience – a series of questioning discourses which still remain with us.

One discourse concerns 'civilisation' and 'barbarism'. A second is about cultural identity, and about where its distinctions and limits should be drawn. A third is a deep self-criticism which imagines that technical and social sophistication entails not only gain but loss – a departure of conscious and rational behaviour from what is 'natural' and spontaneous.

All three themes, provoked by the encounter in the Black Sea,

7

were debated in the classical world. They receded after the dissolution of the western Roman Empire in the sixth and seventh centuries AD. But in the early modern period they returned to European consciousness with a steadily more commanding urgency, prompted by the encounters with the Americas, Africa and Asia and, later still, by the developing ideology of nationalism. On the Black Sea itself, however, these matters were not so much debated as lived. Around the fish-drying screens and the smoke-houses, typical patterns of ethnic and social mingling arose which have still not entirely passed away.

At the outset of his famous book *Iranians and Greeks in South Russia*, the Russian scholar Mikhail Rostovtzeff wrote: 'I take as my starting-point the unity of the region which we call South Russia: the intersection of influences in that vast tract of country – Oriental and southern influences arriving by way of the Caucasus and the Black Sea, Greek influences spreading along the sea routes, and Western influences passing down the great Danubian route; and the consequent formation, from time to time, of mixed civilisations, very curious and very interesting.'

But it was not only around the northern fringes of the Black Sea, and not only in the classical period, that these 'very curious and very interesting' communities appeared. The city of Byzantium (to become Constantinople and finally Istanbul) was such a society through the Middle Ages and up to the fall of the Ottoman Empire in the twentieth century. So was the Grand Comnenian Empire of Trebizond (on the south coast of the Sea) during the mediaeval period, and so was nineteenth-century Constanța near the Danube delta, and the city of Odessa on the Ukrainian coast which was founded only in 1794. So, too, on a smaller scale, were towns like Sukhum and Poti and Batumi on the coast of what was once Colchis, which began as Greek colonies and survived until the end of the Soviet period as sites where peoples of many different languages, religions, trades and descents lived together.

They were 'curious' because power in those places was not concentrated. Instead it was dissolved, like oxygen in the warm upper layers of the Sea, among many communities. The title of supreme ruler might belong to a man or a woman whose family origins were among pastoral steppe nomads, Turkic or Iranian or Mongol. Local government and regulations of the economy might be left to Greek, Jewish, Italian or Armenian merchants. The soldiery, usually a hired force, could be Scythian or Sarmatian, Caucasian or Gothic, Viking or Anglo-Saxon, French or German. The craftsmen, often local people who had adopted Greek language and customs, had their own rights. Only the slaves – for most of these places kept and traded in slaves during most of their existence – were powerless.

Sudak, on the Crimean coast, was a Greek, then a Byzantine and finally a Genoese colony. Now there remains only an enclosure of mediaeval Italian walls and towers, perched on the slanting sea-cliff west of Cape Meganom. Here I was shown a stone tomb, dug among Byzantine foundations, which had contained the body of a Khazar noble.

The Khazars were Turkic-speaking pastoral nomads who arrived out of central Asia in the eighth and ninth centuries AD, and put together an 'empire' around the northern shores of the Black Sea, including Crimea. Offered conversion to Christianity by St Cyril, the Khazars preferred to adopt a form of Judaism. So it came about that this particular warrior, with his ancestry in shamanistic Asia, chose to be buried by the Jewish ritual in a city whose overlords were Greek Christians. And there was one extra touch, neither Christian nor Judaic. The funeral was completed by a human sacrifice, and the victim – brained by an axe blow – was thrown into the tomb to lie beside its Khazar occupant.

Peoples who live in communion with other peoples, for a hundred or a thousand years, do not always like them – may, in fact, have always disliked them. As individuals, 'the others' are not strangers but neighbours, often friends. But my sense of Black Sea life, a sad one, is that latent mistrust between different cultures is immortal.

Necessity, and sometimes fear, binds such communities together. But within that binding-strap they remain a bundle of disparate groups – not a helpful model for the 'multi-ethnic society' of our hopes and dreams. It is true that communal savagery – pogroms, 'ethnic cleansing' in the name of some fantasy of national unity, genocide – has usually reached the Black Sea communities from elsewhere, an import from the interior. But when it arrives the apparent solidarity of centuries can dissolve within days or hours. The poison, upwelling from the depths, is absorbed by a single breath.

9

These lands belong to all their people, but also to none of them. Like the terminal moraine of a glacier, the Black Sea shore is a place where the detritus of human migrations and invasions has been deposited for more than four thousand years. The shore itself, worn and quiet, speaks of the patience of rock, sand and water which have received much human restlessness and will outlive it. This is the voice heard by many writers – Pushkin and Mickiewicz, Lermontov and Tolstoy, Anna Akhmatova and Osip Mandelstam among them – who learned to listen to the slight sounds and large silences of the Black Sea and to measure themselves against a geological expanse of time. They stepped for a moment out of the confines of their own dangerous lives and, in Konstantin Paustovsky's words, acquired 'the love of wisdom and simplicity'.

This book about the Black Sea begins with Crimea. There are sound reasons for this, and some more personal ones. The Crimean peninsula has functioned as a sort of theatre, an apron-stage, for events important to the whole Black Sea region and its peoples. The Greeks made Crimea the centre of their trading empire and so did the Italians a thousand years later; the Crimean War was fought here in the nineteenth century, and Crimea was the scene of some of Hitler's and Stalin's worst atrocities in the twentieth. In 1945, the Yalta conference held on Crimea's southern tip became the code-name for Europe's division during the Cold War.

But I also begin in Crimea because, by pure chance, I first saw the Black Sea there. And, finally, because any child shown a map of the Black Sea would by instinct first put its finger on that pendant, on that funny brown tag which sticks out so rudely into the smooth blue oval.

After Crimea, the book goes in many directions. It is not a guide-book, and I am not a circumnavigator. Turkey, Bulgaria and Romania all get less attention than they deserve. But the intellectual trail I was following led away from those countries on the edge of Europe in the opposite direction, towards the north and east. From Crimea, the investigation of 'barbarism' took me to Olbia, near the estuary of the river Dnieper, and from there – leaping over Crimea again – to the ruins of Tanais and Tana on the delta of the river Don. Soon this trail was approaching the mysteries of nationalism and identity, with all their shameless games with shadows and mirrors and their enormous creative power.

But the track divided. One branch led to the Cossack peoples of south Russia and Ukraine, to Odessa and to Poland, while another turning took me to north-eastern Turkey, where the Pontic Greeks once lived and the tiny Lazi people still does. A journey to Kerch, to explore the 'Bosporan Kingdom' of classical times, again forked into two investigations: of the genuine historical Sarmatians, who commanded this region for a few centuries before and after the birth of Christ, and of the re-invented, fantasy Sarmatians who rode out of the Polish national imagination and were appointed Poland's ancestors. The newest Black Sea state of all, however, is not imaginary; I reached the end of the road in tiny Abkhazia, which broke away from Georgia only in 1992, and I tried there to measure the reality or unreality of Abkhazian independence against all that I had learned on the journey until then.

The prologue and epilogue to this journey are both at the Bosporus. In between is the Black Sea, which is not only the subject but the leading character of this book. The Black Sea has a personality which is not caught by some adjective like 'unpredictable' or phrase like 'friendly to strangers' and which – because it is not made up of traits or epithets but of the interplay of circumstances – cannot be described in detail at all. These circumstances, adding up to an identity, include fish and water, winds and grass, cliffs and forests, migrating birds and human beings. This is not just a place but a pattern of relationships which could not have been the same in any other place, and this is why Black Sea history is first of all the history of the Black Sea.

Chapter One

The death of the contemporary forms of social
order ought to gladden rather than trouble the soul.
But what is frightening is that the departing world
leaves behind it not an heir, but a pregnant widow.
Between the death of one and the birth of the other,
much water will flow by, a long night of chaos and
desolation will pass.

Alexander Herzen, *From the Other Shore*

ON THE BLACK SEA, my father saw it begin. And on the Black Sea,
seventy years on, I saw the beginning of its end.

The Russian Revolution's final victory over its enemies was the
moment at Novorossisk, in March 1920, when British battleships
moved out to sea carrying General Denikin's defeated White Army
on their foredecks. My father was a midshipman there, a boy of
eighteen who then and for the rest of his life understood the
significance of what he saw.

The Revolution ran its course, as the English and French
Revolutions had done in their own centuries, and by the summer of
1991 it was an old and frail thing. Many say that the Revolution
was already long dead: that it perished when Lenin substituted the
Bolshevik Party for direct workers' power, or when Stalin began his
economic acceleration by terror in 1928. But it seems to me that,
while Mikhail Gorbachev still sat in the Kremlin and dreamed of a
clean, modern Leninism which might transform the Soviet Union
into a socialist democracy, the last embers were still warm in the
ashes. In the summer of 1991, suddenly and finally, these embers
were kicked apart and the fire went out. The Russian Revolution –

not as a project but as a phenomenon, as a shape drawn on the paper of time – was completed.

That end was signalled to me by a light in Crimean darkness, a light which I did not understand at the time and recognised only in the days and months which followed. This light glittered at me for no longer than a few seconds. I saw it through the window of a coach making its way back along the corniche highway from Sevastopol to Yalta, after a long day spent in the Greek ruins of Chersonesus. I was the only passenger still awake. Around me slept Italian, French, Catalan and American savants, rolling a little in their seats as the coach began its climb up to the road tunnel which penetrates the range of mountains above Cape Sarich. The moon had set. The Black Sea was invisible, but the white wall of the mountains still glowed above us to the left. Somewhere below us lay the little resort of Foros, where Mikhail Sergeyevich Gorbachev and his family were taking their summer holiday in a villa kept for the sole use of the First Secretary of the Communist Party of the Soviet Union.

At the Foros turnoff, there was a confusion of lights. An ambulance was waiting at the crossroads, its blue roof-beacon throbbing and its headlights on. But there was no accident to be seen, no broken car or victim. For an instant, as we swept by, I saw men standing about and waiting. As the darkness returned, I wondered for a moment what was going on. It was the night of 18 August 1991.

What I had seen was the conspirators' candle, the spark carried through the night by men who supposed that they were reviving the Revolution and saving the Soviet Union. Instead, they lit a fire which destroyed everything they honoured. Five months later, the Communist Party of the Soviet Union – the 'Party of Lenin' – had been abolished, the Union of Soviet Socialist Republics had collapsed and even the continental empire of the tsars which underlay the Soviet Union had been reduced to a Russia with only little windows – a few miles of shore – opening on the Baltic and the Black Sea. At first, for a day or so after the plotters had captured Gorbachev at Foros, the flame of the conspiracy seemed to burn high and straight, and the terrified land was quiet. But then a very few men and women gathered in the streets of Moscow and Leningrad, raising their bare hands against tanks. They blew the flame back over the conspirators, until it consumed not only the plotters themselves but all the dried-out palaces and prisons and fortresses of the Revolution behind them.

In Yalta, next morning, the hotel staff and the coach driver and the Ukrainian interpreter all evaded our eyes. The television in the foyer, which had been working the day before, was now out of order.

Puzzled, we boarded the coach to visit Bakhchiserai, the old capital of the Crimean Tatars, and after a few miles on the road our guides told us. Mr Gorbachev had been taken suddenly ill. A Committee of National Salvation had been established to exercise his powers; it included Gennadi Yanayev, the Vice-President, Vladimir Kryuchkov, head of the KGB, and General Dimitri Yazov, minister of defence. A proclamation had been issued, stressing certain errors and distortions in the application of *perestroika*. They thought that a state of emergency existed, at least in the Russian Republic if not in Ukraine (to which Crimea belonged).

Now I remembered the ambulance guarding the crossroads at Foros and the men standing about. Illness? Nobody among us believed that. But everybody in the coach, and everyone we were to meet that day, believed in the force of what had happened, and to that they knelt down in homage, whatever their private emotions might be. The interval of liberty, that faltering experiment in openness and democracy called *glasnost*, was over. Nobody in Crimea, neither the officials in the provincial capital of Simferopol nor the holiday crowds at Yalta setting out on their morning pilgrimage to the shingle beaches, supposed that the coup might be reversed or resisted. The Crimean newspapers contained only the rambling proclamations of the Committee, without comment. On the coach, the radio by the driver was out of order too.

I sat back and reflected. Would the airports be closed? We were delegates from the World Congress of Byzantinologists which had just taken place in Moscow, and we were near the end of a post-Congress tour of historic sites in Crimea. The biggest group on the coach was Genoese — historians, archivists and journalists. They had come with their families to see the ruins of their city's mediaeval trading empire along the northern Black Sea shore. Now they grew animated, then uproarious. To live through genuine barbarian upheavals on the fringe of the known world seemed to them another way of following in their ancestors' footsteps.

14

The coach ran through the little beach resort of Alushta and turned inland towards the mountain pass leading to Simferopol. I tried to imagine the panic in the world outside, the cancelled lunches and emergency conclaves at NATO in Brussels, the solemn crowds which would be gathering in the Baltic capitals to resist with songs and sticks the return of the Soviet tank armies. There might, I thought, be a few demonstrations in Russian cities; some devoted boy might try to burn himself alive in Red Square. But the putsch – as an act of force – seemed to me decisive. I had seen something like it ten years before, in 1981, when martial law was declared in Communist Poland. That blow had proved irresistible. So, I assumed, would this one.

At that moment in the summer of 1991, the Soviet Union still overshadowed the whole of northern Eurasia from the Pacific to the Baltic. The outside world still believed almost blindly in the reforming genius of Mikhail Gorbachev, and few foreigners as yet understood, or even wanted to understand, that Gorbachev's ambitious programme of *perestroika* structural reform had come to nothing. They could not grasp that his personal following among the ruling oligarchy of the Soviet Union had leaked away during the previous year, nor that the Communist Party – the only effective executive instrument in the land – was now refusing to go further with the political changes which were dismantling its own monopoly of power, nor that the military and police commanders had begun to disobey their orders and act on their own initiative, nor that Gorbachev was no longer respected or even liked by the Russian people.

It was only because I had spent the previous week talking to Russian friends and foreign journalists in Moscow that I had begun to realise how serious Gorbachev's failure was. The phase of reformed, liberalised Communism was over. And the illusion that plural democracy and free-market economy could be simply ordered into existence by the Kremlin – that had collapsed too. But at the same time I knew that this putsch in Moscow could solve nothing. The way ahead was blocked, certainly. And yet the way back offered by Gennadi Yanayev and his fellow-conspirators – a reversion to police tyranny and imperial reconquest – also led nowhere. In the longer term, the plotters had only ensured an even steeper descent into chaos and decay for the Soviet state. But in the short term, I was convinced, they had succeeded and they would be obeyed.

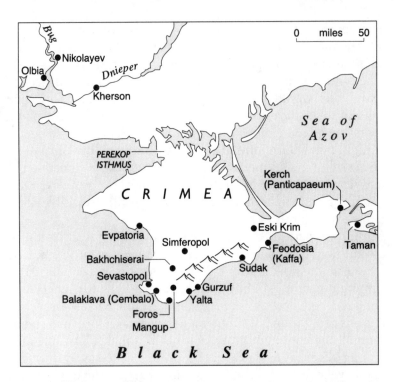

In the palace of the Tatar khans at Bakhchiserai – unloved and faded – I caught the glance of a Russian woman in charge of a band of girl students. It was a dark, hot glance; she halted her girls by pulling roughly on their yellow plaits, as if on a train's alarm cord, and came over to talk. 'This morning, I have two thoughts,' she began. 'The first is for my son, who is in Germany: now I shall never see him again. The second is that there is no vodka in the shops, so I have no way to forget what is happening. You are from Britain? May we please export to you some of our big surplus of fascists?'

Beside us, a fountain carved with a marble eye wept tears of cool spring-water, mourning for a slave-girl who died before she could learn to love the Tatar khan. Alexander Pushkin, touched by the legend, first floated a rose in the basin of the fountain, and they still put fresh roses there for the tourists. All about us I saw Russians uncomfortably looking away. They did not understand our words, but they recognised our tone of voice: a dangerous one. A holiday had ended that morning with the news on the radio, and the season of prudence had returned. Only the students watched us with their round blue eyes, heads cocked, indifferent as birds.

16

Crimea is a big brown diamond. It is connected to the mainland only by a few strings of isthmus and sand-spit, by a natural land causeway at Perekop on the west and by watery tracks across the Sivash salt-lagoons on the north and east. In history, Crimea consists of three zones: mind, body and spirit.

The zone of mind is the coast – the chain of colonial towns and port-cities along the Black Sea margin. For nearly three thousand years, with interruptions of fire and darkness, people in these cities kept accounts, read and wrote books, enforced planning controls with the aid of geometry, debated literary and political gossip from some distant metropolis, locked one another up in prisons, allotted building land for the temples of mutually hostile cults, regulated advance payments on the next season's orders for slaves.

The Ionian Greeks reached this coast some time during the eighth century BC, and under its steep, forested capes, they set up trading-posts – much like European 'factories' on the Guinea coast of Africa two thousand years later – which grew into towns with stone walls and then into maritime cities. The Roman and Byzantine empires inherited these coastal colonies. Then, in the Middle Ages, the Venetians and the Genoese, licensed by the later Byzantine emperors, revived the zone of the mind, enlarged the Black Sea trade and founded new cities of their own.

In the early thirteenth century, Chingiz ('Genghis') Khan united the Mongolian peoples of east-central Asia and led them out to conquer the surrounding world. China fell, and the Mongol cavalry rode westwards to conquer not only the central Asian cities but the lands which are now Afghanistan, Kashmir and Iran within the next few years. But it was not until 1240–1, ten years after the death of Chingiz, that a Mongol army led by Batu reached Russia and eastern Europe (where they were mis-named 'Tatars' after another tribe which had once been powerful in central Asia but which Chingiz had exterminated). Batu's cavalry eventually withdrew from east and central Europe without any serious attempt to make their conquests permanent, and settled on the Volga. There the 'Golden Horde', as this western part of the Mongol-Tatar empire came to be known, remained for three centuries after the death of Batu in 1255. From its capital on the Volga, the Horde controlled both the steppe north of the Black Sea and the Crimean peninsula.

There were times when the Horde burned and looted cities on the Crimean coast. But the Mongol presence also brought those cities great fortune. There was now a single authority in control of the entire Eurasian plain from the Chinese border in the east to what is now Hungary in the west. With stability in the steppes, long-range trade became possible. Trade routes – the 'Silk Routes' – appeared, reaching from China to the Black Sea by land and from there by sea to the Mediterranean. One route led westwards across the lower Volga to terminate at the Venetian colony of Tana, on the Sea of Azov. Later, in the fifteenth century, another Silk Route opened connecting the Persian provinces of the Mongol empire with the Black Sea at Trebizond.

An end was put to all this transcontinental commerce after 1453, when the Turks finally captured Constantinople and destroyed the remains of the Byzantine Empire around the Black Sea, which was closed to Western voyagers. The cities of the coast were mostly abandoned, and their ruins were covered by the dry red earth and the mauve herbs of the Crimean steppe. The coast of Crimea did not begin to revive until the eighteenth century, when the Russian Empire reached the Black Sea, and that revival took a new variety of urban forms. Chersonesus was rebuilt as the naval base of Sevastopol, Yalta as a seaside resort, Kaffa as the grain port of Feodosia.

The zone of the body in Crimea is the inland steppe country, behind the coastal mountains. It is not flat, but a plateau landscape of greyish-green downs, trapezoid and eroded. Its skin is a dry turf woven of sharp-smelling herbs, and if you cut the skin the earth leaks out and blows away in the east wind.

Along the coast, the wind comes off the Black Sea or, very suddenly, in harrying squalls down from the mountains. But inland, behind the mountain ranges, the wind blows steadily out of Asia, across three thousand miles of what used to be level grassland separating Europe from the high Central Asian pastures where the nomad peoples began their journeys. The archaic Greeks crossed a watery ocean to reach Crimea, and their voyage from the Bosporus to southern Russia could take a month or more. But the nomads who came to this coast crossed an ocean of grass, sailing slowly onwards for months and years in their wagons, preceded by their herds of cattle and horses, until they came to rest up against the Crimean hills and the sea beyond them.

The Scythians were already here on the Crimean steppe and

the inland plains when the Greeks first came ashore in the eighth century BC. In the centuries which followed, the period of Greek colonisation, the pressure of westward migration out of central Asia was weak, and five hundred more years passed before the Scythians resumed their westward journey and were replaced by the Sarmatians. Then, in the first centuries of our era, the push of one nomad nation upon another became much more urgent. After the Sarmatians came the Goths, from the north, and then the all-destroying Huns, and then the Khazars who formed their briefly stable steppe empire on the Black Sea shores in the eighth century AD. Turkic-speaking nomads (called variously Kipchak, Cuman or Polovtsy) held the steppe between the eleventh and thirteenth centuries, and were then overrun or driven further west by the oncoming Mongol-Tatars of the Golden Horde.

The Golden Horde's capital was far away from the Black Sea coast, at Saray on the middle Volga. The Horde was always a loose polity which soon began to pull apart, and in the fifteenth century a southern branch of the Horde set up its own independent kingdom on the inland plains of Crimea, settling down to intensive farming and stock-breeding and gradually abandoning the old pastoral life. This was the Crimean Tatar khanate, or 'Crim Tartary'. A few centuries of relative calm ensued in Crimea until the Ottoman Empire, after the capture of Constantinople, reached the northern shore of the Black Sea and Crimea itself. For the Crimean Tatars, who had converted to Islam in the fourteenth century, Turkish domination meant a mere change of allegiance rather than displacement, and the khanate survived until Catherine the Great conquered Crimea for the Russian Empire in 1783.

For the Crimean zones of mind and body to create wealth together, there had to be two conditions: merchants on the coast with secure access to the outside markets of the Mediterranean and beyond, and a stable political situation on the steppe. Sometimes there was turmoil on the great plains; trade routes were closed, cultivation of wheat outside town walls became dangerous, and the city-colonies were occasionally looted and burned. But for long periods, especially during the Scythian time, there was peace. The Greek colonists and the Scythian chiefs near the coast grew wheat for export. Furs, wax, honey and slaves were brought down from the northern forests to the markets in the Greek coastal cities, and for the most part the Scythians let these caravans travel freely across their open grassland to the sea. On the profits of the grain and the slaves, which fed and provided a labour-force for the Hellenic and Roman worlds, both the Greek merchants and the up-country Scythian princes grew very rich indeed.

The Scythians, and then the Sarmatians and Goths who followed them, spent this wealth conspicuously. They bought jewellery and goldwork, made in the city colonies to their personal order and fancy by Greek craftsmen and their native apprentices. They took their treasures to their graves, to lie under tall burial mounds among sacrificed horses, servants and women.

If you travel eastwards across the Crimean steppe, you come to the last of the trapezoid downs and the ground falls away at your feet. You stand on this last ridge, with a battering, restless wind in your face, and look across the Sea of Azov into the infinity of dun-coloured flatness which begins here and reaches away across a continent, past the northern end of the Caspian Sea and as far as Lake Baikal. There is no horizon. Only a long bar of shadow to the east, which is the approaching night.

On this ridge are the foundations of a stone tower. When the Mongol-Tatars of the Golden Horde entered the Crimean-peninsula, splashing their ponies across the Azov saltmarshes, they saw this tower on the skyline above them and called it *Kerim* — fort. They made their first encampment and headquarters below the tower at Eski Kerim, or Krim — 'old fort' — which might be the origin of the word 'Crimea'. From Eski Krim, the Tatars moved to Bakhchiserai and set the palace of the independent khanate in a green valley, near the sound of water and nightingales.

The zone of the body has always pressed impatiently against the zone of the mind. Sometimes the pressure was destructive, as when the Tatars rode down to the sea from Eski Krim in the late thirteenth century and sacked the Genoese metropolis of Kaffa. But often it was metamorphic. The category-fence between 'European' colonists and 'native' nomads was always falling into disrepair or developing large gaps.

Scythians, for example, were not only peripatetic horse-breeders who lived in wagons. They were also capable of laying out fields and growing crops on a commercial rather than a subsistence scale, of designing permanent fortified towns with something like a street-plan, of delicate and innovative metalwork. The Greek or Italian citizens of the trading colonies could be farmers as well as merchants, venturing and working far away from their protective walls. The nomads – there are some well-recorded cases – could live double lives as Hellenic or Italianised gentry within the walls and (literally changing clothes) as traditional steppe chieftains outside them. Rich Khazars, speaking a Turkic language but practising a form of Judaism, lived as respected citizens in Sudak. Much earlier, in the first century AD, Dio Chrysostom visited the city of Olbia, near the estuary of the Dnieper, and found the citizens quoting Homer but wearing the trousers and moccasins of non-Greek nomads.

What we do not know is whether that last process could run the other way – whether there were 'civilised' individuals from the zone of the mind who were magnetised outwards into the 'barbarian' zone of the body, who lived in wagons, drank mares' milk and did reverence before the carcases of impaled horses which guarded royal tombs. Probably there were. It happened on the American frontier, where there were always European trappers and voyaging traders and even the wives and children of colonists who 'went Indian' by choice.

But between the body and the mind, between the steppe and the coast, was a third place: the mountain zone of the spirit. Up on the flat summits of the Shatir Dagh range, or in caves hidden by forest, far above the nomads and the traders, lived communities which had lost all prospects of wealth or conquest.

From Bakhchiserai, the coach drove southwards into the foothills of the coastal range, though a small canyon, and stopped in a meadow surrounded by mountains. The Byzantinologists settled on the grass beside a lake and unwrapped their sandwiches. There were trees, a few tents, a pipe running spring water into an old iron fountain-basin at which two young women were washing themselves and their clothes.

One of them, wearing only a long black skirt, strolled across to us and bent to squeeze the water out of her hair. 'Got a Western cigarette? Our Soviet ones are so awful.'

One of the Genoese offered her a pack. 'Any news?'

She stood upright, shook her hair back, accepted the cigarette and, while the match was being lit for her, said, 'No news. On the

21

radio, only bloody *Swan Lake.*' Behind her, two boys were trying to stretch an aerial from their tent to a tree.

The climb from the meadows of the valley floor to the summit of Mangup Kale takes an hour, two thousand feet of struggling and sweating upwards until a broken city-wall looms up among the trees. From here the going is a little easier. But now the forest becomes a cemetery. Hundreds and hundreds of stone tombs drift on a sea of dead leaves, tilting, listing, capsizing, engraved with deep-cut Hebrew characters.

The tombs belong to the Karaim. They were a Jewish sect which began in Mesopotamia in the eighth century AD and broke with the mainstream of rabbinical Judaism two hundred years later. The Karaim believed that the word of the Lord was to be found in Scripture but nowhere else, and that the additions of the Talmud were impious and decadent. (For that reason Christian Protestants, Germans especially, have always been fascinated by the Karaim whom they imagine, quite falsely, to have been harbingers of the Christian Reformation.)

The Karaim reached Crimea in the twelfth century, dislodged from Palestine and Egypt by the upheaval of the First Crusade. They migrated into the Byzantine Empire and beyond it into north-eastern Europe, where parties of Karaim settled in the lands of the Polish-Lithuanian Commonwealth.

Many sectarians, like the Albigensian Christians of southern France, have felt safe only in remote, defensible places far from centres of power and population. The Karaim shared this existential terror. They withdrew to the tops of the Crimean mountains or, in Lithuania, to the fortress-islands of Trakai in a lake among birch forests. But, like hermit-crabs, they preferred to settle in fortifications already built and then abandoned by others rather than to raise their own, and the Karaim did not take over Mangup Kale until it had been sacked and emptied by the Turks. The oldest Karaite grave in the woods below the summit is dated 1468, a few years before the fall of Mangup, but most of them were carved in the sixteenth and seventeenth centuries.

In Crimea, the Karaim kept their distance from the Christian or Moslem societies around them, living careful Karaite lives, trading and manufacturing small household goods but avoiding service to any government. One historian has remarked that, between about 1200 and 1900 AD, almost nothing happened; Karaite history in

Crimea was a long and peaceful blank. However, by staying aloof the Karaim acquired a reputation for being more upright and more honest than other communities, and in consequence, when the history of the Karaim began to happen once more, it took a curious turn. Gentiles, impressed by their probity, began to invent reasons why the Karaim should be exempted from the general anti-Semitism. It was supposed that they must be converts, like the Khazars. Here was an absurd irony: by attempting to be more intensely and primordially Judaic than other Jews, the Karaim ensured that Gentiles would consider them not to be truly Jewish at all.

After the Russian annexation of Crimea at the end of the eighteenth century, Catherine II took a respectful interest in the Karaim. She had added enormous territories to the Russian Empire: in the west, much of the old Polish-Lithuanian Commonwealth, and in the south almost the whole northern shore of the Black Sea. To develop them, she recruited colonists – Germans, Greeks, Armenians, even French settlers – and the Karaim with their sober energy were suitable to her purpose. Catherine moved some of the Crimean Karaim to reinforce their old settlements in Lithuania; and in the huge new frontier province of Novorossiya (New Russia) in the south she granted them full Russian citizenship, which was denied to the main Jewish population. From Mangup and their other cliff-redoubt at Chufut Kale, above Bakhchiserai, the Karaim began to migrate down to the cities of the Crimean coast, especially to Evpatoria. When the Scottish traveller Laurence Oliphant climbed up to Chufut Kale in 1852, he found only a handful of Karaim left, looking after the old synagogue. The last of them had abandoned Mangup some fifty years before.

During the Second World War, the Nazi racial bureaucracy in Berlin decreed (vainly, as it turned out) that the Karaim should not be included in the 'final solution of the Jewish question', on the grounds that they were not biologically and genetically Jewish but descendants of Khazar converts to Judaism. This was complete nonsense. But the main Jewish communities of the Black Sea, themselves listed for slaughter, seem to have supported the myth in order to save their brethren if they could not save themselves.

Just below the rim of the Mangup summit, there is a spring of chill, delicious water. Then the trees part and you emerge into a tableland of flat, short turf scented with thyme. Ruins stand about, some with towers and arches, others little more than the stone wall-footings which are all that remains of basilicas and gatehouses and synagogues and watch-towers. The world, sea and land, lies spread out below. People came and settled on Mangup when they were afraid or wanted to be alone with God, or both.

That day there was a camp on the flat summit: a line of pup-tents flying the Russian tricolour, an old army cooker on wheels, a blackened bucket full of stewing tea, clouds of blue woodsmoke. An archaeological expedition from the University of the Urals at Sverdlovsk (now again Ekaterinburg) had been digging on the summit for several weeks. Up here, above the world, they knew nothing. The students gathered round gravely, while we drank their tea through thick Russian sugar-cubes. Only light music dribbled from their radio, a long giggle of embarrassment to fill the silence of Russia which grew more enormous as the hours passed.

All human populations are in some sense immigrants. All hostility between different cultures in one place has an aspect of the classic immigrant grudge against the next boatload approaching the shore. To defend one's home and fields and ancestral graves against invasion seems a right. But to claim unique possession – to compound the fact of settlement with the aspect of a landscape into an abstract of eternal and immutable ownership – is a joke.

Crimea, whose beauty provokes almost sexual yearnings of possession in all its visitors, has demonstrated this joke in every century of its history. It has no natives, no aboriginals. Before the Scythians, before the Cimmerians who preceded them or the Bronze Age populations who raised the first burial-mounds, there were human beings who had come from somewhere else. Crimea has always been a destination, the cliffs at the end of the sea or the shore where the wagons must end their journey. Voyaging communities settled in Crimea (the Scythians lived here for nearly a thousand years) but in the end they dispersed or moved on. All that has been constant in Crimean history has been a certain structure which the peninsula has imposed upon its visitors: the zones of mind, body and spirit have often been effaced but until now have always re-emerged. Only in recent times has the Crimean truth – that it belongs to everybody and to nobody – been violated. Two of these violations, which would be merely absurd if they did not imply so much blood and suffering in the past and very probably in the future, are the declarations of two autocrats. In 1783, Catherine II ('The Great') proclaimed that the Crimean peninsula was henceforth and for all time to become Russian. And in 1954 Nikita Khrushchev, a Ukrainian seeking to divert the attention of his own people from their miseries, announced that he was transferring Crimea from Russia to become for all time Ukrainian.

Mangup is about all these Crimean ironies. Most of the ruins on the Mangup summit belong to a forgotten, improbable principality of the Middle Ages. The fortress of Theodoro-Mangup contained an independent Greek principality, ruled by the Princes of Gothia. But what did 'Greek' mean up here, or 'Gothic'?

The Goths came to the Black Sea and to Crimea from an unusual direction, from the north-west rather than from the east. A proto-Germanic confederation of peoples from southern Scandinavia, they had occupied Crimea in the third century AD, in the course of their conquest of most of the Black Sea's northern shore. A hundred years later, the Black Sea Goths were defeated by the Huns. Many headed westward, on the next leg of a migration which in the time of their great-grandchildren would deposit them in Italy as the army of their king, Theodoric the Great. But some remained in the Crimean mountains. Christianised and then incorporated into the Byzantine Empire, they were still there in the sixth century when the emperor Justinian I fortified Mangup as part of a line of strong-points intended to shield the coastal cities against an attack out of the steppes.

When the Khazars conquered Crimea in the eighth century, the remnants of the Christian Goths retreated up into the mountain zone of the spirit. John, Prince-Bishop of Gothia, sallied down from Mangup to lead an unsuccessful rising against the Khazars, but the Byzantine emperors betrayed him. They preferred to come to terms with the Judaised Khazars, recognising them as powerful allies who could form a buffer-zone between the Empire and wilder nomad nations approaching the Black Sea from the steppe; two Byzantine emperors – Justinian II and Constantine V – married Khazar princesses. Gothia went back to its hill and left history for nearly seven hundred years.

Below this 'Lost World' on its plateau, the world continued to change, but Gothia kept on worshipping in its huge basilica and ignoring the turmoils at the foot of its cliffs until – in 1475 – the Ottoman Turks arrived. Mopping up the fringes of the Byzantine Empire, after their capture of Constantinople in 1453, the Turks and their Crimean Tatar allies stormed the Principality of Theodoros on its mountain and brought Gothia to an end.

The Basilica of Constantine and Helen, dating from the ninth century, stood desolate for a time. In 1579, a Polish nobleman scrambled up to look at it. Marcin Broniewski ('Broniovius') had been sent by King Stefan Batory on a diplomatic mission to Mehmet Giray, khan of the Crimean Tatars, and he wrote an elegant Latin account – *Tartariae Descriptio* – which was translated into English a century later by Samuel Purchas. 'Marcopia [Mangup] . . . hath had two Castles, Greeke Temples and Houses sumptuous, with many cleere Rils running out of the stone: but eighteene yeers after that the Turkes had taken it (as the Greeke Christians affirm) it was destroyed by a sudden and horrible fire.'

Broniewski found still standing 'the Greeke Church of Saint Constantine, and another meane one of Saint George. One Greeke Priest and some Jews and Turkes dwell there; Oblivion and Ruine hath devoured the rest; nor are there men or Stories of the quondam inhabitants, which I with great care and diligence everywhere sought in vaine.' Yet Broniewski had been able to question the Orthodox priest, who told him that 'a little before the Turkes besieged it, two Greeke Dukes of the Imperiall bloud of Constantinople or Trapezond [Trebizond], there resided, which were after carried alive into Constantinople, and by Selim the Turkishe Emperour slaine. In the Greeke Churches on the walls are painted Imperiall Images and Habits . . . '

Nothing remains of the basilica but foundations, and the archaeologists from the University of the Urals could only dream of what those 'Imperiall Images' might have shown them. The zone of the spirit is almost empty now. The only inhabitants of Mangup are a colony of Russian hippies, out where the plateau juts to the north-east in a terrifying bowsprit of bare stone overhanging a thousand feet of air. The hippies live in old guard-houses cut into the rock, rolled in blankets on the stone floors, breathing a fog of dope and smoke from fires of green sticks. They growl, snore, fart and sometimes rouse themselves to fits of bellowing. The young girls from the university expedition had learned not to visit this end of the plateau on their own, but groups of students sometimes came and left cans of tea or stale loaves near the cliff-edge. Retreating a few yards, they would wait and watch until the hippies, like bears, dragged themselves out of their tomb and flung themselves on the food.

Gothic, with Greek and probably Hebrew, was one of the languages which continued to be spoken in Crimea as it emerged into the modern period. It was also a written language. Bishop Ulfilas had translated parts of the Bible into western Visigothic in the fourth century, but the tongue survived in Crimea long after the western dialect had died out. In 1562 the Austrian diplomat Ogier Ghislain de Busbecq (more famous as the man who sent the first tulip bulbs from Turkey to Europe) collected a list of eighty-six words and phrases in Gothic which he had gathered from Crimeans he had met in Constantinople, and the last Gothic-speakers seem to have died out in the seventeenth century.

Lakes of ink have been uselessly spilled over Mangup and its 'Problem of the Crimean Goths', which was in truth no problem but an obstinate, perverse attempt to hammer modern definitions of ethnicity onto an ancient society in which they were irrelevant. Excavations began on the Mangup hill-top in the nineteenth century. The antiquaries Uvarov, Brun and Lepier laid out theories. German scholars, excited by the Germanic ethnicity of the Goths, longed to find in Crimea evidence of an ancient Teutonic state which raised stone cities and dominated its neighbours. But the evidence was meagre. The fantasy of an ur-German Crimea, of a Teutonic urban civilisation picking up the torch of culture as decadent Rome let it fall, was thrown away by later scientists.

Then, however, it was retrieved by the Nazi mind – that drain-filter of broken, discredited and putrescent ideas – and recycled into a new version of pseudo-history and political legitimation. Crimea must be reconquered and the Gothic realm restored. Cleared of Tatars, Jews and Russians, except for a temporary labour force of field slaves, the peninsula would be the destination for trainloads of German settlers. Sevastopol was to become Theodorichafen. Simferopol became Gotenberg. Crimea itself was to be known as Gotland.

Hitler himself was, in private, reserved about those departments of the Third Reich devoted to the manufacture of history. He left these enthusiasms mostly to Rosenberg and to Himmler, whose craze for archaeology once induced Hitler to ask: 'Why do you insist on demonstrating to the world that we Germans have no past?' But Crimea stirred him. In April 1941, two months before Germany's invasion of the Soviet Union, it was agreed that Crimea should be separated from Russia and ceded to a puppet Ukrainian state. In July, when the German armies were already penetrating deep into Soviet territory, Hitler himself chaired a meeting on Crimean policy at which the 'Gotland' project was in principle accepted. As for the Crimean Tatars, they were judged to be racially worthless – like the Jews – but their deportation would be delayed in order not to offend neutral Turkey, their protector through so much of their history. The real attraction of the 'Gotland' scheme for Hitler, however, lay far from the Black Sea: it offered a possible way out of his South Tyrol dilemma.

In the mountain valleys of the upper Adige, a German-speaking population had been torn out of the wreckage of the defeated Hapsburg Empire in 1918 and presented to Italy by the victorious Entente. This act was the delivery of a bribe promised some years before in order to enlist Italy into the war against the Central Powers. A few years later, this South Tyrol population posed a delicate diplomatic problem for the new Nazi regime in Germany. The Nazi programme for German minorities abroad was either to annex their territories (as in the case of the Sudetenland) or to transport them *Heim ins Reich* – to resettle them within the expanded Reich frontiers. But Mussolini was Hitler's ally. An exception had to be made over the South Tyrolese. Some tiny pockets of palaeo-Germanic population in other north Italian glens (like the Cimbri, supposedly descended from the horde that Marius slaughtered and dispersed in the Po Valley in 101 BC) were moved to Germany by mutual German-Italian agreement. But the Italian frontier stayed where it was, on the watershed of the Alps at the Brenner Pass, and the South Tyrolese stayed in Italy.

This compromise left Hitler restless. Now he proposed a new solution. The Germans of South Tyrol should resettle Gotland. Why not? Here, too, were forested mountains, fertile valleys, water in abundance. And here already were vineyards, planted by Catherine's foreign settlers or by Russian landowners. Perhaps the quality did not match the red wine from Bozen or Meran (Bolzano and Merano) which had made the Tyrolean peasants rich, but German *Fleiss* and skill would change all that.

In the end, no Germans — Tyrolean or others — were settled in Crimea. But the Gotland project had terrible consequences. Once, it had been the alliance between Crimean Tatars and Ottoman Turks which had destroyed Gothia. Now the Gotland scheme, in its failure, brought down final catastrophe upon the Crimean Tatars.

Field-Marshal von Rundstedt's Army Group South broke into Crimea in September 1941. By November the whole peninsula was in German hands, apart from Sevastopol, which held out until July the following year. At first the Crimean Tatars were inclined to welcome the German conquest — or rather the expulsion of Soviet Russian power — as a liberation. And they had good reasons to feel as they did.

By 1854, after only half a century of Russian colonisation, the Tatars — both reduced in their own numbers and increasingly swamped by Russian and other European settlers — made up no more than 60 per cent of the Crimean population. By 1905, they were a minority in the land which they considered to be their own. A Tatar 'National Awakening' led by intellectuals was launched in the late nineteenth century, and the Tatars greeted the Revolutions of 1905 and 1917 as the overthrow of a repressive colonial empire rather than as a class struggle. They were to be disillusioned. The 1905 Revolution brought forward a hopeful Tatar clamour for independence or autonomy, but the triumph of Bolshevism, between 1917 and the end of the Civil War in 1920, began two generations of atrocity and disaster for Crimea.

After the first massacres of Tatar nationalists carried out by the Bolshevik security police (Cheka) in 1920, there followed the famine of 1920–2 — even worse in Crimea than in southern Russia and Ukraine. Almost half the population of Bakhchiserai, the Tatar capital, starved to death, and by 1923 a mere quarter of the Crimean population was Tatar. Stalin's purges began with the kulaks (the richer peasantry) but soon developed into the liquidation of the whole pre-Revolutionary Tatar intelligentsia and the suppression of the Tatar culture. The historian Alan Fisher, in his book *The Crimean Tatars*, calculates that 150,000 Tatars, half the Tatar population in 1917, had been killed, deported or forced into exile outside the Soviet Union by 1933. A renewed slaughter of educated Tatars, including the Moslem clergy, took place during the Great Purges of 1937–8.

It was therefore scarcely surprising that in 1941 the Tatars looked back with something like nostalgia at their previous German occupation in 1918, at the end of the First World War. Compared with the Bolshevik and Soviet regime which followed, it had been a period of relative liberty. In that year, the nationalist politician Cafer Seidahmet and the Lithuanian-Tatar General Sulkiewicz had organised a Moslem corps to support the German armies in Crimea. Tatar nationalists remembered this German policy of offering a possibility of Crimean independence in return for support against Russia, and they assumed that this bargain might be revived again in 1941. They were wrong. The chaos of Nazi administration – the Darwinian competition of rival institutions, which could be kept within bounds inside the Reich but which flourished uncontrollably in the occupied territories – soon broke up any coherent Crimean policy of the kind that Hitler had contemplated.

Three different power centres were eventually operating three divergent policies in Crimea. The first policy was that of the army. Von Manstein, General Rundstedt's successor in the military command, exploited Tatar resentment of Soviet rule by raising anti-partisan battalions and Tatar village home-guard units, who took over some of the burden of resisting guerrilla groups left behind by the retreating Red Army. But von Manstein was at the same time careful not to suggest that the creation of these militias had any political implications. As a soldier, he had no wish to provoke the majority, non-Tatar population by appearing to favour the Tatars as a community.

A far more pro-Tatar line was taken by the German civil administration. The General Commissar, Frauenfeld, fell in love with the notion of restoring the Crimean Tatars as a *Kulturvolk*. He reopened Tatar schools, for the first time for many years, and spent money on fostering Tatar language and customs. A Tatar theatre was opened, Tatar newspapers were brought back to life and there was a scheme for a separate Tatar university. No doubt Frauenfeld's policy included some 'divide and rule' calculations, but it was essentially a genuine, old-fashioned German intellectual enthusiasm for folk-culture as the foundation of Herder's definition of 'historic nations'. Frauenfeld set up 'Moslem Committees' (some of them including survivors from the pre-1917 nationalist parties), and an ineffectual Tatar mission was established in Berlin, but his approach had little real political content and was well within the bounds of an enlightened colonialism. The Frauenfeld line was, all the same, entirely alien to the spirit of the Gotland project, which had proposed that the Tatars should be reduced to the status of slaves for the Aryan settlers before their final fate – death or expulsion – was decided.

A third policy began to emerge after the arrival, in the wake of the fighting troops, of the SS command structure headed by Otto Ohlendorf. Racial and political extermination squads under SS command had been attached to the rear areas of each Army Group, and in Crimea it was *Einsatzgruppe D* which set about the methodical slaughter of undesirable elements by firing-squad. The savageries of the SS drove more and more Tatars to join the partisans, or, where the Soviet guerrillas would not accept them, to form resistance groups of their own. By the time that the Red Army re-entered Crimea in April 1944, Ohlendorf had murdered some 130,000 people, including the entire gypsy population of Crimea, the remaining Jews and – disregarding those ethnological points so nicely made in Berlin – most of the Karaim. Tens of thousands of Tatars were among Ohlendorf's victims.

The Gotland fantasy stifled in confusion and blood before it was born. All that came from it was Stalin's vengeance on the Crimean Tatars, unfairly accused of mass collaboration with the Nazis. That accusation of treachery to Russia had a long ancestry. Stalin was only contributing to more than a century of Russian propaganda which, in spite of evidence to the contrary, insisted that the Tatars were a form of Turk whose first loyalty was always to the Ottoman Empire and to Islam. During the Crimean War of 1854–6, when British and French troops had fought against Russia in the peninsula, there was no significant Tatar defection to Russia's enemies. But Alexander II, who became tsar while the war was still in progress, was informed that the Tatars had shown themselves to be a menace to Russia's security, and after the war they were encouraged to emigrate. In all the subsequent Russo-Turkish conflicts, large numbers of Tatars served in the Russian armies, fighting against their fellow-Moslems, but their display of loyalty made no impression on the prevailing Russian paranoia about them. Each Russo-Turkish war was followed by another Tatar reaction of despair, another wave of emigration.

The fact is that most of the Nazi collaborators in Crimea during the Second World War were non-Tatars. Perhaps 50,000 Tatars had fought on all fronts in the Soviet armed forces. It was true that

31

some 20,000 had joined von Manstein's village-defence units. Most of them intended only to protect their homes against raids by Russian and Ukrainian partisans, which often resembled racial pogroms rather than military operations. But nearly twice as many Tatars from the Volga region served with the Germans in similar volunteer units, and they suffered no collective punishment.

In Crimea, the punishment began instantly. Some partisan units had already been shooting Tatars who applied to join them. Within days of the Soviet reconquest in April 1944, whole villages had been executed and dead Tatars swung from the Simferopol lamp-posts. But these were mere preludes to Stalin's more measured retaliation.

In the expanses of the Soviet Union, Stalin had space for many different ways of dealing with social groups who displeased him. He could, of course, simply have them murdered, and when it seemed necessary, he did so. But – like a Roman emperor or a European colonial viceroy dealing with recalcitrant tribes on the fringes of the empire – he also had the power forcibly to move a whole people into exile, to banish them a thousand miles from their homes.

The Crimean Tatars were the first ethnic minority to suffer total deportation. A few weeks after Soviet power had been re-established in Crimea, the entire remaining Crimean Tatar population was expelled to Central Asia. Driven into railway cattle-wagons for journeys which sometimes lasted as long as a month, the Tatars were ejected into a wilderness without food, tools or shelter, to survive if they could.

This deportation was not announced for two years. Then a statement was issued in Moscow, quoting Article 58, paragraph 1(a) of the Russian Criminal Code concerning 'treason to the Fatherland', which informed the public that the Crimean Tatars, with the Chechens and Ingush of the northern Caucasus, had been 'resettled in other regions of the USSR where they were given land together with the appropriate government assistance for their economic establishment'.

Eleven years later, in 1956, after Nikita Khrushchev had specifically named and denounced the Tatar deportation in his speech attacking Stalin's legacy at the Twentieth Party Congress, the first timid petitions arrived in Moscow from Tashkent. The Tatars asked for the right to return home. There followed thirty years of appeals, demonstrations and deputations; of official lies and meaningless 'rehabilitations'; of struggle by the Tatars themselves and by their supporters in the Soviet democratic opposition like the magnificent Colonel Grigorenko, a war veteran and steadfast opponent of the Communist regime who devoted his life and eventually sacrificed his freedom and his health to the cause of denouncing the injustice done to the Crimean Tatars. All who took up that cause, Tatar, Russian or Ukrainian, knew what the price of their struggle would be: menaces, beatings, mass arrests, sentences served in labour camps or – this was the fate of Grigorenko – years spent in brutal psychiatric hospitals under false diagnoses of insanity.

But now, at last, the Tatars are returning home. They call it home, although fifty years constitutes more than a human generation and all but a minority of those who return were born in Kazakhstan or Uzbekistan. They call it home, but the small white-plastered cottages smothered in vine arbours which belonged to them or to their parents or grandparents are now occupied by Russian or Ukrainian immigrants who, for the most part, hate them. They are attacked by their neighbours, and there have been murders. They are treated as alien squatters by the corrupt Crimean regional government which currently rules at Simferopol. But on stony valley-bottoms which nobody wants, on the barren waste lots outside the Crimean cities, men and woman are building houses out of home-made clay bricks, reeds and corrugated iron. They measure up and parcel out the barren land between families, and conjure water out of the rocks. There is a haze of green seedlings where once there was only dusty grey turf, and a din of hammering. This is their Israel, their promised land, and they will not be parted from it again.

The morning after Mangup, we set off for the airport at Simferopol and the flight to Moscow. This time, even the Genoese were sombre and silent on the coach. But then a bearded Russian scholar next to me – an Orthodox tsarist conservative, as he had earlier described himself – suddenly blurted out in his deep voice, 'Things could not go on as they were! There was utter anarchy; bandits and mafiosi were devouring the land. Somebody had to act.'

I stared at him in astonishment.

Avoiding my eyes, he muttered, 'Well, what about de Gaulle? The Fourth Republic had fallen into anarchy, hadn't it? And when the integrity, the very life of France was threatened over Algeria, then he took over. Well, then . . . '

'Are you trying to tell me that Gennadi Yanayev is de Gaulle – and that Lithuania or Georgia is somehow like "Algérie Française"?'

I got only a reproachful look.

At the airport in Simferopol, there was *Krimskaya Pravda* to read, no more than a folded poster of the junta's proclamations. All demonstrations were banned, the newspaper told us, and there were curfews in Moscow and Leningrad. The paper carried no news, no commentary, but printed a grotesque 'Appeal' by Yanayev and his fellow putschists in the language of some Latin-American *pronunciamiento*, stinking of aggressive paranoia towards the whole outside world, dripping with references to the 'Motherland'.

In Moscow, dim and green under summer rain, columns of armour were waiting in the side-roads off the long avenue from Vnukovo airport. Tanks from the Taman Division stood beneath the dripping trees around Moscow University with their field kitchens and command trucks. This was not a new sight to me: the Soviet tanks had rested like that beneath the trees of the parks in Prague, late in another August twenty-three years before. Now they had invaded and crushed one more country – their own.

Watching them, I felt a sudden suffocation, a violent swelling of the heart. Was it vindictive joy, or reverence for the hammer-blow of justice with which history very occasionally strikes home? Later, I understood that it had been neither, but rather the breaking-through of a compassion for those soldiers – in their buff combat tunics, their black-and-white striped undershirts – which I had never been able to acknowledge in all the years when they served as the jailers of half Europe. I had been released at that instant from a fallacy, from the ingrained lie which invites us all to identify an army, a thousand or a million anxious and obedient young men and their machines, with the private feelings of a whole nation.

Alfred de Vigny wrote: 'The army is both blind and dumb; where it is set down, there it smites. It has no will of its own, and acts as if wound up. It is like a huge, insensate thing that is set in motion and kills, but it is a thing that can suffer too . . . ' All that has happened since the putsch of 1991 – the use of a reluctant army in 1993 to bombard Boris Yeltsin's opponents in the building of the Russian parliament, the misery of Russian troops during the Chechen war of 1994–5 as they massacred and threatened to mutiny and then massacred again – illustrates that blindness, but also that capacity to suffer.

The bus stopped outside the Oktyabrskaya Hotel. I dragged my case through the puddles, past the guard-house at the hotel gate and up the broad, shallow marble steps leading into the foyer. A loud American voice echoed from one corner, where the hotel staff stood pressed together in a herd. Looking over their shoulders, I saw a television set tuned to CNN: on the screen were barricades, women with armbands carrying loaves and duplicators into the Russian parliament, an orator standing on a tank. Running out into the street again, I waved down a passing car and asked the driver to take me to the parliament building. He stared at me in horror. I showed him some dollar bills. He hesitated a little more, then nodded gloomily. I jumped in.

The final victory of the Revolution took place on Saturday, 27 March 1920. On that day, British, French and American warships covered the evacuation of the White armies commanded by General Denikin from the Black Sea port of Novorossisk. There was more fighting to come: Baron Wrangel held out in Crimea with another White Army and managed a last counter-offensive before he was defeated, but Novorossisk was the real end of the Civil War and of the Allied intervention.

Novorossisk, on the north-east coast of the Black Sea, looks today much as it did in 1920, then as now the port for the oilfields of the northern Caucasus. It stands at the head of a small gulf of deep blue water, still dominated by the chimneys of the old Portland Cement factory spewing smoke across the bay. The hillside above the city is scarred into immense pale rectangles where limestone has been stripped to make cement. In the black-and-white snapshots my father took in 1920, I can still recognise those rectangles – smaller then – above a harbour full of masts and smoke.

The *Admiralty Pilot* for 1920 describes Novorossisk harbour as 'protected by two moles; the eastern one extends in a south-westerly direction from the shore and is about half a mile long; the western extends from the town in an opposite direction for a little over half a mile, leaving an entrance nearly two cables wide between them.' Freighters under British and French escort had steamed through this gap to unload artillery and tanks and uniforms for the White armies – much of it to be stolen and sold by racketeers or, in the case of the tanks, to stay rusting on the quayside. And it was to these moles and to the piers and jetties within the harbour that Denikin's broken Army of the South – Don Cossacks and Russian volunteers and a refugee mass of women and children – took flight when their last front on the lower Don collapsed before the Bolshevik offensive.

General Piotr Nikolayevich Krasnov, a Cossack *Ataman* (chieftain) in the White armies, was among the defeated commanders who fled into western exile. He went to Berlin and then to Paris where, to the astonishment of this tough old soldier's friends, he became a prolific novelist. A four-volume novel, *From Two-Headed Eagle to Red Flag*, was published and translated into several languages within three years of his flight, and that was only his first literary achievement. But Krasnov, who had all the Cossack talent for forgetting nothing, forgiving nothing and learning nothing, came to a bad end.

In Claudio Magris's book *Inferences from a Sabre*, a much more talented writer plays through the pathetic coda to Krasnov's life. In 1938, when he was sixty-nine years old, German agents persuaded Krasnov to move back to Berlin, where the SS flattered and manipulated him, satisfied by reports that his hatred of Soviet Communism was matched only by his contempt for the Judaeo-democratic West. After June 1941, as the Wehrmacht broke out across the steppes of southern Russia and Ukraine, the old man happily agreed to command Cossacks once more against the Bolshevik enemy. But when the tide of war turned and the Germans began to fall back, Krasnov and his men retreated across Europe with a nomadic retinue of men, women and animals to finish up as a legion of the defeated, encamped in the mountains behind Magris's city of Trieste. In April 1945, the Cossacks moved into Austria and surrendered to the British. They supposed that they would be treated as normal prisoners of war, or at least as displaced refugees, and evacuated to some new place of exile.

But this was not Novorossisk. The British Army, after a few weeks of deceitful assurances, seized them and drove them – men, women and children – to the zonal border where Soviet security troops were waiting for them. Among those delivered up were a few – mostly officers – who had been rescued from Bolshevik vengeance by the British at Novorossisk just twenty-five years before.

Many of the Cossacks were shot, at once or within the first year. Most were herded into trains and disappeared into labour camps in the Arctic or the Far East. Piotr Krasnov, tried and condemned as a traitor to the Motherland, was denied the soldier's final tribute of a firing-squad. He was hanged in Moscow on 26 August 1946.

In *From Two-Headed Eagle to Red Flag*, Krasnov had described the retreat to Novorossisk.

The nearer the Polegaeffs [two fictional characters] approached Novorossisk, the greater was the number of dead horses they saw. The bodies of soldiers, volunteers, refugees, women and children, partly stripped of their clothes, were also lying about. One came across mounds of hastily dug graves without crosses or inscriptions; broken carts, smashed cases full of clothes, rags and household goods were lying scattered about . . . a vast, wealthy region suddenly rushed towards the sea in search of salvation, dragging all the riches assembled during many centuries, hoping to save them and to settle with their help in a new place . . . The blue sea, the fairy-story of Russia's children, the enchanted lands which must surely lie behind the sapphire sea, forced many hundred thousands to move towards the shore.

As they crossed the last ridge, the Whites saw Novorossisk ahead of them: the sea, the smoke rising from the funnels of the passenger ships and freighters alongside the piers and the moles, the British battleships at anchor in the outer roadstead. Hundreds and hundreds of abandoned Cossack horses stood about the broad streets running down to the harbour: 'although forsaken by their masters, they continued to stand in rows of six'. At the edge of the sea, the trampling, screaming panic to reach the ships had already begun.

Denikin's orderly evacuation plans were overwhelmed. In his terse, unforgiving book of memoirs, he observes only that 'Many were the human tragedies enacted in the town during those terrible days. Many bestial instincts were brought to light at this moment of supreme danger, when the voice of conscience was stifled and man became the enemy of his fellow-man.'

Only a few hundred yards of water separated the Novorossisk piers from a world as remote as a distant planet: the cheerful, monastic, scrubbed routines of the Royal Navy. Incredulous, the young officers watched the shore through field-glasses. Among them was my father, a midshipman aboard the warship *Emperor of India*.

The Navy List for 1920 describes her as a battleship of 25,000 tons, with a primary armament of ten 13.5-inch guns and a secondary armament of twelve 6-inch guns. Commanded by Captain Joseph Henley, she also carried Rear-Admiral Michael Culme-Seymour, second in command of the Mediterranean Fleet, who was in charge of the evacuation. Denikin, who had few good words for anyone else who witnessed his defeat, called Culme-Seymour a 'fine and kindly man' who 'nobly kept his word'. The Admiral, who was under instructions to use his squadron only to protect the civilian transports, had finally consented to embark troops and refugees on his warships as well. He was taking a risk which, as it turned out, nearly ended in disaster.

Emperor of India had steamed up from Constantinople to Sevastopol in the first days of March, and had been off Novorossisk for nearly three weeks when the advance guard of the retreating White Army appeared over the pass leading to the Kuban and began to pour down to the harbour. On 20 March the ship's log records: 'Hands make and mend. Embarked as passenger Denikin and party consisting of one Russian gentleman, two ladies and one child.'

On Friday 26 March, the panic ashore reached its final intensity as Red Army units began to close in on Novorossisk from the hills and along the shore from Gelendzhik to the south.

11.15: sounded ACTION.

12.00: fired 4 rounds three-quarter charge at village of BORISOVKA.

3.30: fired 8 rounds X Turret at same target.

[A snapshot my father took from the bridge shows the gush of black cordite smoke from the gun-muzzles, the after-funnel blurred by the concussion.]

Saturday 27 March was the last day:

2.40: embarked about 500 refugees.

3.30: embarked 538 refugees.

5.24: weighed anchor (shifted berth). Embarked General Holman [head of the British Military Mission].

9.20: General Denikin left ship. Approximately 850 Russian troops left on board.

10.45: Bolsheviks opened fire on ships in harbour at extreme range.

10.51: weighed, left harbour for Theodosia.

My father saw how near Admiral Culme-Seymour's gesture of generosity came to tragedy. His photographs show the decks of *Emperor of India* as a swarming encampment of ragged, fur-hatted soldiers so tightly packed together that they could not sit down; a few sailors are fighting their way through the mob with tin canisters of bully beef. He used to tell me of the crew's horror when they discovered that the torn greatcoats all round them were heaving with lice and that some of the soldiers were sick with typhus. He told me how the Cossack officers, ominous figures in their black, wasp-waisted tunics with bandoliers and sabres, stood under the bridge and stared wordlessly over the rail at the shore of Russia. It was at this point that a horse-drawn battery of Bolshevik field guns galloped over the low ridge just to the north of the city, took up position and opened fire.

Only one of the guns worked. With this, Trotsky's men engaged a battle squadron of the Mediterranean Fleet equipped with many hundred times their fire-power. Their aim, luckily, was bad, for the refugee mass on deck meant that the big warships were unable to reply. Aboard *Emperor of India*, the main armament – the 13.5-inch guns – jutted out only a few feet above the heads of the crowd, and to have fired them would have blown every human being on deck into the sea.

The field-gun shells came wavering through the air and raised harmless plumes of spray, but it was only a matter of time before the gunners registered the range accurately. The admiral decided to pull out. As the battleship came into the open sea, she encountered a drifting barge crammed with soldiers, towed out and then abandoned by a local tug. A line was attached and the barge was brought alongside *Emperor of India*, which embarked its passengers.

To cover the retreat, a destroyer raced back into the bay and began to shell the field-guns ashore. By now, more Bolshevik troops were arriving from the south, and were engaged by a small White Russian warship off the cement-works jetty. The railway station caught fire, and then the storage tanks of the Standard Oil

Company were hit. My father's last snapshot shows black smoke rolling up from the harbour, white smoke patching the roofs. He wrote under it: 'Town Burning.'

Denikin, who had been transferred to a destroyer, now began to hear the rattle of machine-gun fire as well as the thump of artillery. The Red Army was entering Novorossisk. 'Then silence fell,' Denikin wrote. 'The outlines of the coast, the Caucasian range, became shrouded in mist and receded into the distance – into the past.'

It was halfway through the second night on the Moscow barricades, the second night of vigil around the Russian parliament, that I heard the shooting begin. It came from a few hundred yards away, from the underpass on the Sadovaya boulevard behind the parliament building. When I reached the place, this is what I saw.

A bearded priest was walking through blood. He could have found a way not to tread in the scarlet pools and rivers across the roadway, but that would have meant taking his eyes off the tanks ahead, crouching half-hidden in the underpass tunnel. So he walked straight on, slowly, his head up, not looking at what was under his feet.

Behind the priest came two captured armoured vehicles, each carrying a dozen human beings clinging to the turret, to the gun, to one another. Driven by amateurs, they moved in low gear, in violent lurches which made the riders sway and grab for support. The tracks moved over rubble and burned metal, over the glass of smashed trolley-bus windows, then over the sketchy rectangles of sticks laid down to keep walkers away from the blood. Afterwards, the people came back and rebuilt those enclosures and made them into shrines.

The procession behind the priest went slowly down the slope towards the tunnel-mouth of the underpass, in a deafening uproar of tank engines mingled with the outcry of hundreds of people leaning over the parapets on either side. They went on until the bows of the tanks which had gone over to Boris Yeltsin touched the bows of the lead tank still loyal to the army command. Then the demonstrators sprang on board and raised the Russian tricolour and yelled at the crew inside to surrender.

In that night, between 20 August and 21 August 1991, the coup failed. Most of the foreign journalists wrote afterwards that it had been bound to fail; its preparation had been feeble, its organisation slovenly and chaotic, its leaders drunk and irresolute. But I was there too, and I do not think so. In most of the provinces and republics of the Soviet Union, the leadership submitted or rallied to the plotters. The people, appalled but resigned, for the most part did nothing; if the usurpers had held on for another few days, the coup against Gorbachev might have consolidated. Only the determination of a few thousand people in Moscow and Leningrad, challenging the will of the plot leaders to slaughter them, broke their nerve.

The front line of the Moscow resistance was a chain of women holding hands. They made a cordon across the far end of the Kalinin Bridge, looking up the dark boulevard along which the tanks would come. Every few minutes, somewhere in the distance, tank engines rumbled and bellowed and then fell quiet again. Behind the women, who were both young and old, stood an anxious support group of husbands, lovers and brothers with flasks of tea, transistor radios and cigarettes. When I asked the women why they stood there, and why they were not afraid, they answered: 'Because we are mothers.'

Afterwards, when it was over, a Russian friend of mine who had been at the barricades said simply, 'A handful of good, brave people saved Russia.' I still believe that she was right. The defenders stood around the White House of the Russian parliament and around Boris Yeltsin for two rainy days and nights. On the third morning, the sun came out and the plotters ran away.

The succeeding years have shown that this was not the end of what the good and brave handful called 'fascism'. The monster returned again in October 1993. An alliance of Russian nationalists and neo-Communists, sworn to avenge the 'betrayal' of the old Soviet imperium, tried to launch another coup d'état from the White House itself. This time, the parliament and its defenders were bombarded into submission by the same tank divisions which had refused to open fire in August 1991. But Russia has not heard the last of the plotters, and Yeltsin himself, who had shown such courage and such sureness of leadership in 1991, soon degenerated into one of those erratic tsars – now sunk in apathy and now suddenly lashing out with absurd violence – who have so often misgoverned Russia.

All that is true. And yet, in one important way, the defeat of the Yanayev putsch in 1991 was irreversible. The peasants, the industrial workers, the soldiers had all rebelled in the past. But now, for the first time in Russian history, the liberal-minded middle-class minority had come out into the street, built their own barricades and faced the guns in the name of freedom.

The coup against Mikhail Sergeyevich Gorbachev and his *perestroika* failed, but its consequences destroyed both man and policy. Gorbachev never regained the initiative from Yeltsin and was thrust aside; Party-led *perestroika* was replaced by far more ambitious designs for the introduction of market capitalism and plural democracy. Within days, the Communist Party of the Soviet Union was suspended and the Central Committee building on Staraya Ploshchad was sealed off. The Party was not yet dead, but its great head had been cut off and its limbs had been paralysed. It never thought or moved again.

A few months later, the Soviet Union itself dissolved and the nineteenth-century empire of the Russian tsars fell to pieces, and even the eighteenth-century conquests of Catherine the Great – her glorious province of 'New Russia' curving all around the northern shore of the Black Sea – were almost all lost. Ukraine, which had incorporated Crimea since 1954, now became an independent state, following the Baltic republics of Lithuania, Latvia and Estonia. Russia's broad windows to western seas, won and widened at such cost over so many years, closed to a chink. On the Baltic, Russia lost the ports of Klaipeda, Riga and Tallinn and kept only Kaliningrad (Königsberg) and St Petersburg itself. On the Black Sea – Krasnov's 'blue sea, the fairy-story of Russia's children' – Russia now peered out only through Novorossisk on the Kuban coast, and through the shallow, silting harbours of the Sea of Azov. The port-city of Odessa, the new harbour at Ilichevsk, the shipyards at Nikolaev, the ports of Balaklava, Feodosia and Kerch all passed out of Moscow's control. So, above all, did the naval base of the Black Sea Fleet at Sevastopol, in Crimea.

But there is a sense in which Sevastopol can never be cut out of Russia. It is not just that Russia built it – a majestic stone city full of southern space and air, its blue creeks jammed with warships. Sevastopol also provided some of the inmost mental shrines of Russia. This is twice a 'Hero-City': once for its ten-month siege when it held out against the Nazis, once for its two-year defence against Britain, France, Sardinia and Turkey during the Crimean War. And Sevastopol has a still deeper sanctity. It was here, in legend and perhaps in fact, that Christianity entered Russia.

42

The ruins of Cherson (or Korsun, or Chersonesus) cover a cape on the edge of the city. In summer, families come to swim here, filing down among the tall Byzantine columns and round the honeycomb of excavated buildings to reach low cliffs, a beach of boulders, a green and transparent sea. In its life, as a Greek colony and then as the Byzantine Empire's biggest trading city on the Black Sea, Cherson was periodically wrecked by pagan attackers from the steppe (the Mongol-Tatars finally extinguished the town in the late thirteenth century). In its death, the site has been devastated by fortress-building and bombardment and above all by early Russian archaeologists, ploughing down through the substrata to find 'evidence' of the baptism of Vladimir of Kiev in 991.

The place is dominated by a gigantic basilica, with trees growing through its smashed cupola, which was put up in 1891 to celebrate the millennium of Russian Christianity. It is now agreed that the church is in the wrong place, and pious visitors are directed to the ruins of a small Byzantine baptistery a few hundred yards away. Within its walls there is a deep, circular pit or dry pool and a cross incised on the pool's floor. Here, possibly, it happened: this sacramental moment which re-invented an irritable tyrant as a saint and turned the Russian imagination for a thousand years towards the Black Sea and the city of Constantinople.

Russian state nationalism has always dreamed of parthenogenesis. It has always hankered after a myth of isolated origin in which the Russian people developed its own genius, as a huge seed unfolds its own predestined stem and leaves and fruit. The 'Varangian' interpretation, which emphasises the historical fact that the first Russo-Slav state was founded around Kiev on the Dnieper by Viking raiders and settlers, was roughly treated by Slavophil educators under the last tsars and by the intellectual policemen of Stalinism. The 'Byzantine' version, interpreting early Russian culture and institutions as foreign imports which arrived with Orthodox Christianity from Constantinople, has also had a hard time with those bureaucrats who draw up 'patriotic' or 'progressive' curricula and decide which scholar should be dismissed for unreliable views.

Under Stalin, the myth of parthenogenesis (or 'autochthony') was driven to an insane extreme. Soviet archaeology was purged of the very notion of migration. Cultural change, the new Party archaeological bureaucrats laid down, had come about by development within settled communities and not by the entry of new populations from east or west. The phrase 'Migration of Peoples' (*Völkerwanderungen*) to describe Eurasian population movements after the collapse of the western Roman Empire was banned. The Crimean Goths, for example, were declared to be not Germanic invaders but 'formed autochthonously and by stages from the tribes present here before them'. The Khazars ceased to be Turkic nomads from the east and became the ancient inhabitants of the Don country and the northern Caucasus: 'the results of auto-chthonous ethnogeny [sic] created by the intermarriage of local tribes'. The Tatars were rediscovered as Volga aboriginals. More ominously, the Scandinavian Varangians who had created the first 'Rus' state around Kiev were re-identified as Slavs.

From the early 1930s to the late 1950s, the Party officials in charge of Soviet archaeology designed and reared up a skyscraper of chauvinist imbecility. This was the assertion that the whole area of modern Russia, Ukraine, eastern and even central Europe had been inhabited by proto-Slav populations since the middle Iron Age: say, 900 BC. Stalin fired his revolver in the air and the entire past of the Black Sea steppes, which had been a history of ceaseless migrancy and ethnic mingling, froze terrified in its tracks and turned into a history of static social development.

And the shots were not only metaphorical. Mikhail Miller, a Russian archaeologist who took refuge in the West after the Second World War, recorded in his *Archaeology in the USSR* the fate of his colleagues when the new line was enforced between 1930 and 1934. Some 85 per cent of the profession fell victim to the purge. Most of them were deported to Siberian or Asian labour camps or exile. Some were shot or committed suicide when the NKVD came to arrest them. But most – including Miller's brilliant brother Alexander – died in the Gulag.

It was not until well after Stalin's death that the past of the southern steppe dared to move again; at first, only cautiously. A. L. Mongait was a Party loyalist under instructions to write a book for western consumption which would undo some of the damage done by Miller's revelations. Mongait's own *Archaeology in the USSR*, published in an English version in 1961, tiptoed up to what he delicately called 'the Scythian problem': the patent fact that the Scythians had entered the Dnieper-Don steppe from somewhere else. He let the Scythians migrate – but only a little. 'They would have thrust forward from the lower Volga area', where, Mongait implied, they had originated some time in the Bronze Age. The truth known to scholarship for nearly fifty years – that the Scythians were an Indo-Iranian-speaking confederation which had arrived from Central Asia – was still too much for him.

Today migration theory is securely back in Russian and Ukrainian archaeology, but it has returned with tatters of nineteenth-century nationalist historiography still flapping around it. Unpopular to this day remain those who argue that the whole balance of Russian history-writing about 'civilisation' and 'barbarism' is skewed, who ask why the steppe nomads and the non-Slav cultures, encountered by Kievan Rus and then by the mediaeval Russian state which arose around Novgorod and Moscow, must still be dismissed as backward and 'barbaric'. The centuries of Mongol-Tatar conquest, beginning in the early thirteenth century, remain for most Russians 'the Mongol Yoke': a time in which the leaders of Russia manned the outposts of Christian civilisation against a tide of ultimate savagery and disorder. But this traditional version now shows increasing symptoms of Russocentric myth.

There is no denying the ferocity of the Mongols at war, or the devastation created in a subsistence-peasant society by the arrival of perhaps half a million horses with a single nomad army. And yet the Mongols had access to literacy, and their political, military and administrative institutions were in some ways more sophisticated than those of Novgorod Russia. When Russian cultural pessimists blame their nation's lack of democracy on 'the Mongol inheritance', as they always have, they ignore the tradition of the *quriltai* – the assembly of Mongol-Tatar nobles and clan chiefs who gathered to elect a new khan. This was a limited, oligarchic dispersing of power, but mediaeval Russia did not even have that. (The Poles, whose kings were elected by a mass assembly of aristocrats gathering in a field outside Warsaw, have always brought up this custom to prove their attachment to 'Western democracy'. The practice was introduced into Poland only in the late sixteenth century, and the precedent then advanced for it was the oligarchy of the Roman Republic, but this was also plainly a form of *quriltai*, probably borrowed from the Crimean Tatars.)

Under Stalin, equally hostile to religion and to any suggestion that the Russian state had foreign origins, Byzantinologists had become an endangered species. (Doom was more certain only for 'Varangian' historians, who were accused of inventing Germanic origins for the nation.) But at length, during the rule of Leonid Brezhnev, a sort of corrupt relaxation set in as Jews sacked from other university departments were resettled – whatever their original academic backgrounds – in obscure seminars of Byzantine history. From total suppression, the subject crawled up to the status of an intellectual internment camp.

Now, after the fall of the Soviet state, Byzantine studies are hugely fashionable in Russia. This was why the World Congress of Byzantinology met in Moscow in August 1991, two weeks before the coup d'état, and why it was opened by the Patriarch Alexei with a theatrical obeisance to the heritage of Byzantium. Russia was looking westwards for a new politics and inaugurating a cargo cult to bring Western prosperity and the market economy. But in their search for a new identity, the Russians had gone down to the Black Sea shore and were staring towards Constantinople.

This meant that there were really two Congresses going on. One was the intricate mating and challenging display of Western Byzantinologists who come on heat only once every four years; at this Congress, factions gathered behind the terrifying Professor Armin Hohlweg of Munich, editor of the *Byzantinische Zeitschrift*, or behind Professor Vladimir Vavřinek of Prague, editor of the rival *Byzantinoslavica*. Funny as this was, nobody in the Great Auditorium of Moscow University dared to satirise it in public. These are solemn occasions. As a translated Georgian paper on hagiography remarked: 'in Christianity it is the death that laughs, the devil, the mermaids laugh their hands off, but the Christian deity never laughs.'

The other Congress was the mass of young Russians, some of them in the black robes of priesthood, who pressed into the seminar rooms determined to find nothing less than their souls, their roots, their own Russian path to revelation and holiness. I found my way to one of their meetings, in a small fifth-floor room so crowded that I had to clamber over listeners sitting on the floor in order to lean against a wall. This is what I wrote in a notebook:

Marina is sitting reading in rusty French, the sleeves of her white shirt rolled up. Each sheet of notes is tattered and creased, and she throws each down on the pile as she comes to the end of it.

46

Her hair is long and tangled, greasy. She has big hands, like a man. The room is absolutely rapt. Out of the window, beyond a belt of dark-green woods, I can see the black wall of a storm-cloud and, against it, the rampart-blocks of the Moscow suburbs glittering silver.

She is talking about Russia's Christological conflicts with the West. When she finishes, there is violent applause. Now comes Father Ilarion, young, his smooth hair parted in the middle, grave. He asks: 'Shall I speak in English or Russian?' These audiences are normally so respectful, so considerate to the foreigners among them. But now the whole room is imploring together: 'Po Russki! Po Russki!'

Father Ilarion begins. He is reading poetry, his own verse translation from Greek into Russian of the 'Hymns of Divine Love' by Symeon the New Theologian (an eleventh-century Byzantine mystic and saint). Again, these boys and girls are seized. Some are staring at the floor. Some are biting their fists.

When Father Ilarion finishes, there is silence and then clumsy clapping. Marina, drowsy as if she had just woken from a dream, stares at him. Then she turns her head and looks out of the window, where there is a rainbow.

Many months later, back in Western Europe, I was able to find texts of the 'Hymns of Divine Love'. They are entirely extra-ordinary. Concerned not with man in the image of God but with God in the image of man, they have something in common with the mystical poetry of the seventeenth-century German poet 'Angelus Silesius' (Johann Scheffler). But for young Russians, the 'Hymns' are rain on a parched, forbidden and almost forgotten part of their sensibility:

We who live with God becoming / in our natures living gods,
Finding in our mortal bodies / nothing to provoke our shame,
Every organ, every member / is identical with Christ's,
Who, composed of many Members, / indivisible, unique,
Shows that each part of his body / is the whole perfected Christ.
Now you recognise my finger / as the whole of Christ Himself,
And my testicle . . . you shudder? / Are you blushing and aghast?
God was not ashamed to wear a / flesh identical to yours;
Why should you see shame in wearing / flesh identical to His?

No, I feel no shame, created / in the image of my God.
'Yet to name him in that organ, / in that very part of shame,
Blasphemy you have committed / blasphemy in such a trope!'
   Do not tremble, for my verses / nothing shameful introduce.
For these parts, Christ's hidden members, / covered up and veiled
      from sight,
Are thereby more fit to honour, / more divine than all the rest,
Parts invisible, like members / of the Hidden One's elect,
Whence he gives the sperm of blessing / in the wedding-rite
      divine. . .

Chapter Two

And now, what will become of us without the barbarians?
Those people were a kind of solution.

Constantine Cavafy, 'Waiting for the Barbarians'

ON THE SHORES of the Black Sea, there were born a pair of
Siamese twins called 'civilisation' and 'barbarism'. This is where
Greek colonists met the Scythians. A settled culture of small,
maritime city-states encountered a mobile culture of steppe
nomads. People who had lived in one place for uncounted
generations, planting crops and fishing the coastal sea, now met
people who lived in wagons and tents and wandered about infinite
horizons of grassy prairie behind herds of cattle and horses.

This was not the first time in human history that farmers had met
pastoralists: since the Neolithic Revolution, the beginning of settled
agriculture, there must have been countless intersections of these
two ways of life. Nor was it the first witnessing of nomadism by
people from an urban culture: that was an experience already
familiar to the Chinese on the western borders of the Han
dominions. But in this particular encounter began the idea of
'Europe' with all its arrogance, all its implications of superiority, all
its assumptions of priority and antiquity, all its pretensions to a
natural right to dominate.

'Civilisation' and 'barbarism' were twins gestated and born in the
Greek but above all in the Athenian imagination. They in turn gave
birth to a ruthless mental dynasty which still holds invisible power
over the Western mind. The Roman and Byzantine Empires
sanctified their own imperial struggles as the defence of 'civilised'
order against 'barbaric' primitivism. So did the Holy Roman
Empire and the colonial expansions of Spain, Portugal, Holland,

France, Italy, Germany and Britain. By the middle twentieth century, few European nation-states had not at one time or another figured themselves as 'the outpost of Western Christian civilisation': France, imperial Germany, the Habsburg Reich, Poland with its self-image as *przedmurze* (bastion), even tsarist Russia. Each of these nation-state myths identified 'barbarism' as the condition or ethic of their immediate eastward neighbour: for the French, the Germans were barbarous, for the Germans it was the Slavs, for the Poles the Russians, for the Russians the Mongol and Turkic peoples of Central Asia and eventually the Chinese.

The gestation of the twins was a long one. The first Greeks reached the northern Black Sea coast and set up permanent trading-posts there in the eighth century BC. But the encounter lasted for several hundred years before the Siamese twins were born – before 'different' came to mean 'inferior', and before the 'otherness' of the steppe peoples whom the Greeks met on the Black Sea became a mirror in which Greeks learned to see their own superiority. That event – a sudden conceptual leap – took place in Athens in the first half of the fifth century BC, as the Athens of Pericles beat off the Persian invasions and became itself an imperial power.

Athenian intellectuals, above all the playwrights, devised this change in the way that Greeks perceived other peoples and then they sold it to the wider public. The colonists themselves had little or nothing to do with it. Their ancestors were not from Athens or even from the Peloponnese, but were mostly Ionian Greeks from the islands and towns along the coast of Asia Minor. Anyway, they were obliged to be pragmatists if they were to survive out on the rim of the known world. It was not ideology which had brought them and their fathers through the Bosporus and across the Black Sea, but fish. Even by the seventh century, the Aegean city-states were beginning to exhaust the limited arable land around their walls, and it was hunger which drove their ships to the north and east.

At first, the colonists lived by the stinking, profitable trade of fish-processing. Some of their earliest settlements were at the mouths of the big rivers which empty into the shallow north-west of the Black Sea. Tyras and Niconia were built at the mouth of the Dniester, west of modern Odessa, and Olbia at the outfall of the southern Bug where it opens into the Dnieper estuary a few miles from the sea. These were the wrong sites to intercept the two main deep-water fish-flows of the Black Sea, the migrations of the *hamsi* and the bonito. But all three cities stood on the shores of *limans*, enormous fresh-water lagoons formed by these rivers before they meet the sea, and the early Greeks relied on easily netted river fish: sturgeon and salmon and shad and pike-perch. From these estuaries, the Dnieper delta especially, came abundant salt for curing.

Later, the settlers began to plant wheat for export. For almost three thousand years, until North American wheat conquered the world markets in the late nineteenth century, grain grown in the Black Sea steppe and shipped out through the ports of the north shore went to feed the urban populations of the Mediterranean and beyond: the Greek cities, Rome, Byzantium, Egypt, mediaeval Italy, even Britain in the years of the Industrial Revolution. By the time that Herodotus visited Olbia in the fifth century BC, the Greek colony had already persuaded Scythian communities around it to plough the earth and grow grain for the market. Many city-states, and above all Periclean Athens, became dangerously dependent upon imported steppe wheat for their bread.

Herodotus, for his part, was a relativist. He had spent some time in Athens, although he was an Ionian Greek by birth, and he seems to have been a friend of the tragedian Sophocles. But his *Histories* avoid the cultural supremacism which had become the fashion among Athenian dramatists. 'Everyone without exception believes that their own native customs are by far the best . . . there is plenty of evidence that this is the universal human attitude.'

In spite of his own views, Herodotus could not prevent his work being used as an ethnology-mine by nationalist writers determined to prove that barbarians were not just different but evil and degraded. And, in a much subtler fashion, Herodotus too was concerned to demonstrate that the non-Greek peoples were 'other' in ways which illuminated Greekness and Greek identity in a more brilliant, more flattering light. But Herodotus had actually visited and seen many of these other cultures, which the Athenian intellectuals had not. He would never commit the vulgarity of categorising them all indifferently as 'barbarians', or of demonising them as Aeschylus and Euripides were doing.

'People used to regard Herodotus as a historian, and doubt him. But now we should regard him as a politician – and believe him.'

So says the director of the Olbia excavations, Anatol Ilyich Kudrenko. We stood outside the gates of Olbia — pseudo-Greek gates carved out of white concrete — and talked in the early spring sunshine. Mr Kudrenko, like most archaeological site-directors in Russia and Ukraine these days, is stranded and abandoned. The funds for excavation and museum maintenance and staff salaries which used to flow from the USSR Academy of Sciences in Moscow, and later from the Ukrainian Academy of Sciences in Kiev, have dried up to a useless trickle. He is like one of the captains of the ships tied up and rusting alongside the quays at Odessa, immobilised because nobody can afford fuel. His ruins are defiled by abandoned hulks of agricultural machinery and collapsing sheds. Chickens peck among the shards of glossy black Greek ceramic. Peasants from the local collective farm rob the site so casually that they even leave their shovels in the pits overnight, ready for the next day's looting.

Mr Kudrenko believes that Herodotus was not only a traveller and a historian but also an agent in the service of Pericles. He visited the Black Sea coasts not because of his own independent curiosity, but because he was sent there as part of a Periclean campaign to persuade Athens that the city must expand overseas in order to guarantee its food supplies. Earlier, Herodotus had been associated with Pericles' scheme to found a colony at Thurii, in southern Italy, where he eventually settled and is probably buried. His job in the Black Sea, according to Kudrenko, was to arouse public interest in the Greek colonies there, especially those along the coasts of 'Thracia' and 'Scythia' on the western and northern shores of the Black Sea. The object was to justify Pericles in his project for a naval expedition which would put these cities under an Athenian protectorate, reinforce them against Scythian attacks, and seize control of their wheat trade. It was for this (Kudrenko argues) that Herodotus was awarded the enormous sum of ten talents by the Athenian *polis*: funds for imperial pioneering rather than a mere reward for writing an interesting book.

The Black Sea expedition sailed in 447 BC, and the Greek colonies — including Olbia — became part of the short-lived Athenian maritime empire. But Pericles was not simply a military liberator or conqueror; relations between the Greek cities and the Scythians had already become too complicated and interesting to allow that. Nor did he try to impose Athenian democracy on these cities, as Athens had done a few years earlier with the Aegean city-states which had fallen under its influence. Olbia ('Wealth City') had been a democracy of sorts until the emergency of Scythian pressure allowed a certain Pausanē to establish himself as a peculiar 'elected tyrant'. Pericles, by diplomacy rather than force, negotiated a compromise which guaranteed Olbian political independence as an 'autonomous tyranny', but allowed the Scythian empire to retain part-control of the economy – it was by now the Scythians, rather than the Greeks, who organised the growing of wheat and the transport of furs and hides, and brought them down-river to the city. Democracy and full independence did not return to Olbia until some fifty years later, when both Athens and the Scythian empire were in decline, and even then its politics remained unstable. The citizens of Olbia were a small enfranchised minority in a population which may have become as large as 30,000, and eventually two rich shipping dynasties, the families of Heroson and Protogenes, were in practice managing everything and imposing taxes which reduced many other citizens and merchants to debt and poverty.

But, even if Kudrenko is right or partly right, Herodotus was much more than a Cecil Rhodes of the fifth century BC. In his book *The Mirror of Herodotus*, the French scholar François Hartog deliberately turns his back on the old debates about whether Herodotus was accurate in what he wrote about Scythia and examines his *Histories* as a 'discourse of otherness'.

The centre of the *Histories* is the account of the Persian Wars: the ten-year struggle of Athens to beat off the Achaemenid kings of Persia who invaded the Aegean lands between 490 and 480 BC and were defeated at Marathon and Salamis, and the counter-attack of the Greek states under Athenian leadership which followed. In this supreme crisis of their existence, the Athenians had to ask themselves in a new way who they were, and what made the difference between them and their enemies worth dying for. Their eventual answer was an imperial one: a cosmic 'discourse of superiority' to the 'barbarians'. Herodotus could not go that far, but what he chose to say about the Scythians was intended to heighten his record of the Persian Wars – to define Athenian and Greek identity in the most graphic way possible, by contrasting it to mythic 'opposites'.

Nomadism, for example, was set up against Greek city-state patriotism which was about settledness, continuity, love of place.

53

As Hartog puts it: 'how did such people as the Greeks, who were forever declaring that city life was the only life worth living, imagine this figure of the Scythian, the essence of whose life was to keep constantly on the move?' The Athenians insisted that they were 'autochthonous' –biologically rooted in their own place. 'It is not hard to foresee that the discourse of autochthony was bound to reflect on the representation of nomadism and that the Athenian, that imaginary autochthonous being, had need of an equally imaginary nomad. The Scythian conveniently fitted the bill.'

But Herodotus, like some later classical writers, thought of nomadism as a military strategy rather than as a way of life which was the opposite of Greek settledness. His Scythians were inaccessible – in Greek, *aporoi*. Herodotus wrote: 'I do not admire everything about the Scythians, but in this supreme concern they have invented a system which means that nobody who attacks them can escape, and nobody can catch them if they do not wish to be found.' Instead of standing and fighting, they retreated into their endless land, leading the enemy on until he starved or despaired. As Hartog says, they inverted normal sense by making the hunter into the hunted. Instead of defending the walls of a city or capital against an invader, the Scythians simply dispersed. They had no city, not even the idea of a 'centre', for their only fixed places – like the royal tombs described by Herodotus which lay in the 'land of the Gerrhi', to which their kings were carried by wagon to be buried – were on the distant periphery of their realm.

Why does Herodotus admire this? Here his whole literary operation deftly twists on itself. He admires Scythian strategy because it defeated the Persians. Darius I of Persia, later the invader of Greece, entered Europe for the first time in 512 BC on a punitive expedition against the Scythians. He bridged the Bosporus, then the Danube and then (according to Herodotus) marched across the whole northern shore of the Black Sea as far as the river Don in a vain attempt to bring the enemy to battle and conquer them. Frustrated, he was eventually obliged to retreat and leave the Scythians undefeated.

So the Scythians, who in so many ways have to be presented as the polar opposites of the Athenians, are suddenly in some ways like them – they too have beaten the Persians. Not only that, but they have done so by behaving as the Athenians would later behave, according to Herodotus' description of the Persian Wars: the

Athenians overcame the invaders not by trying to defend their territory but by taking to the sea in ships and becoming *aporoi*.

In the last few years, an exhilarating new pseudo-science has arisen called nomadology. The human race, say its exponents, is entering a new epoch of movement and migration, a *Völker-wanderung* which this time involves not merely Eurasia but the entire world. The subjects of history, once the settled farmers and citizens, have now become the migrants, the refugees, the *Gastarbeiter*, the asylum-seekers, the urban homeless.

Professor Edward Said, in his Lothian Lecture in Edinburgh in 1992, argued that the torch of liberation has been handed on from the settled cultures to 'unhoused, de-centred, exilic energies ... whose incarnation is the migrant'. The Polish artist Krzystof Wodiczko, who has drawn many ideas from the 1980 'Traité de Nomadologie' by Gilles Deleuze and Felix Guattari, perceives how the hordes of the displaced now occupy the public space of cities – squares, parks or railway station concourses which were once designed by a triumphant middle class to celebrate the conquest of its new political rights and economic liberties. Wodiczko thinks that these occupied public spaces form new *agoras* (the paved assembly-square in the midst of a Greek *polis*) which should be used for statements. 'The artist ... needs to learn how to operate as a nomadic sophist in a migrant *polis*.' And he has designed for the displaced a series of strange vehicles for shelter, mobility and communication which sharply – if unintentionally – recall what struck Herodotus about the Scythian nomads and their *aporia*. His 'Poliscar', for instance, has ancestry in the supermarket trolley and even more obviously in the battle tank. But it is also a Scythian wagon, a moving home for those who have no centre but who roam endlessly up and down the public spaces, the concrete urban steppe.

The critic Patrick Wright, a friend of Wodiczko, acknowledges the Poliscar's descent from the tank. He identifies its intellectual godfathers in very diverse thinkers about the tank's mobility, from General J. F. C. Fuller, father of modern armoured warfare, to the French sociologist of speed Paul Virilio. But he writes that 'as a "nomadic war machine" [the Poliscar] is devoted to survival, intelligence and the avoidance of engagement rather than to battle itself ... closer to the hunted animal that learns to co-exist with enemies than to the hunter who goes out in search of prey ... an instrument of "manoeuvre" as opposed to "battle", of mobility and sudden disappearance and reappearance, of intelligence rather than brutal and unstoppable advance.'

Here, precisely, is that 'hunted who becomes the hunter' which François Hartog perceives in Herodotus' account of the Scythians. Here is that technique through which the weak become stronger than their oppressors: by scattering, by becoming centreless, by moving fast across space, by all that is nomadism. It was once the ranked, slow-marching foot army of King Darius of Persia which was outmanoeuvred by the Scythians. Now, for Wodiczko, it is the New York Police Department forming up against the homeless dossers on the pavements around Tompkins Square Park which will be outrun and baffled by his Poliscars. Tomorrow it will be the turn of the customs officers and frontier guards of the European Union to be outwitted and 'hunted' by ten million illegal, inaccessible, fast-moving, *aporoi* immigrants.

Not long ago, a magnificent gold signet ring was picked up near the old Greek colony of Istria, at the mouth of the Danube. It carried the image of an unknown goddess with a diadem on her pony-tailed hair, looking at herself in a mirror, and it was engraved with the name SKYLEO.

This was one of those rare moments in archaeology when something lost and found could be traced to its owner. Scyles, or Scylos, is the man at the centre of a story told by Herodotus. This story is about a different and more ominous kind of *aporia*, about the invisible frontier between ways of life and the inaccessibility of one culture to another.

Scyles was a Scythian prince who became dazzled by the Greek city of Olbia. He became two people. Outside the city walls he was a steppe ruler who commanded a complex traditional society with its wagons and herds and rituals. But within the city walls he became a Greek. Scyles kept a Greek wife in Olbia, and on entering the gates would change his nomad dress for loose Hellenic robes. According to Herodotus, he built an elaborate palace in the town (although no such palace has been found: the private houses of Olbia, as opposed to the huge municipal buildings and temples, are modest one-story structures without much decoration).

One day, a group of Scythians contrived to peer over the walls into Olbia at the time of the festival of Dionysian mysteries. There they saw Scyles dressed in the regalia of the Dionysian order, reeling through the streets at the head of the sacred procession. To them, or rather to Herodotus reconstructing their reactions, this sight meant that Scyles had crossed an uncrossable frontier: by consenting to become a Dionysian initiate, he had betrayed Scythian identity and become a Greek. When they brought the news home, Scyles' brother assumed power in his place, and Scyles took flight. Heading south-west, he sought asylum with the Thracians who lived on the other bank of the Danube, where it formed a border with the Scythian domains. But the Scythians already held a Thracian prince as hostage, and the Thracians agreed to hand back Scyles in exchange. On the banks of the river, near Istria, Scyles was put to death by his own brother.

The golden ring pretty certainly belonged to Scyles. But it was a stray find. Whether he gave it away before his death, or whether it was wrenched off the fingers of his corpse at the time of his execution or robbed much later from his grave, is not to be known.

Scyles perished because he tried, and failed, to inhabit two separate worlds simultaneously and refused to choose between them. He might have survived if he had openly declared himself a Hellene and stayed in Olbia, or if he had led a Scythian army through the city's gates to burn and plunder it, or if he had merely absorbed Greek ideas in order to 'modernise' Scythia. In that third case, he would have been a candidate for heroic status, precisely in the sense of H. M. Chadwick's theory put forward eighty years ago in *The Heroic Age*.

Chadwick thought that the contact between a 'high civilisation' and a 'tribal' society (or between 'centre' and 'periphery') often produced a mutation in the less advanced culture. The traditional chieftain, exposed to 'increased opportunities of trade, travel and the gathering of wealth', might be tempted to escape from the restraining web of traditional custom and obligation and make himself into a new type of leader: a lawless, ruthless voyaging soldier and conqueror who mounted military expeditions with his own band of warrior-companions. Finn MacCumhal with his Fenians, or a Nordic hero with his loyal spear-gang, was for Chadwick an example of this heroic mutation at the periphery which substituted 'bonds of allegiance' for bonds of kinship and custom. And yet Scyles, offered all those 'increased opportunities' at exactly such a moment of cultural contact, displayed not the slightest impulse to take to the road as a muscular gang-leader. Chadwick's theory, taken crudely, might predict that Scyles' inner barbaric nature would hurl itself towards the new horizons opened to him in Olbia. But Scyles, shown two contrasting modes of life, wanted them both to continue as they were and to participate entirely in both of them. Scyles is a hostile witness both against ancient theories of 'barbarism' and against more modern theories about the subservience of 'peripheries' to 'centres'. He resembles, quite closely, certain Highland chieftains of late seventeenth- and eighteenth-century Scotland who lived double lives: polished gentlemen in Edinburgh and (later) London, and at the same time traditional leaders of a customary Gaelic society at home. Macleod of Raasay and 'young Coll' Maclean, encountered by Samuel Johnson and James Boswell on their Hebridean tour in 1773, seemed to have achieved this equipoise in dualism.

But the Scottish Gaeltacht was already in the early stages of dissolution, and within a few decades such a balance was becoming impossible to maintain as the traditional leaders of Highland society surrendered to the temptations and pressures of the central culture and began to exploit their dependents as a source of cash. Only half a century after Dr Johnson's tour to the Hebrides, the Clearances had begun to remove the Highland tenantry and replace them with sheep; by 1820, few clan chiefs retained a command of fluent Gaelic, and their use of Highland clothing and custom amounted to little more than fancy dress. Scythia, on the other hand, survived for nearly five hundred years after the fate of Scyles.

The tale of Scyles is very much a Black Sea story. It is not only about the encounter with the new, but also about the distance between worlds. This distance may be cultural, a frontier in the mind, or it may be physical. The point is that a person cannot be two persons at once, but by traversing such a distance between cultures becomes at the end of the journey a different person. Anthony Pagden, in his book *European Encounters with the New World*, suggests that the very length of the sea journey from Europe to the Americas, the experience of months spent in fear and privation on the enormous water-desert of the Atlantic, gave to the first Spanish colonists a sense of having moved from one universe to an entirely 'other' one in which old expectations and moralities no longer applied. The return journey could be made, eventually, but the traveller could no longer disembark at Cadiz or Barcelona as the same individual who had departed years before. Antonio de Ulloa spoke of the eighteenth-century 'Indies' as 'another world'. William of Rubruck, a monk who made his way to the centre of the Mongol-Tatar empire in the thirteenth century, thought after his first encounter with Golden Horde nomads in the Don steppe that 'I was come into a new world'.

The Greeks who reached the northern shores of the Black Sea also felt that they had crossed between worlds. They probably made the voyage by daily stages, coasting between anchorages rather than heading straight across the open sea. But the Mediterranean had not prepared them for the ferocity of Black Sea weather, for its violent offshore squalls or blizzards or winter ice, and the Sea appeared to them as a hostile void – a black hole in time and space – in contrast to the familiar Aegean with its shoals of islands. And when they arrived and struggled ashore, they found themselves perched on the edge of another sea: the steppe.

Near the modern town of Kherson, on the lower Dnieper, there is a place called Askania Nova. 'Askania' is a fanciful nineteenth-century antiquarian's term for Prussia, and here, before the Russian Revolution, an aristocratic German landowner established a nature reserve to protect for future generations an enclosure of the ancient, unexploited steppe with its herbs and grasses and birds.

He was a wise baron. Today, almost nothing whatever remains of the old Ukrainian and south Russian steppe which was the world of the Scythians and Sarmatians and of all the pastoral nomads who followed them, and which survived intact in many regions into the late nineteenth and early twentieth centuries. The Pontic Steppe, one of the formative environments of Eurasia, has been devoured by the tractor, leaving only a gigantic flatness of ploughland divided by lines of silver poplars which run beside the roads from horizon to horizon.

Even Askania Nova, the last remnant, is now in danger. Collective farms around its perimeter are putting sheep and pigs into it; a nearby canal is draining the water table; low-flying aircraft from a military base scare its creatures; there have been devastating fires. The orderly, tranquil days when a scientific staff looked after the reserve and welcomed school parties from Odessa and Kherson and Nikolaev are long gone. It is the story of Olbia over again: no more state money to pay wardens, no petrol for the coaches to bring visitors, no defence against spreading poverty and lawlessness in which each community grabs what it can.

What was the steppe like? Anton Chekhov grew up a few hundred miles from here, at Taganrog on the Sea of Azov, and as a boy he lay on his back on the wheat sacks aboard a *chumak*, an ox-drawn wagon, and sailed slowly for days and nights across this ocean. The 'ocean' image, somehow never a cliché, came to all travellers who wrote about their voyage as an obvious response to the infinite, apparently sterile and featureless horizon of coarse grassland, rising and falling a little as it approached a river, treeless and marked only by the hill-like *kurgan* burial mounds of vanished nomads. William of Rubruck remembered his journey so: 'We therefore went on towards the east, seeing nothing but heaven and earth, and sometimes the sea on our right hand . . . and the sepulchres of the Comanians [Cumans] which appeared unto us two leagues off . . . '

In the nineteenth century, Western tourists found the landscape oppressive, ugly and insulting to the progressive mind. Others, like Chekhov, were happy to be adrift in the summer steppe and to breathe in the scent of its herbs: tough, blue-green plants like thyme, rue and wormwood.

The term 'barbarian' began as an onomatopoeic Greek world about foreign language: the 'bar-bar babble' sound of an incomprehensible tongue. It occurs once in the *Iliad*, when the Carian army is described as '*barbarophonos*' – barbar-speaking. What the word signifies, whether that the Carian troops actually spoke a foreign language or that they spoke Greek with some accent or intonation that struck other Greeks of the Homeric period as grotesque and alien, is endlessly disputed. But it is fairly clear that at the time of the *Iliad* and for long afterwards the Greeks did not lump all foreigners together under the linguistic definition 'barbarians'. Still less did they use the term as a catalogue of inferior 'otherness' comprising all that the Greeks were not. Victorian scholars in the age of empire misread the *Iliad* as an account of the triumph of civilisation over 'barbarous' and morally inferior Trojans. But there is nothing remotely like that in the text of the poem, in which the Greeks are if anything more cruel and treacherous – epithets later heaped into the tray of 'barbarism' – than the Trojans.

In her book *Inventing the Barbarian*, Edith Hall argues that the great change came at the time of the Persian Wars. 'The story of the invention of the barbarian is the story of the Greeks' conflict with the Persians.' Before then, there had certainly been an 'other': the magical and monstrous half-humans and creatures supposed to inhabit the fringes of the world, like Cyclops or the harpies in the *Odyssey*, the sirens and one-eyed Arimaspians. But in the fifth century BC Athens, above all the Athenian tragedians, constructed a single barbarian world, squeezing peoples as distinct as Scythian nomads and Mesopotamian city-dwellers into a single new species, and opposed it to the image of a single and united Hellenic world. All that the Athenian ideology found alien and repulsive was now transferred from the 'monster' to the 'barbarian'. The 'other' was moved inwards from the unknown periphery of the world to the frontiers of Greekness, to the other shore of the Black Sea or the Aegean. And from this new species were born other oppositions. It was not only the Scythian whose *aporia* was barbaric in contrast to Greek autochthony and settledness. It was the Persian or Asian whose servility, luxuriousness and cowardice were barbaric in contrast to Greek and European qualities of freedom, self-restraint and valour. The first-born twins Civilisation and Barbarism were soon joined by an equally long-lived brother: the discourse of Orientalism.

The Athenian tragedies were performed at the City Dionysia. By the end of the Persian Wars, this old popular festival had expanded into a grand propaganda occasion designed to legitimise Athens and its policies – including the democratic constitution, with which the Athenians now identified themselves against Persian 'tyranny' which threatened them with extinction. The *Persae* of Aeschylus was first staged at the Dionysia in 472 BC, only eight years after the Athenian victory at Salamis. But *Persae* already assumed, as if it were common knowledge, what Edith Hall calls 'the absolute polarisation' of Hellene and barbarian (the word 'barbarian' is used ten times in the text). Hall extracts from the *Persae* a long list of barbarous characteristics. Barbarians were cruel, simple-minded, undisciplined and subject to panic. They had an excessive taste for luxury and ultra-refinement. They gave unrestrained expression to their emotions. They wallowed in *ploutos* (gross and unimaginable riches), as opposed to the *olbos* (respectable wealth) which had given Olbia its name. They swung between boastfulness and cowardice. They gave power to women – sometimes even military command or the leadership of the nation.

This last point obsessed and fascinated the Greeks. In the fifth-century world, their society was unique in its exclusive, nervous maleness, but this Greek exception was transmitted and transformed into the rule for the centralised imperial societies which were to follow. The identification of 'civilisation' with a totally male-dominated society was adopted by the Roman Empire, together with its corollary that political authority for women was a sure mark of barbarism. It was only to be expected that savages like the Iceni in Britain would choose Boudicca to lead their rebellion against Roman occupation, or that Gaulish women with 'huge white arms' – as Ammianus Marcellinus wrote in the fourth century AD – would pitch in to save their husbands in a brawl. From the Roman Empire, the tradition of male authority flowed into the Roman Catholic Church, uniting with the Judaic pattern of patriarchy. In the Church of England today, the addled dregs of a classical education lie at the bottom of the deepest resentments against the admission of women to the priesthood: a woman at the altar is 'uncivilised'.

The final item which Edith Hall dredges from the subtext of the *Persae* is political. Greek citizens were free. Barbarians (in this case Persians) were not, and imposed despotism and unfreedom wherever they went. An Athenian citizen enjoyed several kinds of equality under the constitution of the *polis*, and took part in a continuous limitation of state power. Barbarians and their conquered subjects had to humiliate themselves, by the physical act of prostration, before a royal power which was arbitrary and unlimited. The Chorus in the *Persae*, after hearing the news of the Persian defeat at Salamis, proclaims: 'Not for long now [will the conquered] pay tribute and perform prostration . . . Men will no longer curb their tongues, for the people, unbridled, can chatter freely.'

Over the next few years, this 'discourse of barbarism' begun by Aeschylus was carried on enthusiastically by other playwrights. There were obvious problems involved in this cramming of blatantly different peoples into a single 'barbarian' category. Athens was full of foreign slaves, especially Thracians and Scythians, and their unlikeness to each other was evident to every slave-owner. Logically, it was even more difficult to put them in one category with Persians, whose literate, highly organised, urban culture should have put them closer to Greeks than to Scythians. These difficulties were overcome by emphasising the only feature which these foreigners did have in common: their non-Greekness. The Scythians and other northern peoples, for example, were supposed to be wild, hardy and ferocious, while the Persians were perceived as effeminate and undermined by easy living. Never mind! By swerving between two extremes, barbarians were only showing how far away they were from the Greek ideal of *mesotēs* (measuredness), or from the Greek ethic of nothing-in-excess.

A more serious difficulty was the past of the Greeks themselves. In their own history, mythical or more recent, the Greeks had done everything they now deplored as 'barbaric'. Heroes and kings (and the Greeks could not deny that they had once been ruled by kings rather than democracies or oligarchies) had committed every kind of sexual excess, mutilation and sadistic murder, revelling in spontaneous emotion and showing no sense of *mesotēs* whatever.

One ingenious response was to export this criminal history overseas. For example, Euripides presented Medea to his theatre audiences as the paradigm of barbarian womanhood: domineering, uncontrollably passionate, murderess of her own brother and then of her own children, a witch skilled in the magical preparation of herbs. But Edith Hall shows that Medea entered earlier mythology as a Greek, probably that Agamede in the *Iliad* who was a daughter of the sun and knew 'all the drugs ... which the wide earth nourishes'. Euripides relocated her origins in Colchis, at the south-eastern corner of the Black Sea: 'her conversion into a barbarian was almost certainly an invention of tragedy, probably of Euripides himself.' Tereus was a hero of Megara, on the isthmus of Corinth, until Sophocles (in a lost play) exported him to Thrace to become a barbarian king who raped his wife's sister, cut out her tongue and ate his own son. Euripides seems to have invented many of his barbarian characters in order to display cruelty, mendacity or the propensity to butcher one's closest relations as non-Greek traits, and Hall suggests that he devised the central plot of *Iphigenia in Tauris* — her captivity as priestess to the savage Taurians, on the southernmost sea-cliff of Crimea — around the idea that only barbarians would make a cult of murdering shipwrecked strangers by hurling them over a precipice. This, too, was a shameless imposition of 'political correctness' upon Greek mythology, which abounded with tales of Greeks performing human sacrifices on one another.

But not all Greek 'barbarism' could be exported, and it was also necessary to invent barbarous or 'oriental' origins for traditions which did not fit the new self-image. The cult of Dionysus, which Scyles joined in Olbia, had frenzied, orgiastic mystery-festivals for which the tragedians suggested foreign origins in Thrace or Asia – although the cult had ancient roots in Greece and was central to the state religion of Athens itself. Sadistic cruelty was now presented as a Thracian infection, excessive luxury as a disease floating in from Asia. Aeschylus does not pretend that Clytemnestra was a barbarian immigrant, but before she murders her husband Agamemnon – presented as an un-Greek weakling who can't keep a woman in her place – she is given speeches stuffed with deliberately ornate, servile and 'oriental' language. As Hall says, 'femaleness, barbarism, luxury and hubris are . . . ineluctably drawn into the same semantic complex.'

The Trojans too were called in for ideological reprocessing. The war against Troy had to be re-cast as a first round in the cosmic struggle between 'European' virtue and 'Asian' vice, the perpetual war between the two halves of humanity which was now being renewed in the struggle between Greeks and Persians. The image of the Trojans, once brave enemies whose 'manliness' did credit to their Greek opponents, began to be orientalised. They became subtly 'Asian', emotional to an unseemly degree, alien: such conquered, un-Hellenic Trojans were carved into the metopes of the Parthenon in about 435 BC. The Roman and Byzantine imperial cultures inherited this perception of the Trojan War and this reading of the *Iliad* as the earliest literature on the struggle between civilisation and barbarism. It was an interpretation which was to survive virtually unchallenged for a thousand years.

Autopsy, when the Greeks invented the word, meant seeing for oneself. It is a word about individualism and independence of mind, about the right to make up one's own mind on the basis of what one's own eyes have seen. By the late Middle Ages, autopsy was at war with authority – with the version of the natural world and its geography laid down for all time in the corpus of surviving Graeco-Roman literature. For authoritarians, all further enquiry could only amount to *scholia*: mere annotation and exegesis of this existing body of knowledge. But, for the autopsist, enquiry by voyage or discovery or reasoning might reveal entirely new facts, new worlds unknown to the ancients.

To persuade readers to conceive of something completely unfamiliar, the persuader had to use narrative and to carry that narrative upon the first person: 'I saw', 'I heard', 'I experienced for myself'. When Bartolomé de las Casas began his *Historia de las Indias* in 1527, he declared that he was writing 'out of the very great and final need to make known to all Spain the true account and truthful understanding of what I have seen take place in this Indian Ocean', and he told a minister of the emperor Charles V that he was 'the oldest of those who went over to the Indies, and in the many years that I have been there and in which I have seen with my own eyes, I have not read histories which could be lies, but instead I have experienced.' Pagden quotes the Jesuit historian José de Acosta who went to the Americas and 'on finding himself cold at midday yet with the tropical sun directly overhead – an impossible situation according to ancient meteorology – he "laughed and made fun of Aristotle and his philosophy" '.

In the classical world itself, autopsy-narrative was not unknown, but it was rare. The word *histor* first meant an eyewitness, especially in a trial, and when Herodotus chose the title *Histories* for his work, it carried the implication of 'enquiries', the personal conclusions of an investigator. Yet Herodotus only occasionally descends to declaring that he saw something for himself, and then usually to make clear that the rest of what he has to say is rumour or the unconfirmed product of *historeion* (enquiry). Greek and Roman historians constantly produced 'pseudo-autopsy', in set-piece battle scenes or reconstructed deathbed speeches which were pastiches of genuine first-hand narrative. Julius Caesar planned and led the conquest of Gaul which he describes in *The Gallic War*. But he not only distances his narrator into the third person ('Caesar'), but actually offers artificial reconstructions of events – battles and speeches indeed – of which he must have had vivid and direct memory.

Nobody disputed the value of the eye as the most senior and formidable of all witnesses. But that witness appeared only in court, or very occasionally to settle a dispute about geographic or natural fact. Elsewhere, 'I saw' had a faintly disreputable air about it, less acceptable than 'I believe' or 'I know'. This leads to an apparent reticence, or lack of curiosity, in Greek or Roman writers who could have told us something enormously interesting which they must have seen for themselves, but chose not to.

The poet Ovid is particularly maddening. In the year 8 AD, when he was just over fifty, Ovid was banished from Rome by the emperor Augustus and sent to live at Tomi, now the Romanian port of Constanţa on the Black Sea. Here he spent the rest of his life, a clever, observant man who continued to write fluently and at length. Tomi was an old Greek colony in the country of the Getae, a Thracian people who had lived for many centuries around the delta of the Danube. Ovid met them every day, in the streets and in the countryside outside the walls, and the circumstantial evidence that he had Getic friends is very strong.

He reveals in one poem that he had learned the language well enough not only to write verses in it but to read and discuss them with a circle of Getae ('All moved their heads and their full quivers, and there was a long murmur on the lips of the Getae'). This suggests an intimacy which Ovid was not prepared to acknowledge to his readers. Instead, he disguises the occasion as a half-comic casting of pearls before swine, a Roman holding a poetry-reading for gaping barbarians. About that Getic language, about what the Getae wore or ate or believed or sang, the thousand upon thousand of lines of the *Tristia* and *Ex Ponto* say practically nothing whatever. They say even less about Tomi itself and about Ovid's life there, except to describe it as a hell of snow, wind and barbarians.

Many readers find the *Tristia* absurd, a wail of self-pity and self-obsession. Konstantin Paustovsky, living in Odessa in 1921, 'could never understand why the Black Sea had struck [Ovid] as gloomy. I had always thought of it as one of the brightest and gayest of seas. And how could anyone speak of Scythian cold in a region where it doesn't even snow every winter, and when the snow does come it stays only a few days and leaves the thawed-out earth smelling faintly of spring?'

But there is much more to the *Tristia* than complaint. Even if Ovid's life there cannot have been the uninterrupted misery he proclaimed, everything he wrote from Tomi was a plea for remission of sentence, a lamentation designed to arouse the pity of Augustus and the circle of his favourites. Autopsy about the strange place and its peoples would have struck the wrong note, suggesting that he was finding consolations and stimulations in Tomi.

Probably he was, but *Tristia* is written deliberately from within the consciousness of a Roman living in Rome, ventriloquising as feigned experience all the horrors and discomforts which a cultivated Roman reader would imagine to accompany 'life among the barbarians'.

When Ovid does write directly and candidly about what happened to him, he is writing about Rome and his own disaster there. He was banished partly for *Ars Amatoria*, which Augustus found immoral, and partly for failing to distance himself from some unknown sexual intrigue involving a woman of the imperial family. In the first book of *Tristia*, he remembers the last, long, sleepless night at home, the bewilderment about what clothes or luggage to take with him in the morning, his wife in tears, the stricken household slaves standing about. It was this passage which Osip Mandelstam had in mind when he wrote his own marvellous 'Tristia' in 1920. At one level, Mandelstam seems to be anticipating his own end in the Soviet Tomi of Stalin's labour camps. There the voice is Ovidian and mourning. But then secret joy, un-Latin, unexplainable, begins to rise up like dawn mist from the ground of the poem as if a forced parting were also a rebirth into an unknown land:

I have studied the science of saying goodbye
in bareheaded laments at night.
Oxen chew, and the waiting stretches out,
it is the last hour of my keeping watch in the city,
and I respect the ritual of the cock-loud night,
when, lifting their load of sorrow for the journey,
eyes red from weeping have peered into the distance,
and the crying of women mingled with the Muses' singing . . .
Who can know when he hears the word goodbye
what kind of separation lies before us . . . ?

The site of Olbia is 200 kilometres east of Odessa, a journey across gloomy flatness with nothing to look at until the road ends, the car stops, and you step out into a fresh south-east wind coming off the water. It looks like the sea, but it smells like a pond. This is the *liman*, or estuary-lagoon, of the Bug River, where it joins the estuary of the Dnieper and then flows into the sea. This is fresh water, where pike-perch thrive, which becomes brackish only when southerly gales stack up the river-flow and drive salt water upstream as far as the Olbia ruins. But the rivers are so huge that their far shores are no more than dim lines drawn on the horizon with charcoal.

Olbia began in the early sixth century BC, perhaps even in the seventh century. It was a colony founded by adventurers from Miletus in the Aegean, who had already set up an advance base on the island of Berezan a few miles offshore to the west. The Milesian colony grew into a flourishing city with walls and impressive square towers, at first a trading post and harbour dealing mostly in fish and then, as the grain trade developed, the capital of a farming region whose Scythian suppliers might live as far as two hundred miles away or more. At its height, in about the fourth century BC, Olbia might have had thirty or forty thousand people living inside its walls. But nearly as many must have lived in the *chora*, the inner hinterland of the *polis*. Olbia's *chora* developed into a densely settled network of wheatfields and villages covering the whole shore of the peninsula between the estuaries of the Bug and the Dnieper.

Decline set in during the third century BC. The Scythian people were destabilised by the growing pressure of the Sarmatians, another nomadic Indo-Iranian group migrating westwards out of the steppe between the Volga and Don rivers, and Scythian authority began to break up. The city was raided and the grain supply became erratic. In the second century BC one of the Scythian groups took control of Olbia, probably hoping to restore the export trade which had brought such wealth to the whole north-west shore of the Black Sea. But it was unable to prevent the disaster of 63 BC, when an army of Dacians and Getae came up from the Danube delta, captured Olbia and destroyed the city. The population fell to a mere 2,000–3,000 for the next few decades. Roman occupation a hundred years later made the city once more safe to live in, and there was considerable rebuilding, but Olbia never fully recovered from the Getan storm. It was wrecked again, probably by Goths, in the third century AD, and then – finally – by Huns in about 370. After that, the ruins were abandoned to the grass and the sea-birds.

There is not a lot to see at Olbia. Stone-robbers carted off almost everything which stuck out of the ground except for two huge burial mounds, the 'Zeus Kurgan' and the tomb dedicated to

Eurisia and Arete – two unknown Olbian grandees. These are earth barrows covering majestic stone burial chambers of the second century AD, approached by stone-panelled *dromoi* (tunnels). But little of this can be inspected because the mounds are kept locked up, their *dromoi* blocked by decayed shed doors. The tombs, with hens pecking and hopping about their flanks, look more like potato clamps or abandoned air-raid shelters.

As one walks across the site, a great triangle of unkempt foundations bounded on the east by red-earth cliffs above the Bug estuary, it is hard to realise that this is one of the places where Russian archaeology was born and grew up. But to have dug at Olbia, to have confronted its symbiosis of Greeks, Thracians and Scythians and to have contributed fearlessly to understanding it, is one of the proudest battle honours in the profession.

Engineer-General Suchtelev started exploring the Olbian ruins in 1790, at a time when they were still officially within the Ottoman Empire. In 1839, Mikhail Vorontsov, the grandest and most ambitious of all the governors-general of New Russia, sponsored the establishment of the Imperial Odessa Society of History and Antiquity, the first archaeological society in Russia, which took over excavation at Olbia. It was the Odessa Society which brought in the true father and mother of scientific archaeology in Russia, Count Alexei Uvarov and Countess Uvarova, who gave much of their lives to Olbia. Uvarov, born in 1828, had founded the Imperial Russian Archaeological Society in Moscow, which at once became a deadly rival of the other Imperial Archaeological Society established under the eye of the tsar's court in St Petersburg.

When Uvarov died in 1884, his widow, the Countess, took over the chair of the Moscow society, which she had helped to set up. She carried on the struggle against St Petersburg until the 1917 Revolution, when she went into exile, but by then the Olbia site was in new and safe hands. Boris Farmakovsky, calm and systematic, excavated at Olbia every season from 1902 to 1914 and then, after war and revolution had subsided, from 1924 to 1928. He left behind him a series of meticulous and handsomely illustrated excavation reports which contain most of what is known about the 'material culture' of Olbia.

But the evidence about Olbia is not just 'material'. There is also autopsy. The Stoic philosopher Dio Chrysostom came here in about 95 AD, and this was one of the rare occasions on which a Greek or

Latin observer wrote down, fluently and informally and in great detail, what he saw and what he heard. 'Borysthenitica' is a philosophy lecture, based on Dio's visit to Olbia, which he delivered in his home city of Prusa in Asia Minor. But it is also an extraordinary piece of cinema, a reel or two of actuality shot two thousand years ago, a home movie preserved from the Hellenistic world.

Dio came to Olbia (or 'Borysthenes', as he called it, which was also the word the Greeks used for the Dnieper River) at a bad time. After the Getae had destroyed the place in 63 BC, 'the Greeks had stopped sailing to Borysthenes, inasmuch as they had no people of common speech to receive them, and the Scythians themselves had neither the ambition nor the knowledge to equip a trading-station of their own after the Greek manner.' In time, the Scythians returned to the gutted streets beside the Bug and invited Greeks to come back and reopen the port. But by the year of Dio's arrival, well over a century later, 'evidence of the destruction of Borysthenes [was still] visible both in the sorry nature of its buildings and in the contraction of the city . . . ' The citizens had retreated to the apex of Olbia's triangular lay-out, walling off a much smaller triangle with a row of houses and a low defensive rampart (all of which has been turned up just as Dio describes it, by excavation). The rest of the city had been left to fall apart, and some of the old towers which had formed part of the town wall now rose so far away in the distance that, as Dio put it, 'you would not surmise that they once belonged to a single city'.

Olbia had not lost contact with the Graeco-Roman world across the Black Sea, but its inhabitants had an aggrieved feeling that their city had lost the fame and importance of its good old days. The traders and visitors who bothered to sail into the estuaries were pretty third-rate characters compared to their predecessors. 'Those who come here,' one citizen complained to Dio, 'are nominally Greeks but actually more barbarous than ourselves, traders and marketmen, fellows who import cheap rags and vile wine and export in exchange goods of no better quality. But you would appear to have been sent to us by Achilles himself from his holy isle, and we are very glad to see you and very glad also to listen to whatever you have to say.'

This was a ghost town, with ghosts living in it. Dio Chrysostom found himself in a time warp. The Olbians were determined to impress him with their Greekness, but it was an utterly archaic and obsolete version of Greekness to which they clung. In addition, they seemed to Dio to be as much Scythian as Hellenic. His definition of ethnicity had nothing to do with genetics and descent but – like that of Herodotus – a great deal to do with clothes and customs and language. The Olbians wore Scythian clothes, as often as not, and the Greek they spoke was terrible.

Dio went for a walk down to the point where the Bug and Dneiper come together. On his way back, he met a handsome lad on horseback called Callistratus and started a conversation. Callistratus was a real museum piece. He was wearing 'barbarian' trousers and a cape, but on seeing Dio he hopped off his horse and covered his arms, observing the old Greek rule that it was bad manners to show bare arms in public. Like the other Olbians, he turned out to know Homer by heart and to be immensely proud of it, however poor his spoken Greek was. But Dio was even more fascinated to discover that Callistratus was gay.

At the age of eighteen, he was already famous in the city for his courage in battle, for his interest in philosophy and for his beauty, 'and he had many lovers'. Dio read this not as some fact about sexual orientation, but as a wonderful survival from a lost age. Here, in the time of the Roman Empire, flourished still the ancient Greek veneration for homosexual love as the supreme intellectual and spiritual experience. The Olbians supposed that in the world beyond the sea homosexuality was still the height of fashion. Dio, touched and amused, wondered what would happen if they started converting barbarians to this view of love. 'No good end', he thought. The Scythians would fail to keep 'licentiousness' out of it, and would miss the point.

By now a small crowd of citizens had gathered round Dio and Callistratus. Dio suggested that they could all talk more easily if they went back inside the walls. Olbia was being raided almost daily by small Scythian war-parties, who had murdered or abducted several sentries on outpost duty only the day before. Dio, who had a normal sense of self-preservation, had noticed not only that the gates were being shut but that the alarm-flag had been hoisted on the battlements.

But the Olbians seemed indifferent to danger, and wanted to start a philosophical discourse with their guest on the spot. 'Admiring their earnestness, I said: "If it please you, shall we go and sit down somewhere within the city? For perchance at present not all can hear equally well what is said as we stroll . . . " '

In they went, and in the old Greek manner they all sat down outside the portico of the Temple of Zeus to hold their debate. As the older men settled on their benches, Dio noticed that almost everyone still wore a beard, at a time when shaving had been the fashion in the Roman world for at least a century. One clean-shaven man in the audience 'was subjected to the ridicule and resentment of them all . . . it was said that he practised shaving not as an idle fancy, but out of flattery for the Romans'.

Dio Chrysostom started off on a discourse about the 'good *polis*' and its inadequacy in comparison to divine paradigms of perfection. But he was interrupted by an old man called Hieroson (possibly a descendant of that Heroson ship-owning family who had been so big in Olbia in the third century BC). The old man, who said proudly that he could read Plato, asked Dio not to talk about 'mortal cities', a subject which could wait, but to concentrate on 'that divine city or government . . . stating where it is and what it is like, aiming most closely at Plato's nobility of expression'. He and his friends, said Hieroson, were tremendously excited and worked up in anticipation of hearing something really elevated and Platonic.

So Dio gallantly changed course. The result, the 'Thirty-Sixth Discourse (Borysthenitica)', is an astonishing prose-poem about the myth of the Chariot of Zeus, about the parables of the Zoroastrian Magi, about the celestial harmony of the stars and the creation of the world by a sexual act between Zeus and Hera – the *hieros gamos* or sacred mating. (Was it from Dio Chrysostom that Symeon the New Theologian derived his own version of *unio mystica*, a sacred sexual act in which God impregnates his Elect with 'the sperm of blessing / in the wedding-rite divine'?)

It is a beautiful, baffling piece of work. It is also an eclectic patchwork of cults. For his Olbians, Dio brought in not only the Greek pantheon but his own impressions of Persian mysticism and allegory, and in his creation account there is a strong flavour of Judaism ('the Creator and Father of the World, beholding the work of his hands, was not merely pleased . . . he rejoiced . . . he revealed the existent universe as once more a thing of beauty and inconceivable loveliness'). Somewhere at the core, buried under all this, were the original Stoic doctrines about a universe made of four concentric spheres: earth, water, air and fire.

You can still stand where Dio spoke. The space between the foundations of the Temple of Zeus and the back wall of the colonnaded stoa – the long shed-like building open on one side which served a Greek *polis* as weather shelter or meeting-place – is not as big as he suggests. But it is large enough for a few dozen interested people to gather round a lecturer. This old town centre around the agora (marketplace) was outside the makeshift wall drawn around the remaining living quarters, and the temples must have been already half-ruined when Dio stood there. He remembered from Olbia that 'not a single statue remains undamaged amongst those that are in the sanctuaries, one and all having suffered mutilation'.

Dio's picture of Olbia is a picture of periphery as perceived from the centre. Malcolm Chapman, in his book *The Celts: The Construction of a Myth*, shows how customs, fashions and artefacts travel outwards from a centre like rings on a pond until they reach the periphery and finally vanish. It is just before this moment of final disappearance that the 'central' intellectual suddenly bursts into lament: out there, they still have sound values, nurturing families, organic oatmeal, authentic folk music – which must be preserved at all costs before they disappear for ever.

Once, Homeric Greeks in the Aegean had worn beards and shaggy Athenian philosophers had approved the love of man for boy. The concentric waves sent out by these things were still breaking on the shores of the Bug *liman* many centuries after the razor had conquered Athens and poets had started writing erotic fantasies about girls. Dio was touched by the 'real Greekness' which he found surviving at Olbia. At the same time, he was an unromantic person, not a nostalgic metropolitan intellectual in Chapman's sense. It might be true that Athenians had once lived much as the Olbians now lived, but Dio had no wish to reverse history. He liked the present, and was doing well out of it.

In his own way, Dio Chrysostom was also in the archaism business. He was a Greek trader whose trade was Greekness. His line was to play on the Roman inferiority complex by posing as the voice of ancient Greek wisdom and discrimination. As a Stoic preacher, Dio made big Romans feel coarse and clumsy, a feeling they evidently appreciated. He climbed high in Rome, knowing several emperors personally, but he spent much of his life on the road as a prestigious travelling lecturer. His message was 'virtue' and 'philanthropy', conveyed to a parvenu world whose ruling classes were in the grip of a gigantic wealth boom. In reality, Dio was as much a creature of that boom as the audiences he rebuked for their materialism. In his home territory of Bithynia (in north-west Asia Minor), Dio was a businessman who did well out of property deals. As an old man, long after his visit to Olbia, he was taken to court by the younger Pliny, the emperor Trajan's commissioner in Bithynia, over corrupt tendering for a public-works contract.

Olbia had been abandoned for more than a thousand years when a new port-city was founded on the Black Sea coast, a full day's sailing to the west. In 1792, the Turkish fort at Hadji Bey was conquered for the empress Catherine by General Don Joseph de Ribas. It stood on high red bluffs over a bay with deep water inshore. De Ribas thought this was a good site for a new port. The idea was to name it Odessos, after a Greek colony which had stood further down the coast. Catherine, who admired the Greeks, initially agreed. But then, at a court ball in 1795, she suddenly announced that this city which had been founded by a woman was going to have a feminine gender. So Odessa began.

The main strolling street, where Odessan families with ice-creams inspect goods they cannot afford, is named Deribasov-skaya after de Ribas. One morning I was taking photographs of the old Lycée Richelieu on Deribasovskaya when I was picked up by a sea-captain and his first mate. Their ship had no fuel to put to sea. Bored to death by a daily routine of window-shopping, watching television and getting on their wives' nerves, they wanted diversion. We went to a standup bar to have a 'party': a bottle of vodka, Odessa hot-dogs tasting of horse rather than dog, coffee 'made from popcorn'.

The captain, who had been stranded ashore for nine months, shrugged when I asked him what he thought about Ukraine's new-found independence as a sovereign state. 'We have no history. Only Party history. Anyway, this place is lawless now and nobody is ruling it – not Ukrainians, not Soviets, nobody.'

Drunk, I wandered down the street to revisit the Museum of Archaeology and came to a halt in front of a big photograph of Boris Farmakovsky which commands one wall of the Olbian room. There he sat: calm, benign in his old stick-up celluloid collar, his eyes narrow and crow's-footed by so many seasons of standing in the east wind off the Bug *liman*. Farmakovsky, whom even the austere émigré Mikhail Miller had allowed to be 'a good methodologist', had died just in time. Only two years later, men came in the night with guns for his old friends and colleagues, for the young men and women who had crouched and toiled for him in the Olbia excavations, for his brightest pupils who had tried to understand in new ways the encounter of Greek, Scythian and Thracian.

Why did it happen? Millions perished in the purges of the 1930s, but why this particular small profession – why this black hurricane which exploded over the men and women who led Russian and Ukrainian archaeology, blew them into oblivion and then, only four years later, died down as suddenly as it had arisen? Sir Mortimer Wheeler, the Nestor of British archaeologists in the 1960s, used to say that archaeology was not a profession but a vendetta. His colleagues laughed indulgently, but he was serious.

Soviet archaeology became in two senses a vendetta. In the first place, the disaster of 1930–4 amounted to the assassination of the profession's leadership by a dogmatic, Stalinist minority. Miller remembered how university lectures were broken up by Komsomol students shouting: 'Take off the mask!', or 'What is your attitude to Marxism?' Behind the students came a handful of ambitious older archaeologists who switched to the Party line, denounced their colleagues and inherited their jobs. The ideology adopted by the new Soviet archaeology was 'Marrism', a curious, pseudo-Marxist farrago of linguistic and archaeological doctrine developed by Nikolai Yakovlevich Marr, son of a Scottish immigrant and a Georgian mother, who had been a professor at St Petersburg before the Revolution. Marr introduced the notion of autochthony, the weird proposition that changes in language and culture were never the result of new inward migrations but were instead the products of class chemistry working slow transformations in essentially static societies. In the name of Marrism Professor Vladislav Ravdonikas (to take one example) denounced and destroyed the career of his younger rival Sergei Kiselev. In 1950, twenty years later, Stalin suddenly proclaimed that Marrism was arrant nonsense, and it was the turn of Kiselev to destroy the ancient Ravdonikas in equally murderous terms of Party abuse.

But there exists another, always latent vendetta between all authoritarian nation-states and independent men and women who investigate the past. Archaeology tunnels into the deep foundations on which the arrogance of civilisations and revolutions rests. When the tunnellers enter foundations which should be rock but are merely sand, the floors of the state apartments high above them begin to tremble. Had Farmakovsky and his pupils burrowed their way into a zone of secret weakness, and was that why so many archaeologists had to die?

All knowledge about the Scythians, as it accumulates, has undermined the proposition that the peoples of the Black Sea steppe were primitive and barbarous, and the conclusion that nomadism was a backward form of existence. That conclusion – so central to old-fashioned Russian nationalism – was raised to the level of geopolitics by Germans like J. G. Kohl, who wrote in 1841 that 'from time immemorial down to the present day, [the steppes] have been the dwelling-place of savage nomads and barbaric hordes in whom no independent seed bearing the idea of the state, the building of towns or cultural development ever took place'. His compatriot Roesler thought that the very landscape was reactionary: 'such desolate surroundings, where the wandering imagination finds no point of rest on the shifting horizons and the memory no place whereby it can orient itself'.

Out of this kind of stuff developed the popular assumption – still widespread in Europe – that settled agriculture and the existence of a crop-sowing peasantry represented a huge forward development from an earlier stage of nomadism. Here pseudo-anthropology feeds the basic European nightmare: a terror of peoples who move. This nightmare, inherited from the great migrations during and after the decline of the Roman Empire and renewed by the Hun and Mongol raids into the West, was given an extra dimension of horror by nineteenth-century evolutionist intellectuals. The moving peoples were no longer a merely physical menace emerging from the trackless East. They now also seemed to incarnate a cosmic disorder in which the past rose out of its tomb and swarmed forward on horseback to annihilate the present.

That nightmare survives in the new Europe after the revolutions of 1989. It survives as Western fear of all travelling people, of the millions pressing against Europe's gates as 'asylum-seekers' or 'economic migrants', of a social collapse in Russia which would send half the population streaming hungrily towards Germany.

But nomadic pastoralism was not a 'primitive' condition. It was, on the contrary, a specialisation which developed out of settled agricultural communities. To move large herds of domesticated animals hundreds of miles twice a year, north into summer pastures and south again in winter, requires, above all, horses and high skill at riding them. It requires the wheel, if the population is to migrate with its herds by cart or wagon. This way of life needs many kinds of craftsman or specialist, far more than family subsistence farming. And it cannot be carried on without a central leadership able to take rapid and effective decisions in emergency. That emergency could be economic – a traditional pasture destroyed by drought or flooding – or it could be military. The power to ride a horse created armed élites, who were now able to lead their followers out to plunder farming communities or to migrate and conquer distant regions of grassland.

As Herodotus knew, 'pure' nomadism is a rarity. Recording the various 'tribes' or nations of the Scythian culture, he pointed out that many of them were farmers as well as pastoralists. Some ate what they grew; others cultivated grain for the Greek market. And the Scythians were in no way exceptional; that sort of flexibility has always belonged to the economy of mobile steppe peoples. The vision of mounted hordes living off meat and plundered food-stocks belongs only to times of war or of decisive long-range migration – as opposed to the normal circular journeyings after pasture.

Pastoral nomads, even when they do not settle, can and do raise crops. In the fifteenth century, the friar and merchant Giosafat Barbaro lived for many years in the Venetian colony of Tana, on the Don estuary at the head of the Sea of Azov. He used to watch Tatars from the Golden Horde being sent out each March to plant wheat in patches of fertile soil. When the wheat was ripe, the Horde would pass by and reap it from the open steppe on its seasonal journey northwards to the summer grazing.

And Herodotus, a millennium before, had pointed out that, by his time, there were 'natives' who lived in towns. He described neighbours of the Scythians called Budini, who 'have a city built of wood, named Gelonus'. The Budini were nomads, but the Geloni who lived around the city were – according to Herodotus – farmers descended from Greek colonists. His description of their countryside, with its forests and marshes, makes it sound like the middle Dnieper territory. And in recent years, archaeologists have begun to find town-like sites there: fortified enclosures around large settlements with granaries, potteries, smithies for ironwork and permanent cemeteries outside the walls. One of the most spectacular is at Belsk, on a tributary of the Dnieper, whose ramparts are nearly twenty-one miles in circumference. Belsk, which is claimed to be the biggest inhabited earthwork ever discovered on earth, might plausibly be the 'Gelonus' of Herodotus. A workshop has been found there which manufactured drinking-cups out of human skulls – a custom which Herodotus described in great ethnographic detail.

He has turned out to be right about many things. Especially in our own deconstructive times, new historians contrive to shrivel old historians until their information (and conveying information was the only purpose of all their arduous researching and writing) is practically discounted, if not discarded. All that is held interesting about their work is its discourse, the subconscious patterning of its information to establish certain contrasts and 'oppositions' required by the society in which the historian operated. Herodotus has his discourse too. Hartog has identified it brilliantly enough, in a book which will always be read wherever texts on 'barbarism' and 'civilisation' come under study. But when Hartog declines to examine the quality of Herodotus as reporter, to test against archaeological evidence the verifiable rightness or wrongness of the *Histories*' 'enquiry', he achieves an almost perverse feat of intellectual asceticism. For the extraordinary quality of Herodotus is that his information grows in importance from year to year as archaeology confirms it.

Since the first *kurgans* were excavated nearly two hundred years ago, it has been known that Herodotus was roughly right in his account of Scythian royal burial customs, with their human sacrifices and their concentric rings of slaughtered horses. He was correct, too, about the existence of wooden 'towns' on the fringes of the forest steppe. But Herodotus, the 'old liar' of Victorian classrooms, reached his peak of posthumous triumph in the 1950s when excavations were carried out in the burial mounds of Pazyryk in the Altai Mountains, thousands of miles inland from the Black Sea steppe, on the eastern edge of the Scythian realms.

Pazyryk turned out to be the fulfilment of an archaeologist's fantasy: the past in a deep-freeze. It is high enough and cold enough to have preserved its dead and their possessions in the permafrost.

The skin of one nomad ruler was still illuminated like a manuscript with dense patterns of lamp-black tattooing – stylised gryphons and ibex and catfish, probably an individual pictogram about his lineage, territory and cult. He and the other dead men and women lay among dazzling, many-coloured saddle-cloths, an unsuspected art form whose representations of horses in turn revealed a whole culture of decorative mane-dressing and fantastic crested horse-masks. The bodies had been stuffed with many of the herbs recorded by Herodotus in his account of Scythian burial rituals: 'cut marsh-plants and frankincense and parsley and anise seed'.

In the corner of one tomb lay a fur bag containing cannabis. With it were bronze cauldrons filled with stones, and the frame of a tiny, four-foot-high inhalation tent.

> After the burial . . . they set up three poles leaning together to a point and cover them with woollen mats . . . they make a pit in the centre beneath the poles and throw red-hot stones into it . . . [they] take the seed of the hemp and creeping under the mats they throw it on the red-hot stones, and being thrown, it smoulders and sends forth so much steam that no Greek vapour-bath could surpass it. The Scythians howl in their joy at the vapour-bath . . .

Those sentences, about the importance of cannabis as a Scythian consolation and delight, had to wait two and a half millennia to be confirmed.

The Black Sea has eaten into the old Greek coastal cities. The colony of Tyras, under the walls of the huge Turkish fortress of Akerman, is now partly under the waters of the Dniester *liman*. As much as a third of Olbia lies under the Bug estuary, visited every summer by an enthusiastic Italian sub-aqua club which collects amphoras from the muddy bottom. Chersonesus, sticking out into the open sea at Sevastopol, has lost its southern suburbs by drowning, and Gorgippia, now the handsome *port de plaisance* of Anapa on the Kuban coast, attracts Russian divers searching for Greek columns in the yacht anchorage. Of all the archaeological sites I visited along that northern shore, only Tanais on the lower Don – at the head of the Sea of Azov – was complete under the ground. Here, the main channel of the river had moved several miles across the delta and left the port and colony inland.

The Greeks, as colonists, stayed on this crumbling edge, the physical periphery of a Scythian-Sarmatian world. That world famously had no 'centre' of its own, unless it was the Scythian royal tombs. But the Greeks, for all the cultural allure of the jewellery and decorated pottery and wine which they had to sell, remained guests rather than dominators. Along the coast, they balanced – often precariously. The Scythians, in turn, were occasionally enemies but for most of the time hosts. Talk about centre and periphery, with its implication of the centre's general superiority to the lands on the margins, sounds unconvincing on the Black Sea.

Because the Greeks were literate, there is only a Greek version of their relationship to the peoples of the Pontic Steppe. 'We came, we founded . . .' But there could be a different version. After all, it was the Scythians who set the terms on which the colonies were established, and who – given that the colonies generally had no armed forces of their own beyond a citizen home guard – decided whether they should continue to exist. Usually, they wanted them not only to exist but to flourish. Dio Chrysostom described how the Scythians invited the Greeks to return and reopen Olbia after its destruction in 63 BC by the Getic raiders. This action resembles episodes in mediaeval Europe, when kings invited foreigners to found trading cities on their territory with extra-territorial privileges to make their own laws. But if fourteenth-century England, for instance, had been illiterate, we might now be taught that the Hanseatic Germans who set up the Steelyard in London had taken the initiative of colonising a barbarian shore on their own, and had maintained themselves by their own sheer cultural superiority.

Nobody at Olbia questioned the obvious fact that, ultimately, the Scythians were in charge of the situation. The Greeks made no attempt to conquer and control territory – with the exception of the Bosporan Kingdom, which arose in the eastern Crimea and which was in any case a joint enterprise between Greek colonists and local rulers. In Europe, we are accustomed to the idea of colonists who intend at first to subjugate 'natives' and then, eventually, to make the natives 'like them'. That was the Roman way, but not the Greek. It was normal and acceptable to colonial Greeks that people from other cultures should be attracted to their cities and adopt city customs – as Scyles did, and as many thousands of Scythians, Thracians, Maeotians, Sindi, Sarmatians and Khazars were to do in all the ports of the Black Sea, living within the walls as shopkeepers, labourers, craftsmen and eventually – sometimes – as full citizens. But while Greek colonists could assimilate others, they did not proselytise.

Once we were taught that the classical world was a 'centre' which was ultimately destroyed by its barbarian 'periphery'; then, with a little more subtlety, that the classical world was undone by its own inner failures, moral and even monetary, allowing the nomad hordes to flood over the barriers of the Roman Empire. But there is now a third family of explanations, modish and arresting: that the Graeco-Roman societies destroyed their own environment and then, in savage desperation, moved outwards to destroy the cultures around them –Celtic, Germanic, Thracian, Scythian – which until then had lived in harmony with nature.

The Danish archaeologist Klavs Randsborg, for example, calls the whole centre-periphery image 'an academic mental stereotype'. He sees Greek and Roman imperialism as the consequence of economic failure in the city-states of the Aegean and Mediterranean shores. At first, the outer world was content to import Greek and early Roman goods and to construct its own imitations of the Mediterranean city-state in fortified hilltop 'towns' (like Belsk, or like the Celtic *oppida* settlements in the north and west of Europe). Then the peoples on the margin began to make their own high-quality pottery and metalwork, initially reproductions, until they no longer needed to import them. 'The political systems in the old Aegean centre . . . then found themselves forced into a policy of dominance or conquest in order to secure continued economic advantage.'

Randsborg believes that Graeco-Roman city-states, as they prospered and increased in population, raped the fragile soil around them until its agricultural capacity collapsed. 'A politically developed society . . . could therefore only maintain its centre in a particular area for . . . a couple of centuries at a time.' In the Roman Empire, this meant that wider regions had to be exploited. First Gaul and Spain, then Tunisia and the Levant began to supply wheat, wine and oil for the old central regions and to grow rapidly in population. The consequence was disaster for the 'non-classical' world to the north.

The greater Europe outside the boundaries of the Greek and Roman Empires had developed a complex network of long-range trade routes and exchange connections stretching from the Black Sea and the Baltic to the Atlantic. A decentralised but common culture reached across the continent, in balance with its own natural resources and living on infinitely more productive soils than the populations of the Mediterranean 'core'. Now, though, this system and culture were to be torn apart. The Roman imperial expansion into north-western Europe, the Balkans and the Levant drew a fortified frontier between the inner and outer sectors of this common culture. The old Iron Age Europe was sundered: its economic and social unity was disrupted, and its loose political balance overthrown. The 'barbarian invasions' which followed should be seen, in Randsborg's perspective, as a natural attempt by the outer periphery to rejoin the inner. The differences, the unevennesses of development, which the Roman Empire had created between regions of this once-united Europe were so great that those on the outside were almost sucked inwards, as if by the updraught of a fire.

For Randsborg, the force which drew invaders into the Roman Empire was pull, not push. And what he calls the Migration Period (the 'barbarian invasions') should be understood not as an intrusive disaster but as a necessary pause in a process of development. After nearly a millennium of expansion to compensate for repeated economic failure, this process had brought 'powerful centres' to the point at which they had devastated the whole natural and political world around them. 'The picture of the barbarian as destroyer of civilisation,' cries Randsborg, 'should rather be turned on its head.'

Settled people fear moving people, but they also envy and admire them. In envying and admiring, they are inventing the sort of travelling people they want – once again, holding up a mirror to examine themselves.

The Greek tragedians, when they had invented the barbarians, soon began to play with the 'inner barbarism' of Greeks. Perhaps part of the otherness of barbarians was that, unlike the civilised, they were morally all of a piece – not dualistic characters in which a good nature warred with a bad, but whole. The 'Hippocratic' authors – the unknown writers of the Greek medical treatises wrongly attributed to the physician Hippocrates – asserted in *Airs, Waters, Places* that Scythians and all 'Asians' resembled one another physically, while 'Europeans' (meaning essentially Greeks) differed sharply in size and appearance from one city to another. Barbarians were homogenous; civilised people were multiform and differentiated. The Greek tragedians thought this might be true about minds as well as bodies. If it was, they were not sure that the contrast between Greek and barbarian psychology – the first complex and inhibited, the second supposed to be spontaneous and natural – was altogether complimentary to the Greeks.

Somewhere here begins Europe's long, unfinished ballad of yearning for noble savages, for hunter-gatherers in touch with themselves and their ecology, for cowboys, cattle-reivers, gypsies and Cossacks, for Bedouin nomads and aboriginals walking their song-lines through the unspoiled wilderness. When Euripides began to write, the Athenian dramatists were using the 'otherness' of their new composite barbarian as a mirror for inspecting Greek virtues. But by the time that he came to write *Medea*, in 431 BC, the mirror was being used to show Greek vices as well, or at least to put in question orthodox Greek morality. That play, already, has a chorus of Corinthian women who watch the fearful eruption of Medea's passions with feelings that are mixed: pity and horror at the crimes of this barbarian princess from Colchis, but also a dry regret that we Greeks – inhibited by our *miden agān* principle of 'nothing in excess' – no longer know how to let our feelings free. The chorus shows no sympathy for the chill orthodoxy of Jason, Medea's husband, when he rebukes her:

> Allow me, in the first place, to point out
> That you left a barbarous land to become a resident
> Of Hellas; here you have known justice; you have lived
> In a society where force yields place to law . . .

Herodotus thought the Scythians were the youngest nation on earth. Las Casas fancied that in the Americas the invaders had found not so much a new world as the old world in a sort of arrested infancy. With the presumption of collective youth went the presumption of collective innocence. Much later, after several centuries of European speculation about human origins and the state of nature, Romantic young men in imperial uniforms began to fall in love with the natives they were conquering. From the Aurès Mountains in North Africa to the peaks of the Khyber Pass, sulky young officers went hunting other men whom they supposed to be better and more natural human beings than they were.

Pushkin, Tolstoy and Lermontov all served in the Caucasus, officers in the Russian Army which for two generations campaigned to subdue the Islamic mountain peoples. These writers-in-arms projected onto their enemy all the virtues that St Petersburg seemed to lack: utter conviction and certainty of purpose, wholeness of feeling, asceticism in material needs.

At about the same time, English and Scottish intellectuals were passing through comparable storms of self-disgust, and making similar transferences. As the nineteenth century proceeded, these conquerors were to fall in love with the men of Arabia or the North-West Frontier. Indeed, the first of these passions had already blossomed within the north-western frontiers of the British State itself. The Scottish Highlanders had been finally defeated in the pre-Romantic 1740s, a time when the English officer James Wolfe could propose recruiting their beaten clans into the king's service with the words: 'They are hardy, intrepid, accustom'd to a rough Country and no great mischief if they fall.' But by the 1820s such sentiments had become unspeakable, if not quite unthinkable. The Highlander had become an emblem of simple candour, of selfless valour, of indifference to vulgar commerce and lucre and to most of the other virtues which metropolitan London fancied it had lost as the price of 'polish'.

The spiritual escape route devised by Mikhail Yurevich Lermontov, poet and novelist, tunnelled under the whole continent from Scotland to the Caucasus. Descended from a Learmonth of Balcomie, a Scottish mercenary officer who had served the Polish king and then the tsar, Lermontov imagined for his own roots a Scotland of frowning steeps and lonely heroes which was much like the Daghestan and Chechnia around him. When he went to fight in the Caucasus in the late 1830s, he carried with him a Russian translation of Ossian. The Ossianic poems were eventually exposed as forgeries, confected by James Macpherson and flavoured with ground-up extracts from genuine traditional Gaelic poetry, but Ossian seemed to Lermontov a sort of passport, not only to a special intimacy with the Caucasus but to a second identity which was un-Russian, untamed.

In his poem 'A Wish', Lermontov became a 'steppe raven' and flew to Scotland

where the fields of my ancestors flower,
Their forgotten dust reposes.

He ended in a crescendo of exquisite self-pity:

The last descendant of brave warriors
Expires among alien snows.
I was born here, but I am not of here in my soul —
O why am I not a raven of the steppe?

And these two elements, the vision of a Caucasian Scotland and
the dualistic longing to be a person who was two persons, join again
in his brief 'Tomb of Ossian':

Under a curtain of mist,
Under a sky of storms, in the midst of a plain,
Stands the grave of Ossian
Among the mountains of my Scotland.
My lulled spirit flies towards it
To breathe my native wind,
And from this forgotten grave
To begin my life over again.

Balcomie, where the Learmonths came from, is not at all an
Ossianic or Caucasian place. The house, now a jumble of ancient
towers and modern farm buildings, stands not in the Highlands but
on a flat Fife promontory battered by salt winds from the North Sea.
And yet, if this Lermontov-Learmonth had known it, his sense of
doubleness was at the very heart of a Scottish literary tradition
about divided selves and the sense of dual personality. A few years
earlier, in 1824, the Scottish writer James Hogg had published his
Confessions of a Justified Sinner about a man whose two selves
were not a Russian and a Scot but a man and a demon.

But Lermontov was at once dualist and duellist. He did not find
time to read Hogg. Instead, he 'expired among alien snows' in the
Caucasus in 1841, victim of an absurd duel which he had both
provoked and — in his cruel, perfect novel *A Hero of Our Time* —
prefigured. Their seconds had persuaded both men to fire into the
air. Lermontov went first and did so. But as he pulled the trigger he
said suddenly and loudly: 'At such an imbecile, I will not shoot!'

Enraged, his opponent lowered his aim and put his bullet through Lermontov's chest.

Ossian in contrast died slowly. In the Irish tales, Ossian (Oisín) was supposed to be the son of Finn MacCumhal, leader of the band of heroes whose anglicised name is the 'Fenians'. He was their bard, charged to put all that was done by the Fenians into words and melody which would never be forgotten. In the Ossian stories (which are a sort of sequel added to the main body of the Fenian myth-cycle, as if the listeners could not bear the tale to end), he has survived all his comrades and is living into a Methuselan old age – last of the race of giants. St Patrick comes often to visit Ossian, rebuking him gently for his pride in the old world of pagan violence and freedom which has passed away. But the old giant, unrepentant, curses the new world of conformist midgets and jeers at the Christian ethic of peace and submissiveness of spirit. He longs only to go hunting for one last time with Finn and the other heroes by the falls of Easaidh Ruadh.

There is a compassion, a balanced sense of time's cruelty, in those tales which is extraordinary. Euripides would have liked them. But when James Macpherson re-invented Ossian in the eighteenth century, in the 'epic lays' of a 'Scottish Homer', he left out all that mature irony, as he left out that special joy in the natural world of running deer and rowan trees in berry which gives the best Gaelic literature its quality. Some strange re-inventions have happened to Lermontov, too. He hung a lot on the word *zabvenniy* – 'alone, in oblivion'. Pechorin, Lermontov's 'hero of our times', walked by himself asking for neither love nor pity. Yet I have met Lermontov as the life and soul of a family party.

One evening I came to Anapa, a little port in the north-eastern corner of the Black Sea which had been a station in Lermontov's wanderings about this coast. I was there to see the excavations of the Greek colony of Gorgippia which lies underneath it, but I arrived late, and I found the museum director in her best bronze-coloured dress about to set off for a party. She invited me to come too.

We passed through the palm court of what had been a hotel, now a home for wounded Russian veterans of the Afghan war, and found ourselves in a hall full of tables, noise and people. This was the reunion of the Lermontovs. Some sixty people aged from nine to ninety had assembled from all over the world: from Russia and Ukraine, from France and the Americas, even from Scotland – there was a bearded Learmonth, now resident in Luxemburg, and a Procurator-Fiscal from Dundee who organises a society for the preservation of Balcomie.

They had already begun on the vodka and Kuban champagne, and children clutching lumps of cake were twirling on the dance floor or scrambling under the tables. They made me welcome to this celebration of . . . what precisely? Not Lermontov the writer, for in all the toasts and speeches of the night, there was not a word about literature. This was, instead, a clan gathering, a celebration of *Rod* – kinship and lineage.

Mikhail Lermontov never married and, as far as I know, had no children. His mother died when he was two, his father ignored him, and his only source of affection was a grandmother. Never mind! He had been famous, and around his fame distant relations and indirect descendants had assembled themselves into an enormous, affectionate, uproarious family with Mikhail Yurevich invisibly installed at the head of the table. Perhaps it was true that the great ancestor had been deficient in family feeling, a bit of a loner. But he was forgiven now.

They drank toasts to '*Zemlya, Rod, Rodina*' – Land, Race, Motherland. It was impossible not to like the Lermontov race. They had survived – no mean achievement for twentieth-century Russians. They had remembered kinship across oceans and across the walls of the Cold War. When the world and Russia opened the rusted gates, they rediscovered one another and encountered tribes of unknown children. They had just made a mass pilgrimage to the meadow where Lermontov fell at Pyatigorsk (the Fiscal, still pale, confided that the rail journey had been the worst thirty-six hours of his life), but they were not really interested in Mikhail Yurevich for himself. They were interested in each other, and they were celebrating themselves.

In the end, there was no keeping up with them. I went out into the night, and breathed cold sea air from the bay of Anapa. A Cossack man who had driven down with me from Rostov was angered by it all, by the absence of the 'real' Lermontov. He muttered, 'Fetishism!'

The park at Anapa, once a neat and demure place, is now the home of a pack of feral dogs who scratch all day and howl all night.

Beyond the town begins the Taman peninsula, a long spit of Asia reaching out until it almost touches Europe across the Kerch Straits. Lermontov went there too. He stared at the *kurgan* tumuli which rise like hills over this flat landscape: for him, they were tombs for Ossian, *zabvenniy* places.

He was wrong. Scientific excavation had not begun in Lermontov's day, and he would have known little about what really lay inside these burial mounds. It was true that they were first raised to cover the single, lonely body of a nomad prince or queen, sharing the burial-chamber only with sacrificed horses or slaves. But, as the years passed, the grave was usually invaded by a mob of other skeletons crowding in for company. Under the turf, another sort of family reunion would gather until it spilled over into new, smaller burial mounds nearby. In Russia, as Tolstoy was to find before he was even dead and buried, it is hard to remain at once great and solitary.

Chapter Three

The nucleus of this singular people [Cossacks] were
deserters. . . The course of nature, and the constant
arrival of fresh fugitives, rapidly increased their
numbers. They opened their arms to recruits from
every nation, and were joined by all the outcasts
whose crimes compelled them to abandon civilised
society. In this manner, they ceased to be mere
fugitives, and became a people. As may be supposed, their habits revealed the taint which sullied
their origin.

Henry Tyrrell, *History of the Russian Empire*

ONE COLD AUTUMN, I went to the Don delta and stayed in a
Greek colony. On the ruins of the city of Tanais, there is a small
modern village of archaeologists living in wooden shacks. In
summer, expeditions arrive from Russian or German universities to
excavate, and for a few months the site is crowded with muscular
students who sleep in tents and sing to the guitar round camp-fires.
But out of season, only half a dozen men and women live at Tanais,
their beds squeezed between shelves of broken Greek pottery and
carboys of photographic chemicals. At such times, before the
Scythian frosts trim the Sea of Azov with ice and snow blocks the
road to Rostov, there are empty huts to rent to visitors.

The director of Tanais, commander of the colony, is Valeriy
Fedorovich Chesnok. Like his colleague at Olbia, Mr Chesnok is
stranded in an outpost whose subsidies have been cut off, left to
survive on his own resources as if on some ice-floe forgotten by the
supply ships. Water comes from a well, heating is uncertain,
sanitation is a pit latrine. Some food and any amount of vodka can

be found in the Cossack village of Nedvigovka (meaning roughly 'No-Surrenderville'), a mile away. Vegetables can be bought in abundance from a rich, well-organised Armenian village halfway to Rostov, but only in spring and summer. While I was there, in late September, the scientists were still eating well: breakfast was carp stew and beetroot salad, with gallons of steaming tea made from camomile and steppe herbs.

'Science' is the word Russian archaeologists use to describe the whole profession of knowledge to which they belong. The word in Russian has none of the limitation to physical sciences or technology which it has acquired in English; a philologist or an art historian is as much a scientist as a molecular biologist, in the sense of the French word *savant*. Nothing, neither Stalinist terror nor free-market pressures and privations, has been able to rob this Russian term of its majesty. When Mr Chesnok and his colonists spoke about themselves as 'scientists', I came to understand that they were talking not only about their research but also about something inward and existential. They meant a sort of marble stele in the mind; incised upon it are the moral commandments to which the life of a scientist is dedicated. These commandments include the commitments to truth, to loyal comradeship, to intellectual and personal self-discipline, to an ascesis indifferent to discomfort or money. This is the Rule of a religious order. At Tanais, I heard a love affair between a Russian archaeologist and a foreign scholar condemned as 'unworthy of a scientist', because it had led the woman concerned to re-time an excavation schedule.

Once I watched Mr Chesnok as he put through a telephone call to Moscow. He stood up at his table, his small, energetic figure erect, shouting concise orders to one operator after another through the humming and frizzling of static. I was watching an artillery officer at the battle of Kursk calling down a barrage, or getting through to a threatened battery commander. 'Moscow? *Alloa!* This is Chesnok, Tanais – I repeat: Chesnok, Tanais. Get me Moscow! *Alloa!* . . . ' In this way, across widening crevasses of chaos and across distances which seem to grow longer as Russia's central coherence yawns apart, the integrity of science is defended.

Mr Chesnok remains undaunted. He has written a booklet, available to visitors, entitled 'The Principles of Life', which expresses his own iron optimism through citations from the Decalogue and the American Declaration of Independence. One night, at the end of an enormous row with a Cossack about corruption, Cossack nationalism and the fate of the nation, he tried to communicate his faith to me: 'All this is not such a tragedy. Culture is what matters for identity, not ethnicity and not money either. Russia is going through wild years. But we will survive them.'

For a Russian scientist, the wild years which brought the first wave of primitive capitalists after 1991 have often resembled a new inrush of steppe nomads. But when an unfamiliar horde is seen from the walls of a Black Sea city, there has always been a choice of tactics. The first option is to bolt the gates. The second is to invite the nomad chieftains to enter as honoured guests. In return for a few gold rings or an amphora of Trebizond wine, they may be impressed enough to offer their services as the city's protectors. Tanais, whether as a Greek emporium or as a Russian archaeological colony, has generally chosen the second option.

I discovered this for myself early one morning, as I stumbled over mounds of potsherds to reach the latrine. I had stopped to look at the view. The huts and the Greek ruins stand on the northern shore of the Don delta, above a backwater which was once the main channel of the Don but is now the 'Dead Donets'. In the distance, the Sea of Azov gleamed tin-coloured under low clouds. And then I saw a Bactrian camel. It swayed towards me until it reached the end of its hobble, then bit a piece out of a bush growing on the old rampart. Beyond the camel, I made out an encampment of rusty caravans and towing-tractors, all flagged-out with washing hung up to dry.

This turned out to be the Rostov State Circus, in its new winter quarters. Mr Chesnok had discovered a sponsor: a speculative builder who had fallen in love with the lady who trained the performing dogs in the circus. The circus was in trouble, however, and the dog-lady was inconsolable, for the Rostov authorities had cut off the rent subsidy for their expensive palace in the city centre. The sponsor, knowing Mr Chesnok's problems, saw a way out. He proposed that if Tanais would allow the circus a few hectares of unexcavated Greek suburb to winter on and graze its animals, then he could see his way to constructing a new brick storage and laboratory block for the scientists.

So the deal was made. The builder was happy, the dog-lady was consoled, and the Tanais scientists stepped uncertainly into this new world in which culture is dependent upon the pleasure of private entrepreneurs.

For the urban cultures of the Mediterranean, from the Greeks to the Genoese and Venetians, the Don delta was the north-eastern corner of their world. The delta, at the far end of the Sea of Azov, was a place so distant, so exposed to nomad raiding and so hard to reach across a sea which froze over in many winters, that for long periods the Aegean and Mediterranean traders had no foothold there. But in good times fortunes could be made. When the rulers of the inland steppes were not at war with one another, caravan trails – the 'Silk Routes' – would reach across Eurasia from China to the mouth of the river Don.

This was not just hinterland trade, like the wheat, dried fish and slaves which made Olbia rich. It was long-range exporting in luxury commodities. From China, Persia and India came silks, spices, porcelain, bronze and gold luxuries, which the European colonists at the Don delta paid for in different ways. The Greeks exported wine, red- and black-figure pottery, jewellery and ornaments made first in Greece and later in the Bosporan Kingdom at the Kerch Straits. Both Greeks and Italians did a certain amount of cash business, and their coinages found their way thousands of miles back up the caravan routes into Asia. Most of the Italian export trade was coarse European woollen cloth woven in Flanders, Lombardy or Venice, much of it produced in the earliest versions of a factory system.

To serve these long-range routes into Eurasia, two fortified trading cities grew up at the delta. The first was Tanais (which is also the Greek and Latin name for the river Don itself). Founded around 250 BC, it stood on the north side of the delta on what was then the main river channel; ships were able to enter from the Sea of Azov (several miles nearer than it is today), and tie up under its walls. Tanais stood for some five hundred years, until the Goths sacked and burned it in the third century AD. Some squatters returned to the ruins later, but Tanais was finally obliterated when the Huns appeared out of Asia around the year 350.

Prosperity along the north shore of the Black Sea has always required two conditions: steady peace inland on the steppes, and free passage between the Black Sea and the Mediterranean. These conditions revived in the eighth and ninth centuries, when Khazar nomads established dominion over the whole region between the Black Sea and the northern forests. But the *Pax Khazarica* did not reach far eastwards into Asia. It was not until the conquests of Chingiz Khan and his successors in the thirteenth century, extending a Tatar-Mongol empire over northern Eurasia from the Sea of Japan to the Black Sea, that the overland routes between China and Europe reopened after an interval of nearly a thousand years.

The Tatar-Mongols arrived on the Black Sea when the Byzantine Empire was near its end, weakened by the struggle against the Ottoman Turks and by the pressure of the Crusader kingdoms advancing from the west. Pushing behind the land armies of the Crusaders were the maritime city-states of Italy – Genoa and Venice above all – impatient to break through the Narrows into the markets of the Black Sea. Unwilling to share the Sea with outsiders, the later Byzantine emperors at first offered these 'Franks' and 'Latins' only reluctant and occasional passage through the Narrows. But after the Crusaders had stormed Constantinople in 1204, the two maritime empires were able to slip through the Bosporus and reach the Crimean coast, the Sea of Azov and finally the river Don.

Now the second delta city was built. Tana, as it was named, stood on the opposite, southern side of the delta, looking across ten miles of reeds to the silent ruins which had been Tanais. Founded by Genoese and Venetian colonists in the thirteenth century, Tana began as an open trading-post which only gradually acquired Italian-designed stone walls and towers. In practice, the walls meant little. The survival of Tana remained always a gamble on the tolerance of the Golden Horde, the western division of the Mongol empire which had arrived in the Pontic Steppe only a few decades earlier. Tana's diplomacy, like much of its short-range trade, concentrated on the Horde's 'capital' far away at Saray on the Volga. When the Genoese were finally edged out, Tana became for a time the most profitable of all Venetian colonies. But its dependency on the Mongols, and later on the Crimean Tatars, never lessened. For the most part, the sabre of Mongol power was turned away from the Italians. In the end, it struck them down.

One rainy autumn day, exploring what remains of Tana, I looked down into a huge, untidy pit. Its sides were made of fire-blackened earth, wood-ash and calcined plaster. Out of them spilled human skulls and thigh-bones, white debris against the black soil.

Nearby, the archaeologists had piled their finds into open cardboard cartons disintegrating in the rain: fragments of amphoras imported from Trebizond for shipping caviar, broken bottles of fluted Venetian glass, shards of caramel-coloured Byzantine pottery and of exquisite green-glazed bowls made by Tatar craftsmen of the Golden Horde at Saray. Lumps of black rust turned out to be the shoulder-plates of a Venetian cuirass, lying among iron crossbow quarrels.

This was the wreckage left by Timur (Tamburlaine), whose armies sacked Tana in 1398 during the last of the great nomad invasions from Central Asia. But it was not the final grave of Venetian Tana; Italians remained here until the city was stormed by Tatars and Turks in 1475, as their combined armies mopped up what was left of the Byzantine-Latin presence round the north coast of the Black Sea. The city itself survived as the Ottoman port of Azak, then as the huge Turkish fortress of Azov. Today the town of Azov, with its river port on the Don, covers the whole site of Tana. For some reason, the Soviet authorities decided that Genoese ancestry was less ideologically obnoxious than Venetian; there is a ruined 'Genoa Gate' (it is actually eighteenth-century Russian), and a shabby corner where Genoa Lane runs off Rosa Luxemburg Street. The memory of Venice has been banished.

This Tana of the Italians had a briefer life than classical Tanais, but it was eventful. The Genoese were more powerful than the Venetians on the Black Sea as a whole; they were already well entrenched along the Crimean coast at Cembalo (Balaklava), Sudak and Kaffa when they became partners of the Venetians on the Don. But at the end of the thirteenth century, after the first of several Black Sea wars between the two maritime empires, Venice won exclusive control of Tana – and this happened at a lucky moment in world history. The Mongol-Yuan dynasty, which ruled China until the late fourteenth century, made it possible for the output of imperial China to flow westwards across the continental land mass of Mongol-dominated Eurasia to this western terminus of one of the Silk Routes, and the Tana merchants could for a time monopolise almost the entire China trade for Venice.

But this route, kept open only by precarious agreements among the Mongol khanates along the way to China, was never more than a transient opportunity. It had begun to flow around 1260, but within a few years inter-Mongol feuds were already interrupting it. When the Mongol empire broke up in the fourteenth century, the main transcontinental trade lines were disconnected for good – first the northern route, which ended at Tana, and later the southern branch, which had brought spices and textiles from Asia to the Black Sea at Trebizond.

As far as profit was concerned, the long-range import of Chinese and Persian silks was not the main business at Tana. The Venetians made far greater profits out of other lines of business: furs, caviar, spices and above all slaves. While they were on good terms with the Golden Horde and its successors, the Venetians bought and shipped Russian, Circassian and Tatar slaves who were either sold in Constantinople to local and Levantine buyers or auctioned in Venice itself. Venetian slave-traders travelled from Tana as far as Astrakhan, on the Caspian Sea, or to Tashkent, in Central Asia, to inspect the stock. Back at Tana, a staff of solicitors was kept busy drawing up purchase contracts, while in Venice the *Signoria* (the governing senate) supervised the trade and laid down the maximum costs which could be incurred for transporting and feeding slaves on the three-month voyage between the Sea of Azov and the Adriatic.

Kaffa, a rival Genoese colony which stood on the site of modern Feodosia in Crimea, was exporting an average of 1,500 slaves a year in the fourteenth century, almost all male and almost all destined for the Mameluke sultans in Egypt. Tana was probably slave-trading on much the same scale. But then something happened at Kaffa which not only transformed the terms of the slave trade but changed the history of the world.

In the Genoese sea-wall at Kaffa, there is a tall gateway. Through it you can see blue water and merchant ships at anchor in the roadstead of Feodosia. Six hundred years ago, columns of slaves in irons would enter this gate, and gangs of men carrying bales of Chinese silk shipped across the Sea of Azov from Tana. But one day in 1347, an invisible immigrant made its way under the arch and began to explore Kaffa.

The Black Death came to Europe through this gate, the pandemic of pneumonic plague which within a few years had reduced the European population by one-third or more. One legend asserts that the plague broke out among a Tatar army commanded by the khan

95

Djani-Beg, which was besieging Kaffa, and that the khan ordered the heads of the Tatar victims to be catapulted into the town to infect the defenders. More probably, it came with slaves or Tatar stevedores in time of peace. The disease must have taken hold among the nomad inhabitants of the Pontic Steppe before it infected the 'Latin' cities of the Black Sea coast. And it had travelled a long way, clear across Eurasia from Manchuria or Korea, carried down the Silk Routes by traders, porters and soldiers to the fringes of Europe on the Black Sea.

The Silk Routes brought wealth, but then death. Within twenty years of the plague's arrival in Europe, the Mongol Empire founded by Chingiz Khan more than a century before began to break apart. The graveyards which the onslaught of the Mongols had filled in Europe were insignificant compared to this culling by disease which they left behind them.

Between December 1347 and September 1348, the Black Death had killed three-quarters of the European population in Crimea and the other Black Sea colonies. But it also killed half the population of Venice, the slaves and journeymen as well as the grandees, and suddenly there was a labour shortage. All over Europe, where many villages had perished to the last child, there was a famine of manpower on feudal estates, in baronial kitchens and stables, in urban work-shops. Employers who had never dreamed of paying cash wages for labour found themselves on the defensive. In due course, the rural poor were to press their advantage and demand money or charters of secure tenure, as the English did during the Peasant Revolt of 1381.

Good businessmen do not miss an opportunity. The impact on the slave market was enormous. Everywhere on the Mediterranean littoral, from Egypt to Crete and Spain, the price of foreign slaves rose steeply. Most of the Venetian slavers at Tana had died horribly in 1348, but the survivors were rewarded by a boom in demand and prices which roared on for half a century. By about 1408, no less than 78 per cent of Tana's export earnings came from slaves. Out of their misery, and out of the profits born of the Black Death, one palace after another was raised along the Rialto.

In the Powder Magazine museum at Azov, there is a human hand cast in iron. The breadth and thickness of the palm, the hog-back hump of the fingers, suggest some hominid creature bigger than a man.

This is the iron hand of Peter. The fist of Peter the Great brought Russia to the shores of the Sea of Azov, and drove Dutch and German shipwrights to build the first Russian Navy at Taganrog just three hundred years ago, in the 1690s.

Between Russia and the open ocean, there were three bottlenecks plugged by the Turkish enemy. The first was the fortress of Azov, built by the Turks to command the main channel of the river Don as it reached the sea. The second plug was the stronghold of Yenikale, built by the Ottomans to block the Kerch Straits: Catherine the Great broke through that barrier at the end of the eighteenth century. The third was the Narrows, the double passage of the Bosporus and the Dardanelles which led past Istanbul itself to the Mediterranean. The Narrows have been open to the merchant shipping of the world since the collapse of the Ottoman Empire in 1922, but all the armies and navies of Russia have never been able to capture them.

The Russian struggle south to reach the warm waters of the Mediterranean, and the Turkish struggle to hold the Ottoman conquests around the Black Sea and protect the Narrows, raged for nearly three hundred years. They led to one major European war – the Crimean conflict in the 1850s which involved France, Britain and Sardinia as well as Russia and Turkey – and nearly precipitated several others in the course of the nineteenth century. Generations of illiterate, obedient peasant soldiers died on both sides. So did the innocent inhabitants of wasted landscapes and stormed cities all round the Black Sea, from Azov to the outskirts of Istanbul.

Byron devoted a long section of his poem *Don Juan* to one of these famous slaughters, the battle for the Turkish fortress of Ismail on the Danube:

> All that defies the worst that pen expresses,
> All by which hell is peopled, or as sad
> As hell – mere mortals who their power abuse –
> Was here (as heretofore and since) let loose.

In the end, both sides died of their wounds. Russian hatred of Turkey and Turkish fear of Russian expansion were among the most dangerous ingredients in the mixture of unstable diplomatic explosives which blew up in 1914. Russia invaded Anatolia from the east; Turkey joined the war behind Germany and Austria-

Hungary. The effort broke both régimes. Within a few years, before the First World War was over, both the Russian and Ottoman Empires had collapsed.

The honour of knocking out the first Turkish plug belonged not to Peter, but to the Don Cossacks. The Cossacks were confederations of Russian and Ukrainian outlaws and fugitives – often intermarried with local Tatar or Kipchak nomads – who had settled in the freedom of the steppes during the late Middle Ages. This particular confederation or 'host', the Cossacks who ranged over the plains of the lower Don, had been harassing and resisting the Turks for more than a century before Peter the Great arrived on the Sea of Azov. They had dug a canal across the delta, so that boats could sail or be rowed upriver without passing under the guns of the fortress-town of Azov. Far to the west, on the lower Dnieper, their cousins the Zaporozhe Cossacks had built a form of submarine to evade Turkish guard-posts: covered-in skiffs propelled with oars, supplied with air through wooden pipes and carrying sand-ballast to release when they wished to surface. (Reports that fleets of submarines crossed the Black Sea in the sixteenth century, disgorging Cossack commandos who captured Anatolian cities like Sinop, belong, however, to Russian mythology.)

None of this gave the Turkish sultan serious anxiety. But one day in 1637 a Cossack force prowling in the Don delta approached the walls of Azov and then, on a wild impulse, attacked them. There was a large Ottoman garrison there, behind zig-zag brick and earth ramparts constructed according to the latest designs of European military engineering. But the defenders were taken by surprise. The Cossack regiments burst into the town and then, after three days of fighting, captured the citadel.

They soon lost the place again. The Turks came back to Azov with reinforcements, and many years and sieges passed before Peter finally captured it for Russia. In the end, the job had to be done professionally, with encroaching trenches, regular armies, demolition sappers, mortar batteries and gunboats. When Azov finally fell, the butchery was as sad as Byron's hell, and in the back gardens of the town men digging for potatoes still find collapsed trenches containing Turkish bones and buttons among iron Russian cannon-balls.

Peter did the hard and brutal work here, but the Don Cossacks rode off with the glory. Taking Azov suited the Cossack myth. It was a blow struck for Russia and Christendom, in lands far beyond the limits of the tsar's dominion. It was done without orders from any superior, on the spur of the moment, without fear of the forbidding military odds against them. It was the victory of plains people, poor horsemen from the fens and steppes, over settled and heavily armed people who lived behind walls.

The first time I saw Don Cossacks was in Rostov. In a narrow street with broken pavements, several dozen men in uniform were milling and shouting at one another. In the Russian manner, other people passing down Suvorov Street took absolutely no notice of them except to make a slight detour round their noise.

The Cossacks had seized a house, one of those squat old merchant's houses apparently built of blue-and-white marzipan and crystallised fruit. Before the Revolution, the house at 20, Suvorov Street had belonged to the Cossack millionaire Paramonov. Now, defying the city council's orders to move out, the occupying force proposed to defend it as reclaimed Cossack property.

They crowded across the street to harangue me. When, after a diet of Russian novels, you cast eyes on a knout, you recognise it: this leather knout was shorter than a whip but longer than a rope's end, and one of the Cossacks was slapping it against the big red stripe down his uniform trousers. He wore a red-and-white tramdriver cap, pushed to the back of his sweaty blond curls, and his face and neck were brick-red from sun and wind.

The oldest man, wearing a St Andrew's Cross medal on his military tunic, roared at me, 'We are not bandits, as they say in the West! No, we are the party of ecology, the party of the environment! All the Don Cossacks ask for is that the factories be torn down and the steppe be given back to us. We will restore this land to nature, and bring all the poor little town children to come and breathe our fresh air.'

He invited me to sign a petition which demanded a halt to the settlement of 'non-Slavs' in the Don region. This meant 'non-Christians', he explained. So Georgian and Armenian Christians could go on living in Rostov? 'Well . . . but, anyway, not Moslems from the Caucasus, and not . . . you know. Well, Jews.'

The early Cossacks lived much in the manner of their steppe

predecessors, in mobile cavalry hosts migrating in search of seasonal pasture behind herds of horses and cattle. In a landscape without forests or hills, their refuges in time of trouble were marshes and river meanders: the Don delta or, for the powerful Zaporozhe host, the Sech island below the cataracts of the Dnieper.

But the price of Cossack freedom was eternal manipulation by the neighbouring settled kingdoms. Until the eighteenth century, during the long conflict between the Polish-Lithuanian Common-wealth and Russia, the Cossacks were able to sell their support to one side or the other. But as Catholic Poland declined, they fell increasingly under the influence of Moscow and of the Russian Orthodox version of Christianity. After Peter and then Catherine had annexed the northern Black Sea coast to Russia, the Cossacks began to serve as cavalry in the tsarist wars against the Turks, against Napoleon, against the Anglo-French invaders of Crimea. In time of peace, they came to be used as instruments of government terror: against the Jews during the pogroms of the late nineteenth century, and against revolutionary strikers and demonstrators a few years later.

The Revolution of 1917 and the civil war which followed split the Cossacks into 'Reds' and 'Whites'. Some joined the Bolsheviks, like the Red Cavalry described in Isaac Babel's stories which invaded Poland in 1920 under Marshal Budyenny – the *Konarmia* (horse army). Others followed White Cossack leaders like Krasnov into exile. They left their horses on the quays of Novorossisk, and learned to drive *fiacres* and motor-taxis in Paris. Much later, some of their elderly leaders were tempted into the tragic miscalculation of enlistment with Hitlerism.

To feel oneself a Cossack is to enter an excruciating crisis of identity. It seems to me that the Cossacks belong to the category of 'outpost people': faithful defenders of some tradition whose centre is far away and which, often, is already decaying into oblivion. The Krajina Serbs believe that they are the truest and purest Serbs, uncorrupted by whatever may happen in Belgrade, standing guard against the 'Germanised' Croats and the imaginary onslaught of fundamentalist Islam. In Northern Ireland, the Protestant 'Loyalist' community proclaims itself to be the bastion of true Britishness with an unreconstructed Union Jack fervour which now seems antiquated, even faintly foreign, in London or Manchester. The

Afrikaners, to take a very different example, have in the past understood themselves as custodians of 'Western Christian values', stationed among the barbarians on the direct instructions of the Lord of the Old Testament.

Two delusive mental syndromes afflict such outpost peoples. One is false consciousness: a skewed and paranoid awareness of the exterior world. The Afrikaner extremist faces a godless international enemy directed by the Illuminati, whose leaders are mostly 'crypto-Jewish' American financiers and politicians. The Ulster Freedom Fighter believes in a Papist-Fenian world conspiracy (which, until the Soviet Union collapsed, included a secret compact betwen Old Red Socks in the Vatican and the late Leonid Brezhnev in the Kremlin). The Serbian clairvoyant decodes the names of Bosnia's international supporters as the encrypted titles of Satan's archangels.

The second syndrome is dominance. The outposter must constantly remind himself of who he is by displaying his power over 'the others'. These 'others' are held to be inherently inferior as individuals, usually because of their race or religion. But they are more numerous, and represent a constant threat which can be held in check only by public enactments of domination. In Portadown, in Northern Ireland, the Orange March on every Twelfth of July used to surge down through 'The Tunnel' into the Catholic quarter in order to yell up at the windows and show who was master in the town (in recent years, the police has taken to re-routing the procession and barricading The Tunnel). In Bosnia, Serb militias practised the ritual gang-rape of Moslem women in the same spirit.

The very sense of collective identity may come to hang on this enactment. An Afrikaner is self-defined by a variety of markers which include language and a Calvinist religious culture, but if he can no longer demonstrate physically his mastery over blacks, he may feel no longer entirely an Afrikaner in his own eyes. Similarly, displayed domination over others was indispensable to Russian imperial nationalism. The Cossacks above all – considering themselves distinct from 'settled' Russians and yet, at the same time, appointed carriers of the essential Russian values – display that syndrome with gloomy intensity. A Russian is somebody who subdues non-Russians.

Kazachestvo – Cossackism – developed as the idea of a warrior caste whose mission was to defend and extend Russia at its margins.

Religious and racial intolerance were built into the ideology at an early stage, and both tsars and Soviet rulers knew how to flatter Cossack self-esteem. At Novocherkassk, which is now the un-official Don Cossack 'capital', a triumphal arch commemorates the Cossack part in defeating Napoleon in 1812, a statue of the mediaeval Cossack leader Yermak stands in the biggest square, and the museum displays a golden sword presented to his wild horsemen by Tsar Alexander I. Medals have always rained down, but all the honours were intended to distract the Cossacks from the realities of their own powerlessness and poverty.

It worked. For a hundred years, the Don Cossacks lived in a dream: the dream of a horseman cantering across a world of grass with fear rippling ahead of him like the wind.

There was a sinister beauty here which seized imaginations in unlikely heads. Isaac Babel described how, as a Jewish child in the 1905 Odessa pogrom, he watched his father kneeling in the broken glass of his shop and pleading as a Cossack cavalry patrol came down the street. The focus of that scene is not Jewish humiliation but the fearsome grace of the Cossack officer as he rides by, touching his cap distantly, not deigning to glance down.

A few years later, surrendering to the malign spell laid upon him in boyhood, Babel in his pince-nez hoisted himself into a Cossack saddle. He joined the Red Cavalry after the Bolshevik Revolution and, as a *Konarmia* trooper, rode from the Black Sea into the heart of Poland, his horse pacing down the streets of blazing Jewish *shtetls*.

Force, race and male pride defined the Cossack. Then came two successive world-endings in the same century, the Revolution of 1917 and the death of the Revolution in 1991, either of which should by its own manifesto have sent those three values to a museum. But Stalin's imperial state, Great-Russian chauvinism belted with a red star, found a use for them. So has post-Soviet, pre-capitalist Russia in the 1990s. Force, above all, is in demand all round the Russian borders and frequently in the cities. And, because the Cossacks see in this confusion a fresh crisis of the Russian race, they have rediscovered the male profession of warrior.

Volunteers from the Don Cossacks have fought and been killed in the newly independent state of Moldava, defending the Russian minority in 'Transdniestria' against the Romanian-speaking majority. Kuban and Don Cossacks have turned up in the battles of the northern Caucasus, professing to be defending the margins of Russia by supporting the Abkhazian or Ossetian rebellions against Georgia. In the name of Slavic brotherhood, more than five hundred Cossack volunteers joined the Serbian militias fighting in Bosnia.

How can this defence of Russianness be at the same time the defence of a distinct *Kazachestvo*? Here the Cossack muddle about identity solidifies into a dead-end of contradiction. On the one hand, the Cossacks are impatient to take up arms against non-Christians and non-Slavs who have the impudence to claim a right to rule over Russians. On the other hand, Cossacks themselves have been seduced into the bazaar of ethnic and linguistic nationalism which is selling quick identities all around the Black Sea. They have proclaimed their own distinct ethnicity as the Cossack *narod* (people), and in several regions, including the lower Don, they have pegged out an autonomous territory of their own.

The seven million Cossacks in Russia (ten million, according to their leaders) are in theory descendants of separate 'hosts' settled across Eurasia from the Don to the Ussuri River on the Chinese frontier and even on the Pacific coast. After the Bolshevik Revolution, the hosts were disbanded. The Cossacks lost their old freedoms and became collective-farm workers – a parody of the Cossack system of holding land in common – or industrial labourers in Soviet cities. Stalin manipulated Cossack patriotism in time of war, but their history of independence displeased him; they suffered intensely during the south Russian famines of the 1920s and the purges of the 1930s, and the political control over *Kazachestvo* was tight. The *atamans*, traditional host chieftains, were retained, but only as servile officials nominated by the Party.

When the Cossack revival began, after 1991, the resources of the *Kazachestvo* heritage were wretchedly depleted. Most of the movement's new leaders were townees, or minor Party bureaucrats who had defected to make an expedition to their own roots. All over Rostov, for example, wives and sisters were ordered to sew together uniforms modelled on faded sepia photographs, while their men, no less clumsily than Isaac Babel, learned how to mount and then how to stay attached to a horse.

Yet Cossack military strength is real. So is the danger that any convincing revival of old-fashioned, reactionary Russian nationalism will enlist that strength. Early in 1993, Boris Yeltsin resolved to outflank his enemies by playing the Cossack card: a presidential decree offered the Cossacks the return of their customary lands, the revival of the local self-government which they had enjoyed up to the 1917 Revolution, and the restoration of purely Cossack units to the Russian Army, complete with their classic uniforms, ranks and decorations. But the Russian parliament, at this stage dominated by a nationalist-Communist coalition moving into confrontation with President Yeltsin, rejected the decree. Even after the parliamentary forces attempted their coup in September 1993 and were crushed by troops loyal to the presidency, the Cossack laws remained in limbo; nobody could remember whether they were in force or not. Instead, the Cossacks acted on them. That October, three thousand miles east of the Don, armed Ussuri Cossacks on ponies rode up to the frontier guards on the mountain-line which divides Russia from China and began – without orders – their first patrol. They had returned to their old duty: the watch at the outpost.

All these contradictions found a home in the house at 20, Suvorov Street in Rostov. Paramonov, who built it and lived in it, was a Cossack. But he was also a great urban capitalist, an industrial and commercial magnate who owned grain elevators and coal mines and barges on the Don. His rival, Panchenko, owned paper mills, and early this century the two dynasties solved their differences with a wedding: a Paramonov daughter married a Panchenko son.

After the Revolution, many of the Paramonovs and Panchenkos retreated into exile in Western Europe. For the next seventy years, both families were categorised in the land of their birth as bloodsucking monopolists, White terrorists and merciless exploiters. But any conversation in modern Rostov reveals that in spite of three generations of propaganda they are still remembered and revered. Today they enjoy a reputation, golden in hindsight, as fathers of their city, as builders of schools, embankments, parks and churches, as patrons of the arts.

Cossack achievement which is neither a heaped battlefield nor a street of broken glass is rare and precious. So it was with awed excitement that the Don Cossacks learned a few years ago that the granddaughter of Paramonov and Panchenko was alive and living in France. They hit on the idea of seizing and occupying her grandfather's house, which had become a municipal office. They would hold it until they could hand it over to her – a true-blood Cossack and the house's rightful heiress – as a symbol of the Cossack right to all their 'stolen' properties and lands.

I met her on her first visit to the land of her fathers. Madame Nathalie Fedorovsky was born in Belgium, raised in Katanga and now dwells at Roissy, near Paris. But her Russian is perfect. More important, this wise and polished lady possesses a French sense of proportion. She was aware of all the ironies: that Cossack male machismo should be constructing a cult round a woman; that pre-capitalist steppe horsemen should be making a shrine out of an industrialist's city mansion. She walked through the streets of Rostov like a queen, with a small, fluttering retinue. Madame Fedorovsky was not to be manipulated.

When I first saw her, she was in the treasure-cabinet of the Rostov Museum, inspecting the diadem of a Sarmatian warrior-princess. Later, at a lunch given in her honour by the museum director, she told me about her visit to the Don Cossacks on Suvorov Street. 'I said that I sympathised with them and their demands, but I warned them above all to avoid violence. Then their *ataman* made a great welcome speech about "we, the Cossack people". I interrupted him to say, "There is no such thing! I am proud to be a Cossack, but I am a Russian – and so are you." I turned to all the others, and I dared them to tell me aloud that they were not Russians. And, do you know, they looked so hangdog, and they mumbled to me, "Yes, we are Russians . . . " '

The Cossack revival is a disaster of the human ecology. Not all the ecological catastrophes of the Black Sea happen in water. Just as the inrush of pollutants into the Black Sea has decimated the variety of marine species, allowing certain algae and the marauding jellyfish *Mnemiopsis* to multiply on an explosive scale, so Stalin's deportations created a social void, a monstrous demographic impoverishment into which the Cossack movement now expands uncontrollably.

'New Russia', the imperial province established by Catherine around the northern coast of the Black Sea, was a colonial territory of many peoples. Before the Revolution, a traveller would have experienced this land as a succession of ethnicities: Tatar villages; colonies of Russian veteran soldiers and their descendants; settlements of Polish exiles; neat farming districts where almost everyone was German; Cossack *stanitsas* ('stations' or villages); Jewish *shtetls*; Greek towns and rural regions, like Mariupol or Anapa; Armenian villages and even cities, like Nakhitchevan, which was a separate town before it became the Armenian quarter of Rostov.

Between 1930 and 1950, this proliferation of human societies was systematically destroyed. First came the suppression of cultural rights, which had on the whole been well cared for in the first years after the Revolution. Greek and Tatar schools, newspapers and publishing houses were closed. The anti-religious drive shut down the synagogues and churches and mosques, and in the central square of Nakhitchevan, the Armenian cathedral was dynamited – to be replaced by an immense concrete and glass building designed in the shape of a caterpillar tractor. Finally came the deportations, reaching their peak in the post-war years when the Germans, Tatars and Greeks were driven out of their homes and removed to Central Asia. Immigrants from Russia and Ukraine were brought in to occupy their houses and their land. The Armenians and the few Jews who had survived the Nazi occupation lived cautious, unobtrusive lives.

The Cossacks alone remained with a confidence of deep-rooted belonging. They had been persecuted and robbed of possessions and liberties, but they were still in their own country, and – given their curious ideology of imperial patriotism – they could understand the inflow of millions of uprooted Russians and Ukrainians as a sort of reinforcement rather than as a threat of dilution. When the Communist régime fell apart, and with it effective central control over what happened in distant provinces and on the margins of Russia, the Cossack claim to mastery and domination was unimpeded. Most of the rival, 'alien' populations had gone (few Cossacks wish them back, or regret the Russification of the Black Sea coast). So had the authority of Moscow, which had once used the Cossacks as a whip to control the nationalities of New Russia but which had never, ever, offered the Cossacks political power over others.

A mile away from Tanais is the village of Nedvigovka. It is an old Don Cossack *stanitsa*, a single street between wooden cabins and cottages of plaster washed blue or white. The women wear headscarves; the men have long, soft leather boots stained with clay. The children, climbing in and out of the gaps in the broken plank fence along the street, are very thin.

The only new thing is the inside of the church. The priest stands in the yard among his own calves, geese and kittens, while his son and a black-bearded deacon lug scaffolding poles up the church steps. For many years, the Church of the Death of the Madonna at Nedvigovka was boarded-up or used as a storehouse. Now the restoration is almost complete.

They brought a young woman from Rostov to renew the nineteenth-century frescoes in the cupola. Finding them almost effaced by damp and frost-flaking, she settled down to painting her own. St Andrew, patron of Russia and of the Cossacks, is there, and so is St Cyril who crossed the Don near Nedvigovka to preach to the Khazars. But they are now the only men in the scene. The young woman from Rostov, who had advanced views, felt that Russian Orthodox androcentrism was due for revision. The Madonna's family is entirely female, the congregation of martyrs is composed exclusively of women, the angels leaning down from the cupola to stare and laugh are all girls with Russian faces.

The scientists from Tanais come here to pray or – in one case – to be christened into the Orthodox faith after twenty years of education in atheist materialism. They find delight in a church so unexpectedly dedicated not only to the Mother of God but to all women. But in Nedvigovka, where women are held to know their place, people are less certain about what to think about the frescoes. They are one of many ripples from distant revolutions which reach the lower Don and leave the Cossacks baffled, uneasy.

The priest asked me, 'What are we to think of this new Russia? In this village of ours, people are beginning to come from outside and sell things which they have not made themselves. To travel in order to stand on the street and sell carrots which you have grown, a toy which you have carved, a kettle which you fashioned in your own workshop – why, yes, that is natural and even good. But these new people do nothing beyond buying and selling. They buy an article in one place, and then they come here to sell it for a higher price. They do not work, they do not make anything! I have told my congregation that it is a wickedness, a sin, to make money out of what you have not produced.'

The transition to a market economy in the lower Don requires more than laws made in Moscow. It needs nothing less than a cultural revolution, an overthrowing of inherited moral codes no less complete than the transformation which St Cyril intended for the Khazar pagans. (St Cyril failed. The Khazars chose Judaism instead.)

Once, in a hotel room at Anapa, I argued late into the night with a Cossack who had decided to start a tourism business. He was eating salted Azov herrings as he sat on his bed, pulling off their heads and splitting their bodies with a horny, expert thumbnail. His idea was to invite rich foreigners down to the Don country for holidays. 'You could bring them from Moscow on charter flights,' I suggested. 'And you could build a dude ranch out in the steppe beyond Novocherkassk, with comfortable chalets with running water, and offer them Cossack Heritage Experience.'

He shook his head. 'That would cost money. To bring them down by train would be far cheaper. They could stay with local people who have apartments and could rent them a room for dollars.' But surely, I said, you had to make some sort of investment first to attract foreign customers, so that you could recoup the start-up costs and make a profit by charging high prices.

'No, no,' returned the Cossack entrepreneur. 'The foreigners will pay very high fees, and we will spend as little on them as possible, and in this way we will make more money.'

There were two other people in the room. One was a young archaeologist from Tanais, herself of Cossack ancestry. She had been listening to this conversation with rising disgust. Now she said, 'We are talking about the sharing of our culture with guests from other lands. For that, we do not need this vile commercialism!'

The other person was an Armenian, a Rostov worker who used his car as an unofficial cab. He said nothing. But he caught my eye. A gold tooth glinted. He rolled his gaze upwards, and very gently shook his head from side to side in disbelief. Russians!

Barbarians, by definition, are so-called; they do not consider themselves to be barbarous. It was not until the last hundred years that certain Europeans undertook the experiment of describing themselves as barbarians. As part of a ferocious modernist critique of 'effete' and restrictive civilisation, they proposed to reverse all the headings over the conventional value-table. 'Barbarous' characteristics changed file from bad to good. Violence, spontaneity, youth, the leadership-cult and Nature became positive. Tolerance, maturity, rationalism, democracy and urban culture itself became negative and decadent.

In January 1918, as his poem 'The Scythians' began to form in his head, the Russian poet Alexander Blok 'felt physically, with my hearing, a great noise of the wind – a continuous noise (probably the noise from the collapse of the old world)'. What he wrote then was addressed to that old 'civilised' world, to Europe, from a Russia made young and returned to its barbaric self by the Revolution:

> Yes – we are Scythians. Yes – we are Asiatics.
> With slanted and avid eyes. . .
> For the last time – come to your senses, old world!
> To the brotherly feast of work and peace,
> For the last time to the bright brotherly feast
> The barbarian lyre calls.

When Blok snatched up the 'barbarian' conceit for revolutionary Russia, it had already been well-worn in the service of imperial nationalism, above all in Germany. Emperor Wilhelm II had invited his troops in China to fight the Boxer rebellion with the ruthlessness of Huns, and throughout the Second Reich, from its foundation in 1871, the fashion of barbarity had been embodied in monstrous state monuments: the neo-pagan colossi inside the Leipzig memorial to the Battle of the Nations, or the pseudo-Aztec kitsch of the Deutsches Eck, the imperial ziggurat raised at Koblenz over the confluence of the Rhine and the Mosel rivers. The Third Reich hardened this fashion into a full cultural dogma. It is enough to remember the project for mausolea to commemorate the SS dead who fell in the Russian campaigns: artificial mountains of earth towering over the steppe in the manner of Scythian or Sarmatian *kurgans*, lonely and *zabvenniy*, the barrows of a barbarian warrior caste.

To proclaim oneself a barbarian can amount to a licence for acts of unspeakable savagery. But at the same time it is to state that one is not, in fact, a barbarian, but a 'civilised' person who is borrowing costumes from civilisation's theatre-wardrobe of counter-values in order to make some point about the decadence of the times. Under the verbal surface, the old Athenian antithesis between barbarians and 'our sort of people' remains intact.

This is why the neo-Cossack discourse of brutality and primitivism is so revealing. One of the new *atamans* of the Don Cossacks, Yevgeni Yefremov, said recently to Bruce Clark of *The*

Times that sending men into battle in Moldava was 'like drinking a cooling glass of water after a long walk through the desert'. In that remark, which is a fair sample of Cossack rhetoric, Yefremov showed what the new Cossackism really is: a parade of negations, an adolescent Black Mass whose celebrants repeat the liturgy backwards – not to raise demons but to appal liberal piety.

There are Don Cossack settlements where illegal village courts now inflict public whipping, frequently on visiting Armenians. Superficially, this is a return to custom. In reality, it is a self-conscious performance, a 'heritage' pantomime of atavism laid on to impress other Russians.

The Cossacks were the last of many steppe peoples to inhabit the Black Sea plains in the old way. And yet they were in some respects unlike their predecessors. The Cossacks were never true nomads, who migrated in wagons behind their herds as the Tatars of the Golden Horde did, or the first Scythians and Sarmatians. The Cossack hosts were ramshackle rafts onto which all kinds of fugitives and adventurers had scrambled, and their economy was mixed: they were as much village-based free peasants as they were horse- and cattle-breeding pastoralists.

Politically, Cossack unity was never more than a matter of short episodes in history. Nothing emerged with the stability and complexity of the Scythian kingdoms, or of the Crimean Tatar Khanate. When commercial port-cities revived again along the Black Sea coast after the Russian conquests of Peter and Catherine, the Cossacks were not capable of acting as partners and protectors, as the Scythian steppe lords had been to the Greek cities and the Tatar khans to the Italians, but fell instead into subjection. Compared to the Indo-Iranian peoples of antiquity, and to some of the Turkic peoples who followed them, the Cossacks were primitive. Force, race and maleness are seldom the values of a stable and traditional society, but rather of bandits.

Chapter Four

Wax for women, bronze for men.
Our lot falls to us in the field, fighting,
but to them death comes as they tell fortunes.

Osip Mandelstam, 'Tristia'

WITHOUT A MAN upright on a horse, the landscape of the Black
Sea grasslands seems incomplete. The novels, from Tolstoy's to
Sholokhov's, have been read; the films watched. But this was once
Amazon country, and the very maleness of the Cossacks is in reality
a discord with the past.

Among the nomads of the Pontic Steppe, women were at times
powerful: not in the condescending male sense of silky persuasive-
ness in beds or over cradles, but directly. They ruled; they rode with
armies into battle; they died of arrow-wounds or spear-stabs; they
were buried in female robes and jewellery with their lances, quiver
and sword ready to hand.

In their graves, a dead youth sometimes lies across their feet. A
man sacrificed at the funeral of a woman? This could not have
happened in the Graeco-Roman tradition we call 'European
civilisation', where – as the German film-maker Volker Schlöndorff
once said – every opera about human transcendence requires the
sacrificial death of a woman in Act Three.

To say 'the Amazons existed' is too easy. What is fair to say is that
the Greek story about a race of virgin women warriors, mounted
and firing arrows from the saddle, still looks like myth but no longer
entirely like fiction. A hundred and fifty years ago, those same
Victorian scholars who taught that Herodotus was a liar dismissed
his and other versions of the Amazon story as childish fantasy. Since
then, archaeologists and structuralist critics have both concluded

III

that Herodotus was more sophisticated than the Victorians supposed. His statements about material and spiritual culture in the Pontic Steppe continues to be confirmed by research, as we have seen. Where he did invent, it has become clear that he did so in a secondary, 'non-fictional' way: assembling shreds and tatters of diverse narratives from the past (which would otherwise have perished entirely) into a collage, a new presentation whose impact he had calculated with some care.

Writing in the fifth century BC, Herodotus started with old Amazon tales known to most Greeks and then assimilated them to new narratives which had come to him – second-hand, third-hand – from his oral sources, most of them apparently colonial Greeks on the Black Sea coast, if not from Olbia itself.

After the Trojan wars and the death of their queen, Penthesilea, the Amazons living on the south shore of the Black Sea had been overcome by the Greeks and herded into prison-ships. But they mutinied, killed their guards and finally landed somewhere on the Sea of Azov. Here they at first fought the Scythians but eventually mated with them, settling 'three days' journey from the Tanais eastward and a three days' journey from the Maeotian lake [Sea of Azov] northwards' and becoming the nation of the Sauromatae. 'Ever since then the women of the Sauromatae have followed their ancient usage; they ride a-hunting with their men or without them; they go to war, and wear the same dress as the men.' Thus wrote Herodotus.

It was not until the middle of the nineteenth century, when archaeological techniques were still perfunctory, that Russian excavators in the Pontic Steppe began to register that some of the warrior skeletons under the *kurgans* were female. The first of these discoveries was made in a tumulus in Ukraine, near the middle Dnieper, by the amateur Count Bobrinskoy who knew a bit about skeletal anatomy. But gradually the bones of the women warriors, as they were recorded on the map, began to cluster in the region north-east of the Don, the land of the Sauromatians in the time of Herodotus. Further east, in the plains between the Ural and Volga rivers, nearly a fifth of the female Sauromatian graves dated between the sixth and fifth centuries BC have been found to contain weapons. Scythian graves all over southern Ukraine have revealed women soldiers, sometimes buried in groups, equipped with bows, arrows and iron-plated battle-belts to protect their groins. Later

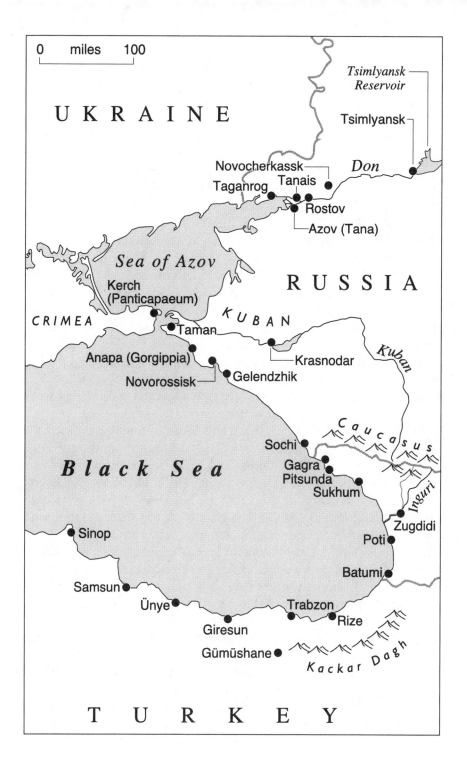

still, it became clear that the Sarmatians, who began to displace the Scythians from the Black Sea coast in the fourth century BC, also shared military and political authority between men and women. Sarmatian women burried by the Molochna River lay in scale-armour corselets, with lances, swords or arrows. The young Sarmatian princess buried at Kobiakov on the Don with her treasury of cult jewellery – a whole Iranian pantheon of animal and human figures made of gold – had her own battle-axe placed in the tomb beside the harness of her own horse-team.

Two conclusions seem to emerge. One is that Iron Age societies inhabiting the Black Sea-Volga steppes in the time of Herodotus and afterwards provided for a least some military and political parity between men and women. Not all of them did: Thracian women were not as free to ride, fight and govern as the women of some neighbouring nations were. Nor is it sensible to talk about 'equality'; knowing that both women and men were trained to use weapons and to ride as aggressive cavalry does not reveal much about how men and women behaved to one another or divided labour when they were out of the saddle. All the same, the Greeks were right to think that the Scythian-Sarmatian world had an attitude to women and power which was quite unlike their own. They found that attitude horrifying and fascinating.

The second conclusion is that Herodotus, knowing this fascination, catered to it. The Amazon legend had been around for years, always shocking and titillating to Greek male sensibility. What Herodotus heard about Sauromatian society could be appropriated to the Amazon stories by a neat myth about how the Amazons got from Anatolia to the Volga steppe. No doubt the voyage myth already existed somewhere, perhaps in several forms conflated by Herodotus. What matters is that he 'Amazonised' the Sauromatians into a mirror-game – a complex one, as François Hartog observes, in which the 'otherness' of the Amazons' original preference for war over marriage is well paraded for the Greek reader, but which ends with a sudden coming-together of those two opposites.

By consenting (in the Herodotus version) to make love with the young Scythian warriors, the Amazons open the way to a new society in which marriage and war no longer exclude one another but may both be practised by a woman. This society – Sauromatia – is in the physical sense formed by the children whom the Amazons bear to the Scythians. But it is also formed by a unique treaty

114

between men and women. The Amazons refuse the patrilocal suggestion of the young Scythians that they should all return to Scythia together, and instead insist that the young men must forsake their own families and follow them across the Don into that empty land 'three days' journey from the Maeotian lake northwards'. In that new place called Sauromatia, the two gender-halves of the community will each retain some of their own distinct rights. The language is to be the male choice of Scythian, which the Amazons (according to Herodotus) never learn to speak correctly. But the rights of women to hunt with or without men and to ride into battle are entrenched for ever. Women also retain control over sexuality and the reproduction of the nation, because the unwritten compact gives priority to Amazon tradition which prescribes that 'no virgin weds till she has slain a man of the enemy; and some of them grow old and die unmarried because they cannot fulfil the law'.

There remains a gap between archaeological evidence and all the various Amazon narratives of Herodotus, Strabo, Diodorus Siculus and the others. It we think that there were Amazons, in some sense, and if we cannot swallow classical explanations of how such societies of female power arose, then we owe ourselves a more 'scientific' set of hypotheses. Many modern savants have been tempted to provide them.

Mikhail Rostovtzeff (1870–1952), the father of Black Sea historiography, thought that he was looking here at one of the decisive stratifications in human spiritual history. He held the Sauromatians to be a pre-Indo-European population which had preserved the social pattern of matriarchy and the ancient cult of the Mother Goddess. But then 'Semites and Indo-Europeans (Rostovtzeff, writing in 1922, meant Scythians and Sarmatians) brought with them patriarchal society and the cult of the supreme god.' The Mother Goddess none the less survived, in a covert way, and 'the Amazons, her warrior priestesses, likewise survived'. The Sauromatians also preserved older ways: they 'impressed the Greeks by a notable peculiarity of their social system: matriarchy, or rather survivals of it: the participation of women in war and government; the preponderance of women in the political, military and religious life of the community.'

Not all of this has stood the test of time and of another seventy years' excavation. The Sauromatians were not pre-Indo-European: they were Iranian-speakers, the first contingent of the nomad conglomeration we call the Sarmatians to arrive on the Black Sea. And the Scythians – the previous Iranian-speaking wave – were not strikingly more patriarchal. Their cults, as Herodotus recorded, centred on goddesses like Tabiti, the hearth-goddess, or on the 'Great Goddess' so often shown on Scythian goldwork giving a sacred 'eucharist' drink to a king or warlord.

Since Rostovtzeff's time, it has been contended that as pastoralism developed from 'primal' Neolithic settled agriculture, it imposed a new division of labour which was sharply to the disadvantage of women: with men constantly in the saddle on the track of the herds, women were confined to domestic work in the tent or the moving wagon. Behind ideas like that lies the enormously influential work of the late Marija Gimbutas, whose work on the origins of the Indo-European language-family has become something of an orthodoxy – and an indispensable text for feminist historians.

Gimbutas believed, roughly, that in south-eastern Europe in the fifth millennium BC there lived a peaceful, highly artistic, matrilineal population of farmers. This settled late-Neolithic society was then disrupted by the arrival of quite different people from the steppes to the east: warlike, pastoral, nomadic and patriarchal invaders who overthrew the farmers and installed their own more 'primitive' and male-dominated patterns. Gimbutas named these intruders the *Kurgan* tradition, after their custom of steppe burial in mounds, and she identified the *Kurgan* peoples as the core of the 'proto-Indo-European' speakers, spreading out east, west and south from a homeland somewhere in the expanses of the Pontic-Caspian steppe.

This alluring theory would solve a lot of problems for archaeologists and linguistic historians. Even more alluring is its offer of a 'herstory', which would furnish a scientific basis for the association of peace, culture, religious reverence and agriculture with femininity, while categorising war, inequality, philistinism and cattle-ranching as phenomena of male domination.

Not everybody is comfortable with the Gimbutas version, however. There is agreement that there was a 'Late Neolithic Crisis' in south-eastern Europe, and that a densely settled agricultural population gave way to sparser patterns of settlement which were more reliant upon cattle and horses for food, traction and transport. With this change, religious cults or outlooks which involved the manufacture of thousands of clay female figurines were replaced by a different belief system which preferred solar symbols and engraved them upon vertical stone stelae. But there is not much hard archaeological evidence that this revolution was the direct result of a male-led invasion from the steppes. Critics of Gimbutas suggest that the great change could have happened for other, internal reasons. The population may have grown too large to support by crops alone; the introduction of the plough and greater reliance on stockbreeding may by themselves have changed and enhanced the male role.

Whatever the truth here, the Gimbutas link between pastoral nomadism and male-dominated social forms does not help to understand the Indo-Iranian nomads – the Scytho-Sarmatian peoples who began to arrive in the Black Sea steppe nearly three thousand years later. By then, the settled farming peoples of the Mediterranean region were stiffly patriarchal, while nomads and other 'barbarians' often showed signs of matrilineal authority. Timothy Taylor, of the University of Bradford, suggests that the position of Scythian women may have been very free and strong indeed until the pastoral-nomad economy began to make its first contacts with the earliest Greek colonies, in perhaps the seventh century BC, and it was that encounter with Hellenic colonialism which sent the authority of women into decline.

It is not hard to see reasons why Taylor could be right. The symbiosis with the Greeks transformed a large part of Scythian society into a wheat-farming export economy, in which the muscle-power of paid labourers was decisive. At the same time, Greek prejudices and inhibitions about women – their astonishing invention of a society in which women actually had no power or civic participation at all – may have exercised a growing and fashionable influence on Scythian male élites.

One Scythian myth of origin, which has come down to us in a queer, Grecianised form, tells how Hercules went searching for his lost mares in the Hylaea. This was a region of dense forest, now entirely vanished, which seems in classical times to have covered the left bank of the lower Dnieper, near the modern city of Kherson.

There, in a cave, Hercules met the Mixoparthenos, a creature who (as Herodotus put it) was a woman above the buttocks and below them a snake. She insisted that Hercules must make love to her before she returned his horses, and when he was gone, she bore three sons. The youngest, Scythes, being the only one who could bend the bow which Hercules had left behind him, became king in the land and ancestor of the Scythians.

The Mixoparthenos became a symbol. In spite of the Hercules element in her story, she belonged originally to Iranian rather than to Hellenic spirituality, and her effigies have turned up on the metal decorations of horse-harnesses in Scythian nomad burials. But then the Mixoparthenos reached the cities of the coast. She became, in the end, the crest of the rich, hybrid culture which arose in the Bosporan Kingdom, where the ruling families and dynasties were descendants of Sarmatian and Thracian chieftains while the merchants were Greeks and the soldiers Scythians, Sindians or Maeotians.

She is always full-face. Below her navel, her body splits into two serpent-trunks which coil up either side of her; she grasps the two coils with outstretched hands as if to keep her balance. On her head is a many-tiered oriental crown. Her pubis, thrust forward by the separation of her snake-thighs, is covered by a vine-leaf.

In a cave, under a shaggy wood, a female monster entraps a male hero to drag seed from him. It was blatantly not a woman who imagined the tale of Hercules and the Mixoparthenos, but neither was it a male 'barbarian'. As Herodotus takes care to point out, the details of how and why the snake-woman coupled with the hero were grafted onto an originally Scythian story which was processed and repackaged in the imagination of Greek colonial settlers – 'the story of the Greeks who dwell in Pontus'. (No doubt different Scythian communities had different, even competing, myths of origin. The one Herodotus tells as 'the Scythians' account' is a beautiful, mystifying story of how a golden plough, yoke, sword and flask fall from heaven. When the three sons of Targitaus go to pick them up, the gold bursts into flame at the approach of the first two. The third son, Coloxais, takes them safely, and becomes the founder of the Scythian 'kingly' line.)

The Mixoparthenos, Mother of Scythia, was present in the Scythian mind long before the 'Greeks who dwell in Pontus' embroidered her into the pattern of their own fear and dislike of women. In the centuries which followed, she slowly lost whatever function she may have had in the rites of steppe nomads and turned into the badge and protectress of the whole Bosporan Kingdom and the city of Panticapaeum. 'Scythia' as a Greek term ceased to mean one particular language-group of Indo-Iranian nomads: it expanded to denote a whole region of the world and a mixed Iranian-Hellenic culture which embraced the Black Sea Greeks, the Thracians, the Scythians and the Sarmatians alike.

At Panticapaeum, capital of the Bosporan Kingdom and the richest and most successful of all the Black Sea colonies, two statues of the Mixoparthenos flanked the main gate of the city (one of them is now in the museum of Kerch). But her effigy turns up in large and small versions, in stone but also in gold, silver or bronze, all round the north-eastern shore of the Black Sea. She was the patroness of the first genuinely and freely multi-ethnic culture on the Black Sea (for the Bosporan Kingdom was plural and 'Iranianised' in a way that even Olbia was not). She was the Mother of Scythia as the place where, for a time, the old Athenian polarity of 'civilised' and 'barbarian' appeared to be growing obsolete.

But the Mixoparthenos lived on in another, entirely practical way. She became a handle. Her slender body, curving outwards but held in again at head and serpent-legs, became an ornamental lug baked onto the rims of pottery cups, riveted or welded to the necks of bronze and glass vessels. She remained nameless but useful long after her city had burned down and her children had left history.

No longer recognised, the Mother of the Scythians still lives among us. The other day, in one of the old Habsburg railway stations in Budapest, I felt something unusual as I pulled open the heavy double-door of a ticket-office. There in my hand, in worn-away brass polished by millions of travellers, was a naked woman divided below her navel into two coiled serpents.

Renate Rolle, the German archaeologist who is now the best-known Western interpreter of Scythian research in Russia and Ukraine, is a true believer: she uses the word 'Amazon' without qualification. She has looked at the bones of the young women warriors, and she recognises them with joy. But after writing of their skill and balance in the saddle, of the dazzling co-ordination of eye, arm and breath required to shoot from a reflex bow without the support of stirrups, Rolle suddenly and touchingly feels that her readers require to be reassured that these warriors were feminine as well as female. She is an intellectual German woman of the late twentieth century; she wants women who are free physically and socially and politically but who have in no way modified their 'femininity'.

When she wrote her book *The World of the Scythians*, she was also a West German in a still-divided nation. Rolle evidently felt that her image of Scythian girls trained to muscular and nervous perfection had to be walled-off from the contemporary triumphs of East German women athletes, hardened and unsexed by anabolic steroids. 'Because their physical training was so varied, the physique of these fighting women would in no way have resembled that of the "mannish" women sometimes produced nowadays by intensive training for one particular competitive sport . . . These "man-killers" were, however, for all that no less aware of their femininity and wished to retain their charms in the land of the dead . . . they all have jewellery and mirrors, decorated according to the women's individual social rank; those interested in cosmetics also have make-up of various colours and also scent bottles.'

Amazons, if that is what we call them, belonged to the unmodified steppe life of pastoralism. When the symbiosis with Greek colonies began to change that way of life, the women warriors seem to fade away as a caste or institution. But something survived; the Greeks and later the Romans were constantly reminded of the Amazon tradition by the confidence and militancy of queens and princesses in these more settled societies. In 529 BC, Tomyris, queen of the Iranian-speaking Massagetae, was said to have killed Cyrus the Great of Persia and to have taken his head home as a trophy. Tirgatao, a Maeotian princess, raised and led an army which defeated Satyrus, tyrant of the Bosporan Kingdom. Amagē, wife of a Sarmatian king near the Sea of Azov, seized power from her own husband and led a cavalry commando into the Crimean Scythian kingdom next door, where she seized the palace, killed the king and imposed a peace settlement between the Scythians and the Greek city of Chersonesus (now Sevastopol). A few years later, the Emperor Augustus was forced to compromise with Dynamis, queen of the Bosporan Kingdom, who was supposed to be a Roman vassal: she gathered a Sarmatian army in order to overthrow and kill the man whom Augustus had proposed as her husband.

But beyond the Amazon problem, which is about what femininity may have meant to the Indo-Iranian nomads, there is an altogether more unsettling question. What did masculinity mean to them?

How 'male', by the standards of our own culture, were masculine Scythians or Sarmatians?

The Hippocratic manuscript *Airs, Waters, Places*, written in the fifth or fourth century BC, claims that Scythian men had low fertility and an equally low libido, in part because of their 'constitution' (in terms of humours) and in part because of their way of life. 'The men have no great desire for intercourse because of the moistness of their condition and the softness and chill of their abdomen ... moreover, the constant jolting on their horses unfits them for intercourse.' A little later, the pseudo-Hippocrates returns to the subject of Scythian impotence, which is 'also because they always wear trousers and spend most of their time on their horses, so that they do not handle the parts, but owing to cold and fatigue forget about sexual passion, losing their virility before any impulse is felt.'

Whatever this may mean, the Hippocratic authors are much more interesting about the mysterious Enareis or Anaries, who are also mentioned by Herodotus. The manuscripts portray them as a category of Scythian men who have become – in their social behaviour – women. 'The great majority among the Scythians become impotent, do women's work, live like women and converse accordingly.' These men are explicitly described as cross-dressers: they 'put on women's clothes, holding that they have lost their manhood'. They take this step after finding that they are unable to have sexual intercourse, thinking that 'they have sinned against Heaven'.

Herodotus, in the first book of his *Histories*, retails a legend that the Enareis were originally members of a Scythian war-party which sacked a temple of Aphrodite at Ascalon, on a retreat after raiding Egypt. The goddess retaliated by afflicting them and their descendants with menstruation which endures to this day: 'those who come to Scythia can see the plight of the men they call Enareis.' In the fourth book, he remarks that 'the Enareis, who are androgynous, say that Aphrodite gave them the art of divination which they practise by means of lime-tree bark. They cut this bark into three portions, and prophesy while they plait and unplait them between their fingers.'

Representations of magical androgynous figures do appear on Scythian, Sarmatian and Indo-Iranian decorations. A tiara from a grave in the Kuban shows such a figure serving the Great Goddess, and another occurs on a drinking-horn found in Romania. A third – Timothy Taylor is convinced – appears on the Gundestrup Cauldron, that stupendous silver mystery covered with repoussé scenes of unknown gods and rituals which was found in a Danish bog a hundred years ago, but which was probably made in Thrace during the second century BC. This is the beardless but male 'Horned God', cross-legged and crowned with antlers.

Here is a belief-world in which men can acquire the power of prophecy and become spirit-possessed mediums only by relinquishing their masculinity. Timothy Taylor refers to 'gender-crossing shamanism', something 'well-documented among recent Siberian pastoralists'. He suggests that, for men no longer able to ride to war, the abandonment of virility to become a shaman was an escape from the expectation that a man ought to die in battle.

All this means that the time has come for a new Count Bobrinskoy. In his own day of revelation, the count realised that so many of the young warriors at the end of his spade were not men (his predecessors had been so sure of the warriors' maleness that they had not bothered to examine or, often, even to keep their bones) but women. Now it is time to take a much closer look at the bones of queens, priestesses and important women in general, lying among their cosmetics and the remains of expensive dresses and tiaras. Some of them could turn out to be men: Enareis transvestites and gender-crossing mediums who have deceived another generation of far more sophisticated archaeologists.

Volodya and Yura Guguev are still young men. They were brought up as children at Alexandrovka, a new housing scheme on the north-eastern fringes of the city of Rostov. In those days, the 1960s, some green open space was still left there, and the boys used to play on the mounds of Kobiakov, a few hundred yards from their home, on the road to the old Don ferry at Aksai.

They both became archaeologists. Volodya was introduced to his career at Tanais, where he used to join the visiting expeditions each summer, but the burial mounds at Kobiakov never let his imagination rest. He went back to them after graduating, mapped the whole site and obtained permission to begin formal excavation.

It was the last possible moment to do so. Rostov was expanding again; the Kobiakov site was to be levelled for a new riverside expressway, and it was already being destroyed by garbage-tipping and temporary barracks for construction workers. Volodya did what rescue-archaeology he could: he found traces of settlements and kitchen-middens as well as several hundred graves dated between the Bronze Age and the Roman period. In the summer of 1988 he started work on 'Kobiakov 10', a burial site which had been flattened out in recent times but which had once been covered by a small *kurgan* three metres high.

Almost all *kurgans* have been robbed, some repeatedly, some within a year or so of the burial, but Kobiakov 10 had been left alone or overlooked. Volodya Guguev found a square pit – a room cut into the earth – and on its floor lay the skeleton of a young woman on her back.

She was a Sarmatian, aged between twenty and twenty-five, who had died some time in the second century AD. Her head had been crowned with a diadem of gold-foil stags, birds and trees. She had bracelets, a ring, an axe and horse-harnesses. Around her neck was a huge rigid collar of pierced and chiselled gold, encrusted with turquoises and decorated with a series of unknown magical creatures: dragons fighting with what seem to be monkeys in armour who hold clubs. In the centre of the collar was one of those works of art which, once seen, carry out a small but irreversible coup in the mind: a serene, golden, cross-legged man, his beard and hair carefully combed, a sword laid across his lap, a cup nursed in his two hands.

All these objects are now to be seen in the treasury of the Rostov Museum. Volodya Guguev studies the antecedents of the jewellery, which he recognises to be Central Asian – the great collar perhaps drawn from some distant central treasury between Tashkent and Afghanistan – and of the Indo-Iranian mythology represented by the golden man and the armoured monkeys. The Kobiakov find has made him well-known and respected in his profession. But when I met him at Tanais several years ago, he was still working as a disc-jockey in Rostov in order to earn a minimal living. (At that time, to change a £50 traveller's cheque into roubles was to have the annual salary of two professors of Byzantinology in your pocket.)

She was a princess or a queen – a woman from some great family who had attributes of a priestess, for almost everything left in the darkness with her had magical significance. Yet I have heard Volodya and his brother Yura speak with deep emotion of 'the poor princess'. Archaeologists are not immune to unscientific feelings about the dead, and this was not a usual case.

123

As a child, Volodya Guguev had run and played on the grass over her head. As a boy, he had wondered who and what might be hidden under the Kobiakov mounds. In the end, when he had grown into a good-looking young man, a flower in the chivalry of Russian science, he had found his way to this sleeping princess who had given him everything: fame as an excavator, national respect as a scholar, moments of incredulous joy and revelation of the kind which do not come twice in a lifetime.

She had given him her treasure which, had he been a wicked man, could have been melted down and transformed into enough bullion to buy him a Manhattan penthouse and a life of leisure. She had given him her faith, a puzzle which might, if he chose, preoccupy the rest of his days. In the end, when there was nothing else left at the bottom of the pit, she had given him what was left of her twenty-year-old body.

Not quite all her bones were there. Some of the very smallest phalanges, the most delicate finger-tip bones, were missing. I saw that this was distressing to Volodya, and we did not pursue it. But his younger brother Yura, one rainy day at Tanais, showed me the colour video of the excavation at Kobiakov 10, and mentioned that he and his brother were divided on this problem of the phalanges. His own view was that they had been gnawed off and removed by mice soon after the burial, something fairly common in chambered graves without coffins. Volodya, however, did not accept this. He preferred to think that the finger-tips had been ritually severed just after death, perhaps in some ceremony to exorcise the living from the touch of the dead. He could not bear the idea of the mice.

Chapter Five

We therefore went on towards the east, seeing
nothing but heaven and earth, and sometimes the
sea on our right hand, called the sea of Tanais, and
the sepulchres of the Comanians [Cumans], which
appeared to us two leagues off, in which places they
were wont to bury their kindred all together . . .

The Comanians build a great tomb over their
dead, and erect the image of the dead party there-
upon, with his face towards the east, holding a
drinking cup in his hand, before his navel.

Friar William de Rubruck, 'Journal', 1253

THE FIVE BROTHERS are *kurgans*. They are a group of burial
mounds standing on a patch of dry land in the middle of the Don
delta. From the summit of the tallest Brother, still some twenty feet
high, you can see the golden onion spires of Rostov Cathedral seven
miles to the east, and to the south, the cranes and grain elevators of
Azov.

Under this *kurgan*, although it had been looted by tomb-robbers
in antiquity, Soviet excavators found part of the primary burial
intact. It was 'royal': the tomb of a male Scythian ruler who had
died some time in the fourth century BC. It contained a huge
gorytus, the combined quiver and bow-case which Scythian men
and women carried slung on their hips, made out of silver and gold
and embossed by a Greek goldsmith with scenes from the myth of
Achilles.

But when I went to see the Five Brothers, expecting the usual
Ossianic setting of emptiness and loneliness, I was astonished to
find that this biggest Brother is still in use as a village cemetery. A

wavering plank fence surrounds its base. The *kurgan* itself is covered with weeds, bushes and Russian Orthodox graves: white stones leaning at all angles, many decorated with little photographs under glass, some topped with double Cyrillic crosses of rusty ironwork. The most recent of these graves, still strewn with faded flowers, was only a few months old; the first burial on this site, well before the mound was raised to cover the Scythian and his *gorytus*, had been dated to the Bronze Age. This mound has been in use as a necropolis for some four thousand years.

The continuity puzzled me at first. Even in southern England, where villages like to think that they have an unbroken collective memory reaching back at least to the Saxon invasions, I have never seen a Wiltshire long-barrow – for example – still in use as a Church of England graveyard. By contrast, the Pontic Steppe, with its open, oceanic horizons, had been a place of constant movement and change; each new population might have been expected to wash away all traces of its predecessors rather than to accumulate its own debris on theirs.

But in the end I saw where I had gone wrong. Crossing the steppes behind Olbia, looking at the burial mounds notching the infinite straight skylines, I realised how *kurgans* concentrate meaning. In a featureless place, they are the only features. Once they have been raised, it becomes inevitable that any act with human significance will be done on them, under them or around them. To lay a dead body anywhere else on the steppe would be an abandonment, a burial at sea. And the *kurgans* are not only funerary monuments but also beacons of hope. This is in part because they have always served as landmarks to lost travellers. But it is, above all, because in the *kurgans* there is gold.

The presence of treasure was always known. Many *kurgans* were looted by tunnellers soon after they were built; their sheer size and wealth made robbery inevitable, once the clan-relatives of the dead had moved away or lost control of the region. The Sarmatians, especially, took this into account and often constructed secret recesses for gold and jewellery sealed into the walls of the tomb chamber.

The scale of the bigger *kurgans* required professional mining skills from the robbers, some of whom left their own corpses in collapsed tunnels. These mounds could be sixty feet high, and fifty-foot vertical shafts gave access to long horizontal passages leading to the central chamber. Such an underground 'house' and its anterooms often contained human sacrifices: servants and guards or – sometimes – wives killed in a form of suttee. Food was left for the dead inside the chamber, and consumed in gargantuan quantities during funeral feasts around the *kurgan*: the Tolstoya mound in the Kuban held in its outer ditch cattle and horse bones which corresponded to almost six and a half tons of meat. Herodotus, in his famous account of the details of a Scythian royal funeral ritual, described how the mound was surrounded by a ring of dead, straw-stuffed riders mounted on dead horses and all impaled so that they would not collapse as they decayed. It is very possible that, when he was at Olbia, Herodotus heard a version of the gigantic ceremonies which had taken place some decades earlier at the Ulskii Aul *kurgan* in the Kuban. When the Russian archaeologist N. I. Veselovsky opened the Ulskii mound in the nineteenth century, he found the remains of 360 horses, tethered around stakes in groups of eighteen and forming a ring under the outer circumference of the mound.

It is not easy to disentangle the two attitudes of later populations to the *kurgans*: the impulse to 'desecrate' and plunder them, and the impulse to accept them as sacred places and re-use them for burials. The mounds were plainly a resource of treasure, but extracting it would usually have been too long and difficult an operation either for casual nomad visitors or for gangs acting in a clandestine, 'criminal' context. Many of the tomb robbers may well have been official concessionaires charged by some recent conqueror to gather bullion for him.

At the same time, it was obvious that the gold and jewellery had been deliberately placed in these mounds by some vanished race. The general taboo against disturbing the dead must have discouraged local initiatives to break into the *kurgans*, apart from the technical problems of gaining access. It may be that a certain pattern developed: that in new conquered steppe territory there would be a wave of officially sanctioned digging for treasure, but that afterwards the *kurgans* would be assimilated to the cults of the incomers and would reassert their 'sanctity'. The re-use is striking enough. The Scythians, or at least some Scythian groups, had erected life-sized stone figures on the top of their burial mounds. This was imitated more than a thousand years later by the Kipchaks (Cumans), a Turkic-speaking nomad people who arrived from

Central Asia and controlled the Pontic Steppe during the eleventh and twelfth centuries. Adding their own burials to Scythian mounds, the Kipchaks carved their own crude and sinister stone colossi, sometimes set upright on the summit of the tumulus but on occasion buried horizontally just under the surface. As late as the nineteenth century, many *kurgans* were still crowned by these stone 'babas', men or women with flat, scowling features and tall headdresses who hold cups in their lap. Then the new landowners began to remove them as 'idols' or 'curios', and today few south Russian or Ukrainian museums lack a row of Kipchak giants, usually parked in the museum garden.

The mediaeval Italian colonists on the Black Sea had no inhibitions about the sanctity of the *kurgans*. The stories of buried treasure obsessed them. Giosafat Barbaro, a Franciscan monk, was a prominent businessman in the Venetian community at Tana when, in 1437, an Egyptian acquaintance told him about the great treasure of 'Indiabu', last King of the Alans (Sarmatians). This treasure was supposed to be hidden inside a tumulus called 'Kontebbe' (possibly a version of the Turkic words for sand-mound), some twenty miles up the Don River from Tana near what is now the site of Rostov.

Barbaro (whose travel memoirs were wonderfully translated in the sixteenth century by William Thomas) at once organised a treasure venture. He signed up a partnership with a few other Venetian and Jewish merchants, took a hundred and twenty labourers up the frozen river by sledge, and tried to dig into the 'little hyll' of Kontebbe. Defeated by the frost, they retreated to Tana and returned in March after the start of the thaw. Barbaro and his men were now able to drive an enormous railway-cutting of a trench into the mound with pick and mattock, but they were completely disconcerted by what they found.

> Next unto the grasse the earth was blacke. Then next unto that all was coles . . . under this were asshes a spanne deep, and this is also possible, for having reades there by which they might burne, it was no great matter to make asshes. Then were there rynds of MIGLIO [millet] an other spanne deepe, and bicause it may be said that they of the cuntry lyved with breade made of miglio and saved the rynds to bestowe in this place, I wolde faine knowe what proportion of miglio wolde furnishe that quantitie to cover

such an hill of so great a breadth with the onlie rynds thereof for a spanne deepe? Under this an other spanne deepe were skales of fishe as of carpes and such other.

The treasure never showed up. Barbaro and his partners had to be content with 'halfe the handle of a little ewer of silver, made with an adders hedde on the toppe'. Meanwhile the weather had broken. 'Finally in the passion weeke the east winde beganne to blowe so vehemently that it raysed the earth with the stoanes and cloddes that had been digged and threwe them in the workemens faces that the blowwde followed. Wherfore we determined to leave of and to prove no further.'

It turns out that Barbaro was not digging into a burial mound or treasure cache at all. Without knowing it, he was cutting into a huge kitchen midden raised over centuries by Maeotian river fishermen and their families, and when the Russian archaeologist A. A. Miller excavated the settlement in the 1920s, he found the remains of the Venetian pit in exactly the dimensions given by Barbaro in his book. The fish scales and ash were still there, though the millet husks could no longer be found. Barbaro at least deserves admiration for the quality of his recording and measuring. But he is also entitled to some sympathy. The Kontebbe mound is at Kobiakov. Only a few hundred yards away, as Barbaro's team shovelled away in the frost and east wind, a Sarmatian princess was lying in the darkness among enough gold and jewellery to pay for a new basilica in Venice. But she was waiting for Volodya Guguev.

Barbaro failed. But the narrative of his failure contributes as much to knowledge as any 'Alan gold' he might have unearthed. It demonstrates, once again, that treasure-hunting in *kurgans* was a serious economic activity in the Pontic Steppe as early as the fifteenth century. It also confirms that breaking into a Scythian *kurgan* (as opposed to the later activity of looting Greek sites, which was far easier) was a substantial enterprise which required, and could be worth, a big investment of time and labour.

The *kurgans* came to be regarded as a natural resource – a form of mine. This was not true at all times nor for everyone, as we have seen. It is striking, for example, that Barbaro implies that only foreigners went on organised treasure expeditions, whereas the Tatar-Mongols appear to have left the *kurgans* alone. But all inhibitions broke down when Russian power expanded into Siberia and then to the Black Sea and the southern steppe zones. Russian officers and landowners, followed by huge settlements of discharged soldiers, exiles or transported peasants from central and northern Russia, treated the burial mounds as if they were mineral outcrops. In our own time, especially in the West with its frantic concern for historical conservation and 'national heritage', it has become unimaginable that anyone could treat monuments of the human past as a geological resource available for exploitation, like a gravel-pit or a peat-moss. But these are recent, sophisticated distinctions. Few beyond a tiny, educated minority drew such distinctions in the past, and the truth is that, in spite of the way in which archaeological 'heritage' has been assimilated into nationalist ideology, few outside Europe and North America draw them even today.

What took place in the steppes of the Russian Empire was one of the catastrophes of Eurasian culture. By the late seventeenth century, large armed bands of Russians were already living as professional tomb-robbers in the new Siberian territories. In 1718, Peter the Great decreed that all archaeological artefacts should be remitted to local governors, accompanied by a sketch of their place of discovery; little notice was taken of this, although enough was recovered from *kurgan*-robbers to form the nucleus of the imperial collections at St Petersburg. But when Russian settlement began along the Black Sea shores at the end of the eighteenth century, plunder became a regular occupation not just for magnates or bandits but for ordinary immigrant villagers. The Cossacks especially found a new source of wealth here, and they violated not only the *kurgans* of the grasslands but the more accessible and vulnerable remains of the Greek coastal cities and their hinterland. The magnificent stone-built tombs and catacombs of the Bosporan Kingdom were vandalised and their contents stolen; the surviving walls, towers and monuments of colonies like Tanais and Olbia were pulled down and used as building material. Landowners had title to what was found on their estates, and as Mikhail Miller wrote in his *Archaeology in the USSR*, 'a large number of landowners, having serf labour at their disposal ... excavated *kurgans* all through the nineteenth century out of boredom or curiosity'. Captain Pulentsov, a Cossack, became famous because he dreamed of a buried treasure and then spent the next twenty years frantically digging holes in the Taman Peninsula wherever the lie of the land vaguely recalled his dream (in the end, by pure accident, he found a valuable and unusual coin hoard). In such a climate, it was little short of a miracle that a class of devoted archaeologists emerged in Russia, at first amateurs but later scientifically minded professionals, who were able to rescue so much material and knowledge and to introduce systematic excavation and recording.

All the same, the cultural treasures and scientific data which Russian archaeologists saved have to be measured against all that simply vanished. Much was melted down for bullion or sold abroad. Russian archaeologists still remember the charlatan D. G. Shulz, who pretended that he had official authorisation and excavated some of the magnificent burials at Kelermes, in the Kuban. Shulz had the *chutzpah* to pose as the scourge of the tomb-robbers, and he persistently denounced plunderers to the local authorities until, in 1904, he was himself caught in Rostov selling Scythian gold to a jeweller who melted it into ingots. Further west along the coast, Odessa was the centre not only of this illegal antiquities trade but of forgery – the highly skilled and impeccably scholarly confection of Scythian and Sarmatian articles custom-made for the tastes of individual Western museums. The most famous victim was the Louvre in Paris which bought, at enormous cost, the 'Tiara of Saitapharnes'. This was manufactured by the Odessa goldsmith Ruchomovsky. He had studied a famous Olbia inscription – incomplete – describing how King Saitapharnes of Scythia was to be propitiated with an 'honour' from the city, and he used all his craft and imagination to supply this honour to the Louvre. The talent represented by Ruchomovsky has not yet died out. Exquisite 'Greek' cameos and brooches can still be bought from young men who hang around the museum in Odessa.

An almost equally frustrating problem for archaeologists is the mass of material that survives without any certain facts about where and how it was found. Looking along the showcases of gold ornaments in the town museum of Novocherkassk, I noticed how few of them had any information about provenance. The interpreter, herself an archaeologist, smiled ironically. 'They come from lucky people,' she said. As we travelled on across the Don country and into the Kuban, visiting museums wherever we stopped, I heard a great deal more about 'lucky people'.

Schastye is a Russian word that means both luck and happiness. It is the sort of happiness which is not planned or earned but which falls from heaven or jumps out of the earth: a blessing. It is the feelings of a Russian peasant whose mattock grinds against a jar crammed with Bosporan gold coinage or a bundle of Sarmatian horse-harnesses studded with emeralds and garnets. His poverty is over; his life is transformed as if by the Last Judgement. Those who found wealth in the ground in this way became known as the *schastlivchiki* – the lucky, happy ones. The term appeared among the inhabitants of Kerch, the Crimean port built on the ruins of Panticapaeum where much of the 'Scythian' goldwork was made, and spread throughout New Russia.

In Chekhov's short story *'Schastye'*, two shepherds lying out on the steppe at night with their flocks fall into conversation with a stranger, a passing estate foreman who has stopped to get a light for his pipe. The talk is of buried treasure. They are all certain that gold is stowed away in the earth all about them, in *kurgans* or in pots dug into the banks of streams, but they are almost equally certain that they will never find it. Why is it denied them, who need it so badly?

The older shepherd complains at one point that the treasure is under a spell, which makes it invisible to all seekers except those who have acquired a special amulet. But then he begins to talk as if the rich and powerful were immune to the spell and needed no amulet. 'It will come to this, that the gentry will dig it up or the government will take it away. The gentry have begun digging the barrows ... They scented something! They are envious of the peasants' luck.'

Dawn comes up, and they all stare into the 'bluish distance' where 'the ancient barrows, once watch-mounds and tombs . . . rose here and there above the horizon, and the boundless steppe had a sullen and death-like look'. The foreman slowly mounts his horse.

' "Yes," he says, "your elbow is near, but you can't bite it. There is fortune, but there is not the wit to find it . . . Yes, so one dies without knowing what happiness is like." '

One of the three inalienable rights in the American Declaration of Independence is the pursuit of happiness. Can this also mean the right to seek luck? The right to the pursuit of *schastye* – that liberation which happens when the earth suddenly opens and gold blazes around the end of the spade – has always seemed inalienable to the poorest people of many lands and times. A man's fate had little to do with his ability; hard work or natural talent or entrepreneurial flair could not free an English villein, a Russian serf or a Mexican peon from inherited slavery. On the contrary, the whole human world seemed fashioned in order to perpetuate their unfreedom. If there were to be an escape from misery, it must therefore come either from the superhuman or from the inhuman; from God in the sky above, or from whatever force ruled the darkness under the earth.

'Lucky people' were chosen to find treasure by a sort of grace. And yet, as Chekhov's old shepherd was suggesting, the ruling-class could be cruel enough and greedy enough to lock even that last door of hope against the poor, and to pocket the key. This fear survives, its origins scarcely understood, not only in Russia but even among sophisticated urban populations in the West. In Britain, for example, during the 1980s, a war of words and often of fists raged between the metal-detector clubs and bodies like the Council of British Archaeology. Superficially, this appeared to be a contest between responsible scientific authorities defending the material evidence of Britain's past, and rapacious scavengers (some of whom could be justly described as tomb-robbers) interested only in ripping 'valuable finds' out of the context which made them significant. But under that surface lay, on the one hand, archaic popular attitudes to traditional rights and, on the other, a complacent and authoritarian possessiveness with almost equally ancient roots.

The metal-detector lobby, whose club members were largely working-class, pronounced that its supporters were exercising a natural liberty of free-born Englishmen to seek treasure. That liberty was now being dismantled by a middle-class professional élite with the insolence to proclaim itself the rightful guardian of Britain's 'heritage'. (Here the treasure-seekers were offering bad history: treasure in England belongs to the landowner unless the Crown exercises its right to 'treasure trove' and appropriates it, rewarding the finder rather than the landowner.) But there was, all the same, something authentic in their sense of the emotional importance of 'luck' to ordinary people in the past. Equally, there was something penetrating in their question to the State's official heritage custodians: Who do you think you are? Why should a university degree in archaeology and a government excavation licence allow you to assert ownership over the buried treasures of Britain, and to deny the opportunity of 'luck' to the vast majority of the population?

Cossacks have been especially lucky, and their descendants still fantasise about where their ancestors may have hidden their luck. In that Chekhov short story, there is hungry speculation about the treasure supposedly buried by Don Cossacks on their way home after the Russian victory over Napoleon in 1812. And all over southern Russia and Ukraine tales are told about the hidden wealth of the Zaporozhe Cossacks, the 'Treasure of the Sech'.

The powerful Zaporozhe host, which had dominated Ukraine and the debatable lands between Poland and Russia for hundreds of years, was finally suppressed by Catherine II in 1775. A Russian army, pretending to be paying a peaceful visit on its way to harry the Turks, attacked the Cossack stronghold on the Sech island in the Dnieper in the middle of the night. The Cossacks, taken by surprise, surrendered without resistance. Their *ataman* Peter Kalnishevsky and his lieutenants were arrested (the Russian records of confiscation show that Kalnishevsky had in his barns 162 tons of wheat and personally possessed 639 horses, 1,076 long-horned cattle and over 14,000 sheep and goats). The rest of the host were disarmed and allowed to disperse quietly. Some forty thousand of them moved into Crimea, still then under Turkish-Tatar control, and settled near the Cimmerian Bosporus around Kerch.

This was not the way a Cossack host preferred to end. Within a few years, more flattering myths about the Zaporozhe Cossacks began to circulate. One of the most persistent claimed that Peter Kalnishevsky had escaped from his Russian captors and, with a few comrades, had driven sixteen peasant wagons loaded with treasure across the steppe from the Dnieper to the Don country. There he had buried the wealth of the Zaporozhe Cossacks in a secret cache.

There was not a world of truth in this. Kalnishevsky and his chancellor Globa were taken off to Moscow under guard, and the *ataman* was then imprisoned in the Solovetsky Monastery, on an island in the White Sea which was still a penal settlement in Khrushchev's time. There Kalnishevsky was kept until his death, reputedly at the age of 112. As for the treasure, it seems never to have existed. Catherine's favourite Potemkin, who was in charge of the raid against the Cossacks, stole the gilded decorations from the Pokrovsky Church on the island, which were found in his palaces after his death. The herds and the grain were sold for a large sum of money which was used as founding capital for a municipal bank in the newly built port of Novorossisk. The Cossack artillery, with any petty cash and valuables found in the Sech by the empress's officers, was removed to St Petersburg.

But these facts were not allowed to impede the Cossack dream. Only five years ago, a Rostov newspaper announced that the 'Treasure of the Sech' had been located near Azov. A Rostov town councillor named Anikeev insisted that it had been buried in a field belonging to a Cossack named Zabarin, which lay between the town of Azov and the sea at Kagalnik. Here a hidden well had been discovered, close to a mound which contained six barrels of treasure hanging from oak beams. Councillor Anikeev gave no information about when the discovery was made, or even about what happened to the contents of the barrels – the book of local legends from which he turned out to have plagiarised the story had given no details either – but he added helpfully that while this treasure might have been Kalnishevsky's, it might equally well have belonged to 'Indiabu, Tsar of the Alans'. At all events, the indifference to this great discovery shown by the head of the Azov museum was an example (Anikeev declared) of disgraceful bureaucratic sloth.

The local archaeologists at Azov, enraged by Anikeev's article, chose the scientist S. V. Gurkin to reply. In an eight-page essay entitled 'Field of Miracles in a Land of Imbeciles', Gurkin proceeded to devastate the wretched Councillor Anikeev for credulity and ignorance. 'Here on the open spacious steppe,' Anikeev had written, 'with its scent of grass and the incessant voices of birds stood, more than 250 years ago, the persecuted *ataman* Kalnishevsky with his comrades.' Gurkin pointed out mercilessly that Kalnishevsky had not been an *ataman* 250 years ago, that he had demonstrably never been near the Don in his life, and that if he had been there when Anikeev said he had, he would have been burying his treasure in Turkish-held territory under the noses of the Azov garrison. The only 'lucky' Russian in the whole of this story, Gurkin concluded, was the man who had looted the Pokrovsky Church on the Sech, Prince Potemkin himself.

Chapter Six

We [Russians and Poles] started from different
points, and our paths only intersected in our
common hatred for the autocracy of Petersburg.
The ideal of the Poles was behind them; they strove
towards their past, from which they had been cut off
by violence and which was the only starting-point
from which they could advance again. They had
masses of holy relics, while we had empty cradles.

Alexander Herzen, *My Past and Thoughts*, Part VI

I am these two, twofold. I ate from the Tree
Of Knowledge. I was expelled by the archangel's
    sword.
At night I sensed her pulse. Her mortality.
And we have searched for the real place ever since.

Czesław Miłosz, 'The Garden of Earthly Delights'

THE OCEAN TERMINAL, which is Odessa's new gateway to the
Black Sea, juts out into the harbour at the foot of the Odessa Steps.
When I went there, the great modern building was desolate and
silent, its concrete decks and curtain walls scarred and holed as if
the place had been bombarded.

The indicator board had jammed many months before, showing
still the previous summer's ship departures for Yalta, Ochakov or
Sevastopol. The plate-glass windows lay in shards across the floors.
The sea-wind gusted in past ranks of passenger ferries and launches
rocking uselessly at their moorings, the blue-and-yellow Ukrainian
ensigns already fraying at their sterns. Only one ship showed signs

of life: the big motor-vessel *Dmitri Shostakovich*, which had taken most of Odessa's Jews away to Israel when emigration became easy in the late 1980s, was tuning up her engines for the voyage to Haifa.

Inside the terminal, a few embers of activity still glowed. The parade of tourist shops and duty-free booths was shuttered up, and some had clearly been looted. But on one of the upper decks, next to a roped-off chasm in the floor, I discovered a small coffee bar was open. Better still, it was selling coffee, which had become almost as rare as petrol and diesel in Odessa. A Ukrainian family had found its way to the bar, picking its way through the unlit concourse and up a staircase impeded with rubble, and was cheerfully drinking Crimean champagne.

As I left, walking along the quayside, I saw ahead of me an exquisite grey Honda with lightly smoked windows, parked on the edge of the dock. It was crate-new, so fresh from a Japanese freighter that it had no licence plates. Coming up to the car, I saw through the darkened glass two men on the front seats, each bent forward to sniff lines of powder off a board spread across the facia top. I saw them and one of them, pulling himself upright in an unhurried way, saw me. It seemed wise to walk faster. Fifty yards further on, I passed the maritime police post. An officer inside, drawing on a cigarette, watched me and the Honda without apparent interest.

Odessa has experienced times like these before, intervals – sometimes lasting for years – when its heartbeat runs down and the streets fall quiet, when some disaster freezes the harbour and its shipping like January ice and separates the city from the Black Sea. But these intervals are in the city's nature: a port thrown up hastily on a barren shore to bring New Russia into the capitalist age of slump and boom. It has always been feasting or famine with Odessa.

Foreigners built Odessa and ran it for the Russian Empire, and it was more than twenty-five years before a Russian became governor-general there. Most of the planners were French émigrés – the Duc de Richelieu who was to become the father, benefactor and tutor of Odessa's childhood; the Comte de Maisons who had been the president of the Rouen *parlement* before the French Revolution; Alexandre Langeron who left his name to the headland and the wide beach east of the harbour where children still swim and fish. The architects were usually Italians, as was the first generation of grain dealers, and Italian was the official language of commerce in the early years. Much of the shipping business was Greek. The suppliers of wheat, for the first hundred years the reason for Odessa's existence, were the great Polish landowners whose estates lay far up country in Podolia and Galicia. Their nation had been finally obliterated by the Third Partition in 1795, the year after Odessa's foundation, but now, sometimes quite cheerfully, these eastern Polish magnates were adapting to life as subjects of the tsar.

The city went up with a rush. Two years after its official inauguration, held on a dusty building-site on the cliffs between the steppe and the sea, Odessa had a cathedral, a stock exchange and a censorship office. There were just more than two thousand settlers at the end of the first twelvemonth, in 1795, and by 1814 there were 35,000. That was the year when Richelieu, the true founder, climbed into his coach among lamenting crowds and set off back to France. He took with him one small trunk containing his uniform and two shirts. Everything else had been given away. His salary was paid into the fund for distressed immigrants. His books were left behind to form the library of the Odessa school which he had founded, and which later took his name: the Lycée Richelieu.*

This was a man of the Enlightenment: energetic, austere, universal, lonely. Richelieu, whose statue notches the sky at the summit of the Odessa Steps, was happier among immigrants than among the Russian bureaucrats whom he commanded. As the city prefect and then as the governor-general of New Russia, he looked forward to creating another America in which the displaced and the ambitious of all countries would gather to live and to trade in freedom. Serfdom did not follow Russian and Ukrainian peasants who arrived as settlers, and Richelieu carefully embedded them among German, Greek, Moldavian, Jewish and Swiss colonists who would teach them both modern agriculture and the practice of liberty. In all, more than a million human beings emigrated to make their homes under his protection. Richelieu was especially fond of the contingent of Nogay Tatars who had fallen under his persuasive influence. It pleased him that he had induced these steppe nomads to

* Richelieu became prime minister of France in September 1815, less than three months after Napoleon's defeat at Waterloo, and his friendship with the tsar helped him to secure the withdrawal of Allied occupation troops after only three years. Before his time in Odessa, he had taken part on the Russian side in the storm of Ismail in 1790. (see p. 97), where he is said to have rescued a Turkish child from Cossacks about to murder her. Byron used this incident in *Don Juan*, but attributed it to his eponymous hero.

settle. For them, among their new vineyards overlooking the Black Sea, he had stone mosques erected and houses for their mullahs.

Odessa's first disaster happened in 1812, while Richelieu was still there. Plague broke out that August. Richelieu shut down every public institution, including the new Italian opera house, and ordered the population to remain at home. He segregated the city into five sealed districts, each with a doctor and an inspector (four out of the five doctors died). A few carriages still passed through the wide, dusty streets, bearing black flags for a corpse, red flags for an infected passenger. Patricia Herlihy, in her *Odessa, A History* records that 'convicts dressed in black leather suits soaked in oil, and still wearing chains, were sent into the contaminated houses to clean them out twenty days after the dead were removed.'

But the plague was only a waver in the Odessa boom which was now under way. Exports through the port had tripled in value between 1804 and 1813. Then a coincidence of crop failures in Western Europe with breakneck rearmament after Napoleon's escape from Elba sent grain profits up in a geyser of easy money which only began to falter in about 1818. Through the Treaty of Adrianople, in 1829, the defeated Ottoman Empire conceded free passage to Russian shipping through the Narrows; Odessa went into another boom in the 1840s and into yet another, following Britain's abolition of the Corn Laws in 1847, which lasted until the outbreak of the Crimean War.

This was the beginning of more disasters. The war itself, bringing maritime trade to an instant halt, was serious enough. An Anglo-French naval squadron bombarded Odessa on 10 April 1854, killing a number of citizens and hitting some of the large public buildings, like the governor-general's palace, which were built along the low cliff-top above the port and made an easy target. A ball lodged in the plinth of Richelieu's statue, where it still remains. Honour was saved, however, by a gun battery on the end of one of the moles, commanded by Ensign Shchegolov, which managed to disable the British frigate *Tiger*. She was beached somewhere near Langeron Point. One of her cannon, taken as a trophy, now stands mounted at the end of Primorskie Boulevard, the majestic terrace which runs along the cliff-top at the summit of the Steps. But the Crimean War was also the beginning of Odessa's decline. Although the competition of American wheat was becoming serious, Odessa – coddled by free-port status which assisted trade but also meant that the harbour was cut off from the Russian domestic market by tariff frontiers – had not bothered to industrialise or to diversify.

Odessa began to rejoin the Russian economy in 1859, when the free-port privilege was withdrawn and New Russia lost its autonomy within the Empire. After the European slump of 1873, which brought the grain trade temporarily to its knees and caused a wave of bankruptcies in the city, a new influx of foreign capital began to exploit Odessa as the main port for the Ukrainian hinterland; the Belgians, above all, set up sugar-beet refineries and invested in the huge coal and iron deposits being opened up in the Donets basin. The Belgian entrepreneur Baron Empain, the world's pioneer of electric transport, laid down a tramway network. The British built a waterworks (Odessans, drinking the foul water of the Dniester estuary, had been subject to outbreaks of cholera almost every summer), while the Germans provided gas lighting for the streets. After the eruption of Mount Etna in 1900, some of the seaward boulevards were re-paved with black Sicilian lava.

At the same time, Odessa's demography began to change. In the first years of the century, Richelieu had worked to bring in Jewish colonists from Russian-occupied Poland. By the 1860s, and especially after the 1882 'May Laws' restricted Jewish business activity in the countryside, the population of the Jewish *shtetls* in the west of the Russian Empire began to flow down to the Black Sea in a broadening torrent. A census of 'native language' in Odessa taken in 1897 suggested that more than 32 per cent of the population spoke Yiddish, while the figure for Russian was only just more than 50 per cent. The third mother-tongue was Ukrainian which – in a city now proclaimed to be ancestral Ukrainian territory – was spoken by a mere 5.6 per cent; almost as many Odessans spoke Polish. This new Yiddish Odessa, whose people were overwhelmingly artisans and small shopkeepers, took over the city's already Mediterranean culture and gave Odessa its special raucous, parvenu brilliance which survived until the Bolshevik Revolution. Most of the Jews were poor, and many were revolutionary. In this intellectual and physical turbulence, punctuated by pogroms organised by the Russian authorities themselves, were formed the minds of Isaac Babel, Leon Trotsky and Vladimir Jabotinsky.

The inner city is divided between crows and doves. The crows rule the district by the railway station, where Richelieu and Catherine Streets – for fifty years disguised as Lenin and Karl Marx Streets – set off on their dead-straight march to the sea. In spring, twigs clatter down on the broken pavements of Richelieu as the rookery nests pile up in the plane trees. White bird-lime draws a line round the feet of the beggars in the cathedral porch on Pushkin Street: Russian beggars with matted fringes and buniony faces, who cross themselves continuously with shaking hands.

The crows make enough noise in the mornings to wake the guests in the cheap hotels near the station; their quarrels are louder than the grinding and crackling of the trams. Further on, in the streets between the station and the Moldavanka quarter where the Jewish gangsters used to live, is the real heart of crow territory. No dove or pigeon would survive long here, for this district is the site of the crows' food supply, the Privoz market. In the mud between the market halls, they hop and haggle over shreds of calf-muzzle, crumbs of brinza cheese, carrot-tops and the skeletons of anchovies. Gypsies passing with jam-jars of hot tea shout at the crows, and the Tatar women selling grated carrot slash at them with sticks if the birds sidle too close to their stalls.

About halfway down Catherine Street towards the sea, as you approach Deribasovskaya, the doves begin. They do not hustle, but get a living by charm. They sit in rows along the cornices of the opera house, whirring down prettily to beg from children in the Palais Royal gardens or by the monument to the *Battleship Potemkin*'s mutineers. The families mooching along Deribasov-skaya shed trails of sunflower seeds and fragments of ice-cream wafer for the doves.

The doves disdain the trees, although there are huge old planes all along Primorskie Boulevard – a street which is really a long esplanade garden with palaces down one side and an open view over the port and the Black Sea on the other. A few years ago, at the end of the Soviet period, a planner decided to improve this view by cutting the trees down, and it was the first sign of changing times in Odessa when dozens of young people came down to Primorskie and clung to their trees until the workers with chainsaws grew ashamed and went away. But the doves prefer to feel marble and bronze under their pink feet, on the ledges of the ancient London Hotel and the governor-general's palace, on the *Tiger* cannon, on the sculptured forehead of Pushkin's statue or on the shoulder of Richelieu at the top of the Steps.

Konstantin Paustovsky, who wrote about Odessa as a man writes about a wife who died young, used to sit here on the low wall. Giddy with hunger – it was 1920, a year of blockade and famine – he would rest in the early morning on his way to the newspaper office where he worked and breathe the wind.

> Apart from decks, it smelt of acacias, dry seaweed, the camomile in the cracks of the sea wall, and of tar and rust. Occasionally, all these smells were washed away by a special after-storm smell from the open sea. It was quite unlike, and could not be mistaken for anything else. It was as though a girl's arm, cool from bathing, were brushing my cheek.

When I first read those words, nearly twenty-five years ago, I knew at once that this could no longer be true about the sea wind on Primorskie, and that Paustovsky had known that it would not be true. The air at the top of the Steps now smells of oily brine, low-octane petrol and fatigued cement. But those words cannot be unwritten. I have remembered them in other Black Sea places, like the harbour at Anapa at dawn after a night of wind. They are accurate because nothing can be added to them and nothing taken away.

The Odessa steps, the *Escalier Monstre*, are enigmatic. To see them, for anyone who cannot forget how Eisenstein in *The Battleship Potemkin* made them into the most famous flight of stairs in the world, is like seeing a famous actress: smaller, drabber, less purposeful than in the movie. The Steps seem to go nowhere in particular. Once they leaped straight down from the city to the harbour, a triumphal strut towards the sea and the southern horizon. Now the main dock highway cuts across the foot of the Steps and the view is blocked off by walls of stained cement: the dilapidation of the Ocean Terminal.

And, from the top, the Steps seem short and neglected. They are so constructed that a glance down them sees only the landings between each flight, suggesting a mere set of terraces. The grass on either side is unkempt. On one flank an ugly metal funicular railway is broken down and rusting. It is all a disappointment. But then, as you start off down the 220 granite steps, there arises a sense of entering some process of illusion, rather like going into a maze or walking up to a Greek column.

There is even some legerdemain about who built the Odessa Steps; they were certainly started in 1837, but not by the Italian architect Boffa whose name is engraved on them. So is the name of an Englishman called Upton, but his Steps numbered only 192 and were made of Trieste sandstone.* At some point, the design, the material and the master of works all changed. The Steps were re-planned in granite by Boffa, or possibly by Rossi or even Toricelli who both built much of Odessa, with a sharply diminishing width from base to summit.

So it happens that at the bottom you turn around and are amazed. From here only the risers are visible; the Steps, extended by a false perspective, race up to heaven. At the top is Richelieu, with clouds streaming past his head. In reality, his statue is dwarfish, smaller than lifesize. But from the foot of the Steps he is a colossus.

After Richelieu, Langeron governed in Odessa. He was a pleasant, witty old soldier who found the New Russian salad of races too much for him and said so: 'a territory as big as France and populated by ten different nationalities.' He was succeeded by the first Russian Governor-General, Ivan Inzov, who lasted only a year and in 1823 was replaced by Count Mikhail Vorontsov.

With Vorontsov, a new magnificence arrived in Odessa. Educated in England, where his father had been ambassador, this was a gentleman of enormous public and personal ambition. He helped to make New Russia and Odessa rich, and the Vorontsovs offered splendid official hospitality in their white palace at the end of Primorskie. He also made himself spectacularly rich on the profits of private land speculation (while he was still Governor-General) and of new Crimean vineyards equipped to produce champagne. At Alupka, on the Crimean coast, he converted Richelieu's old villa into a Tudor-Moorish palace with 150 rooms.

* Upton was a civil-engineering genius who could not keep his hand out of the till. Raised in Daventry, he got into trouble for running a post-office and embezzling the postal fees; he then became one of Telford's most trusted road-builders and developed the main highway to Holyhead. In 1826, he was charged with pocketing construction funds by forgery – a capital offence. Upton jumped bail and escaped to Russia, where he became chief engineer at Sevastopol and built not only the sluice tunnels for the naval dockyard but many of the forts whose capture cost thousands of British lives during the Crimean War a few years later.

It stands there still, a monstrosity in perfect taste, chilly on the hottest summer day. The British delegation stayed there during the Yalta conference in 1945.

Alexander Pushkin thought Vorontsov was a marmoreal prig. Vorontsov inherited this cross, untrustworthy poet from Ivan Inzov when he took over Odessa in 1823. It was then nearly five years since Pushkin, at the age of twenty-one, had been rusticated from St Petersburg. He was officially a member of the Foreign Service, so that he could be discreetly punished by being sent on an official journey; Pushkin was handed over to Ivan Inzov, a tolerant guardian who took the poet with him on a succession of appointments in Ekaterinoslav and Kishinev, and allowed him to wander off on a prolonged 'convalescence' in Crimea and the Caucasus. When Inzov was transferred to Odessa, Pushkin went too, and took up enforced residence in the city.

This was not exactly a serious punishment for a dissident writer suspected – accurately – of anti-state activities. But Pushkin, who could not know what worse fates would fall upon other Russian poets in the two centuries ahead, felt himself a martyr. Part of his punishment in Odessa was to be taken up by Vorontsov and bored stiff. He resented having an eye kept on him, and still more the governor-general's suggestions for little jobs to keep him busy.

One reason for Pushkin's resentment was that he was already busy. In May that year, he had started writing *Eugene Onegin* in his dark apartment behind Primorskie. But there was another reason. Soon after the new governor-general's arrival, Pushkin had started a love affair with his wife, the Countess Vorontsova. In Odessa, nothing stays secret. Pushkin met the cold, English gaze of the count and did not like what he fancied he saw there. Early in 1824, Vorontsov overruled the poet's noisy protests that he was dying of a heart aneurism and was too sick to move, and appointed him to a travelling commission to study locust damage in the Dniester country. Pushkin never forgave him. His report is supposed to have consisted of a four-line poem:

> The locusts flew and flew over the plain.
> They landed on the ground,
> Ate everything they found,
> And then the locusts flew and flew away again.

This may be apocryphal, but by now Pushkin was becoming unbearable to Vorontsov, who wrote to his friends in St Petersburg and secured Pushkin's dismissal from the Foreign Service. This meant that he had to leave Odessa and live on his father's country estate for two years of boredom and loneliness, in the course of which he wrote most of his best verse. He took with him a gold talisman-ring with a cabalistic Hebrew inscription, which Countess Vorontsova had slipped onto his finger one day after they had made love on a Black Sea beach. Pushkin wore the ring for the rest of his life. It was removed by friends after his death thirteen years later in a duel, and survived until 1917 when an unknown looter took it from the Pushkin Museum in Moscow in the early months of the Revolution.

Pushkin was expelled from Odessa in July 1824. Less than a year later, Vorontsov was sent another poet to keep an eye on. In late February 1825, after a journey, mostly by sledge, from St Petersburg, three young Poles arrived in Odessa. They were Franciszek Malewski, Józef Jezowski and Adam Mickiewicz.

They were all under sentence: banned from the Polish provinces of the Russian Empire and subject to orders of enforced residence. A few months before, they had been released from imprisonment in Vilnius and transferred to the Russian capital, where they had persuaded the authorities to let them be redirected to the south, hoping to wind up in Crimea or the Caucasus. As a compromise, they were sent as far as Odessa.

All three had been involved in a plot, or more correctly in a secret society, devoted to the restoration of Polish independence. The Filarets ('lovers of virtue') had arisen in the early 1820s among students at the Wilno (Vilnius) University, some twenty-five years after the final suppression of Poland by the Third Partition. Before the Filarets, there had been a much smaller grouping called the Filomats ('lovers of learning'), to which all three exiles had belonged: something between a Masonic lodge and a debating club in which romantic students discussed Byron, sex (they invented an 'Erometer' for measuring passion) and the liberation of Poland. But too many people heard about them and wanted to join.

The Filarets started as an overflow organisation from the Filomats. Soon, however, they became much larger and bolder, not to say reckless. Prominent Polish conspirators, sought by the tsarist police, came to Vilnius and talked insurrection. So did a few young

Russian friends of liberty, who later became members of the 'Decembrist' conspiracy. Russian informers kept note of words and names. But the explosion, when it took place in 1823, was expected by nobody, touched off by a stroke of pure Polishness.

It started in a classroom at the Vilnius Lycée. One lesson was over, but the next teacher had not turned up. A boy called Plater, in the fourth form, sidled to the blackboard and wrote *Vivat Konstancja* in chalk. He had some girl in mind. But another boy in the form, a serious-minded youth called Czechowicz, rubbed out the end of the second word and wrote *Konstytucja* – Long Live the Constitution.

Every boy in the room knew what that meant. It meant the patriotic Constitution of the Third of May, 1791, the charter of Polish national enlightenment and liberty which had been erased by the tyrannous partitioning powers. Somebody else drew an exclamation mark. Then yet another schoolboy got hold of the chalk and added: 'Ah, what a sweet memory!' Hubbub broke out in the classroom and spread down the corridors.

It was too late to contain the outbreak. The school authorities arrested three of the boys and were then arrested themselves by the Russians. All over the pink, yellow and white walls of baroque Vilnius, graffiti unreeled themselves: 'Long Live the Constitution! Death to Tyrants!' Senator Novosiltsev, who had been sent to Vilnius to investigage rumours of sedition in the university, was roused from a drunken coma and signed an order licensing the police to act on the Filaret files. Within a few days, most of the leading Filarets and Filomats, including Adam Mickiewicz and his companions, were locked up in a dungeon in the cellars of the Basilian Monastery.

It was October when they were arrested, already disagreeably cold, and they remained in the dungeon for most of the ensuing winter. They got through the weeks and months by drinking mugs of hot tea, arguing about what sort of Poland they intended to restore, singing to the distant sounds of the monastery organ at Mass, and listening to Adam Mickiewicz while he read his own poems. They lived, in other words, through the essential experience of every generation of young Poles from that day to this.

Mickiewicz, who was to become the 'national poet', even the lay patron saint of his country, was then twenty-four: about a year older than Pushkin. He was already a famous young man. With his collection *Ballads and Poems*, he had introduced Romanticism into Polish literature: 'Faith and feeling more reveal to me/ Than the sage's lens or eye . . .' In an occupied, demoralised nation whose hope of new life seemed to be a matter of visionary faith rather than of reason, the book had instantly sold out. He had written the long poem *Grazyna*, and in Vilnius he had composed two acts of *Dziady* (Forefathers' Eve). This was the beginning of an extraordinary poetic drama about love, magical religion and political sacrifice which is unlike anything else in European literature and which was never to be completed. The writer Ksawery Pruszyński has compared it to a cathedral of which 'an aisle, a chapel, a presbytery, part of the choir' were raised but never united under a single roof.

It is not easy to come close to the young Mickiewicz. He became too important to Poland. Even his friends from the Filomats wrote about him with an undifferentiated awe, as if he were a Romantic icon: a one-dimensional figure of passionate emotions and immaculate patriotism, a profile with wind-blown locks and burning eyes brooding among crags and eagles. Only much later in life, in the long years of his exile in Paris, does a human being emerge from contemporary descriptions. This middle-aged Mickiewicz, thickset and with bushy grey hair, was solemn in speech, endlessly patient with friends and strangers, short-tempered with his own family. Disappointments and a difficult marriage had marked him. His last great work, the narrative poem *Pan Tadeusz*, had been finished in 1834, and for the last twenty years of his life he wrote little of lasting value. Instead he gave his energies to organising the vain struggle for Polish independence, travelling up and down Europe to summon up support for the cause and to raise armies from Polish communities in exile. In Paris he fell victim to the religious charlatan Towiański, who for many years exploited the poet's fame to bolster his worthless mystical sect and drove a wedge between Mickiewicz and the political leadership of the Polish emigration.

It is hard, too, to comprehend the nature of his Polishness. Adam Mickiewicz was born in Lithuania, in the town of Nowogródek which is now in Belarus (Byelorussia). He opened *Pan Tadeusz*, the most beloved work in the Polish language, with the words: 'Lithuania, my fatherland . . .' The national poet of Poland, sent into exile at the age of twenty-four, never visited the country we now know as Poland at all, apart from a brief foray into Prussian-occupied Poland near Poznań during the insurrection of 1830–1. He never saw either Warsaw or Kraków, the two capital cities of historic Poland. It is as if Shakespeare had never visited England. A little more accurately, it is as if Shakespeare had been an Anglo-Irishman brought up in Dublin, driven to take refuge in Paris before he could find his way to London.

These ironies did not seem ironic to Adam Mickiewicz. They derived from the nature of the archaic, pre-ethnic Polish imperium which had collapsed just before he was born. The Kingdom of Poland and the Grand Duchy of Lithuania had been united into a royal 'commonwealth' in the Middle Ages. And this 'Lithuania' was not the small Baltic-speaking nation of today, but a huge, decentralised sprawl of territories reaching southwards almost to the Black Sea – and at times touching its coast. Its peoples included not only Balts in the far north, but Slav-speaking nationalities who were later named Byelorussians and Ukrainians. Among the inhabitants of the Grand Duchy were Cossacks, Nogay Tatars and – in the towns and villages – the main Jewish population of the world at that time.

As generations passed, the dominant culture of the Grand Duchy became Polish. Below the level of the gentry, the lower orders – including peasantries which had often been reduced to serfdom – preserved their own languages and their own rich folk cultures. But by the time that Adam Mickiewicz went to university, Vilnius was a Polish- and Yiddish-speaking metropolis, while almost the entire landowning class – the princely families, the squirearchy, the 'bonnet lairds' of the petty aristocracy – considered themselves to be 'Lithuanian Poles'.

This was a tenacious identity. It produced many of Poland's best writers in the century-and-a-half after Mickiewicz, and the con-temporary poet Czesław Miłosz, raised in Vilnius, can still describe himself as a 'Lithuanian of Polish speech'. It gave Poland a series of national leaders and patriotic conspirators, like Józef Piłsudski who led the nation to its regained independence in 1918. Especially after the Partitions, its political tradition was fiercely anti-Russian, and its Catholic faith – in a countryside where the peasant majority was often Orthodox or Uniate – was embattled and mystical.

In the Literary Museum at Odessa, in a cabinet which once

belonged to a Polish family in the 1820s, there is a miniature portrait of a woman. She is blonde, blue-eyed, conventionally pretty, with flowers in her hair and a low-cut 'peasant' dress. The women who sit on chairs keeping an eye on the visitors say that this is a picture of Karolina Sobańska, the lover of Mickiewicz.

If it is a portrait, it is not a likeness. She was anything but a little shepherdess. Another Pole who fell for her in Odessa wrote much later, after he had decided to loathe her: 'She was about 40 [a slander: in fact she was about 30], coarse-featured, but what physical appeal, what a voice, what a manner!' Other, more believable portraits, some of which vanished during the German occupation of Poland in the Second World War, showed bronze-coloured hair, dark eyes full of amusement, a slightly snub nose with big nostrils. The younger, more cheerful part of 'good society' in Odessa adored Sobańska, and crowded to her receptions and tea-parties. Older and more respectable people, including the Vorontsovs, detested her. This was partly because she was promiscuous even by Romantic standards. But for some of the Polish families in Odessa, there was another reason. They thought her a traitor.

Karolina Rozalia z Rzewuskich Hieronimowa Sobańska, to give her full married name, was not just an aristocrat. She came from the Rzewuski family, one of the oldest and most influential clans in Poland. Her own branch of the family was firmly located in what we would now call Ukraine; her father had been a member of parliament in independent Poland and then, after the Third Partition, a Russian senator and Marshal of the Nobility in the province of Kiev. Karolina, one of a clutch of brilliantly clever and attractive sisters and brothers, was educated in Vienna. Her sister Ewa was to marry Balzac in 1850, after besieging him by letter for many years. Her brother Henryk Rzewuski, in Odessa a good-natured chatterbox with vaguely revolutionary ideas about the fate of Poland, later became ultra-conservative and even pro-Russian in his views and took to writing historical novels. (One, *The Recollections of Seweryn Soplica Esquire*, is still worth reading as an ironic portrait of the eastern Polish nobility.)

But Karolina lived with the chief of the Russian secret police. She had been married, almost a schoolgirl, to Hieronym Sobański, a rich landowner who had set up an export business at Odessa for wheat from his own estates up-country. Then, in 1819, she met a much more interesting man.

Colonel-General Jan Witt was in his forties when Karolina became his mistress. His mother was a famously beautiful Greek woman who had been 'acquired' in Istanbul as a possible mistress for Stanisław August Poniatowski, the last king of Poland. His father was a Dutchman who managed to abduct her on the way to Warsaw. Jan Witt himself was small, shrewd, with Greek good looks; even those who hated his profession found it hard to dislike a man who was such good company. That popularity was the centre of his operation. By acquiring Karolina, and by making their house a place to which any restless young person or visitor would gravitate in search of a party and perhaps a woman, he became irresistible. It was before the age of microphones. It was still an age in which a fine fellow was a fine fellow, and his politics came second. So it came about that when the conspirators of Odessa felt like a good time – an intellectual argument, a drink, a dance – they would go round to the house of the tsar's chief of police.

Witt's assignment in Odessa was what we would now call counter-intelligence. He had to build up and maintain a net of informers, and to gather intelligence about conspiracies. As far as he knew in 1825, there were two lines of enquiry to be followed up in Odessa. One was the jumble of Polish secret organisations, some more imaginary than real, which were planning an insurrection and the restoration of Poland's independence. The other was the evidence, already solid, of a Russian conspiracy against Tsar Alexander I, a plot among intellectuals and young officers to overthrow the régime and instal liberal and constitutional government. Witt knew the names of some of these conspirators, now remembered as the 'Decembrists'. He suspected – and he was on the right track for much of 1825 – that they would initiate their revolution by assassinating the tsar.

Vorontsov, perhaps having learned something from his attempt to be fatherly with Pushkin, passed Adam Mickiewicz and his two companions to the care of Witt. Mickiewicz and Jezowski were lodged in the Lycée Richelieu, on the first floor of the long, two-storey school building which still stands in Deribasovskaya; they were supposed to teach, but in practice were never invited to enter a classroom. Instead, they set about amusing themselves.

This is an uncomfortable period for the poet's more pious biographers. The saintly patriot is held to have let himself down. Mickiewicz, though not a virgin, had led a fairly repressed life until then. He had fallen chastely and deeply in love with the young daughter of a landowner near Nowogródek. When he had been posted to Kaunas (Kowno) as a teacher after his graduation, he had become involved in an earthier way with Madame Kowalska, the local pharmacist's wife. But in Odessa, where northern conventions counted for little and most people lived for the moment, he let himself go. In poems and letters, he wrote about 'Danaids', the girls who took him to bed just to score a poet or to see how much money he had, and he described himself – a bit self-consciously – as a 'pasha' with a harem. But among the Danaids, there were four Polish women in Odessa who mattered more. One was a young married woman known only through a group of erotic poems as 'D.D.', with whom Mickiewicz for a time thought he might be in love. The second was Eugenia Szemiotowa, a married women with a family, whose small house was used for meetings of Polish exiles. Eugenia had nothing to do with Odessa social life, and her importance for Mickiewicz seems to have been her unwavering Catholic patriotism. Another close friend, steady and supportive, was Joanna Zaleska who, with her husband, kept the poet fed and comforted when playing the pasha grew too much for him. The fourth woman was Karolina Sobańska.

A great many letters which might have answered questions about how the poet and the policeman's mistress came together have been burned – many by Mickiewicz's son after his father's death. This lack leaves behind two mysteries. The first is what they felt for one another. The second mystery is how much they really knew about one another's secret activities, for, with both of them, there was a great deal to be known.

This was not a grand love. It began, evidently, with physical attraction and mutual curiosity, and quite possibly with a suggestion from Jan Witt. He used Karolina, before and after Adam Mickiewicz, to find out what men were up to, and if that meant going to bed with them, he accepted it. But the affair between Sobańska and Mickiewicz led to something which in the circumstances was unlikely: they became friends. Mickiewicz found in this grand and wicked young lady somebody he could talk to without making allowances; his nickname for her was 'Donna Giovanna', the bold adventuress who was more Byron's Don Juan than Mozart's. She, in turn, was touched by his awful provincial manners, which seemed to put her in her place as just one more

Vilnius student comrade. When she was an old lady, the thing she remembered best about Adam was how boorish he became when he was fully launched into a speech in her drawing-room. He would stick out his empty tea-cup at Witt, as if he were a passing lackey; and when they first met and she enquired what he would like to drink, he really did talk to her as if she were a waitress: 'I want coffee, but it's got to be with double cream and a thick head on it!'

Others found the relationship horrifying on moral but above all on political grounds. For them, Karolina was a Russian informer and collaborator, no more. But Mickiewicz, then and afterwards, insisted that she was a good human being finding her own way through impossible difficulties. There were things about her which he resented; she was unfaithful to him, and he could not accept it when she tried to explain that he must always be 'one among others'. She could be a nuisance, pestering him to write her into poems or badgering him – probably at Witt's request – to show her his work journals. But, unlike everyone else, he never said that she was corrupt. Many years later, when he was in Paris, the American writer Margaret Fuller met Karolina on a ship and wrote to ask Mickiewicz who she was. He told her about the jealousy ('I was too romantic and too exclusive'), and expressed hope that he would meet Karolina one day in Paris; he would give her some good advice and consolation 'if she is still as she used to be: kind and sensitive'.

These were odd words to use, but his view of their relationship was that he had done most of the taking. As a writer he took her life and unpicked it in his imagination. The theme of outer treachery concealing inner loyalty, of the betrayer who is really working in the enemy camp for the cause of those who think he or she has betrayed them, fascinated him and stayed with him. It inspired the narrative poem *Konrad Wallenrod*, which he composed soon after leaving Odessa, a mediaeval story about a Lithuanian double agent who joins the Teutonic Knights in order to destroy them. From this work the term 'Wallenrodism' arrived in the Polish language, to describe the sinister ambiguities and double-bottomed loyalties which most Poles know about from experience. But this theme also gave him the little-known play *The Confederates of Bar*, a melodrama about an episode in eighteenth-century Polish history. Mickiewicz, by then an exile, wrote it in French to pay his family's bills; the Paris theatres turned it down and lost most of the manuscript, so that only two out of five acts survive. What remains turns out to be a thinly disguised account of Witt, Karolina Sobańska and some of the ominous police agents in Witt's pay. Here Karolina is plainly a 'Wallenrod'. As a Polish countess who is the mistress of the Russian general in Kraków, she is hated and despised by most other Poles, including her own family. But in reality the countess is working to save her fellow-countrymen from arrest, exile to Siberia and the gallows.

It looks as if this was the way that Karolina explained herself to Mickiewicz. It also looks as if he believed her. About now, he wrote 'The Hawk', a sonnet which is either unfinished or has lost its last line to some pair of scissors. It is about a bird of prey which has taken refuge from the storm by clinging to the yard of a ship; 'let no godless hand seize him . . . ' Then the sonnet goes on:

> He is a guest, Giovanna; whoever seizes a guest,
> If he's at sea, let him beware the tempest.
> Remember my own, remember your own story!
> You too on life's sea – you saw monsters,
> And the gale drove me astray; the rain drenched my wings.
> Why these sweet words, why these deceitful hopes?
> Yourself in peril, you're a snare to others . . .

But Karolina Sobańska, although she may have been a bird of prey, was not the loyal countess of *The Confederates*. She was no Wallenrod, either. Sobańska was a skilled and devoted agent of the tsar, who did untold damage to her own country in the next few years.

In 1830, the Poles rose once again against foreign occupation. The November Insurrection began in Warsaw and spread throughout Russian-occupied Poland and Lithuania in the following year, a desperate struggle fought in pitched battles against Russian regular armies and by partisan campaigns in the forests. As the rising began to fall apart in defeat, Witt was transferred to Warsaw in 1831 as military governor of the reconquered city, and he took Karolina with him. There she is said to have saved many captured Polish officers from deportation to Siberia, and to have visited the Polish wounded in hospital. But her main task was espionage. Witt sent her to Dresden, in Saxony, to infiltrate the leadership of the insurrection and the mass of Polish refugees who had gathered there. In Dresden she posed once more as a patriot and sympathiser, and she won the confidence of at least some of the refugee community. She not only reported political and military intelligence to Witt, but, if she thought it safe, tried to persuade demoralised Polish officers to make their peace with the tsar.

Curiously, and in spite of her reputation from Odessa, the Polish insurgents were more inclined to trust her than Witt's Russian masters. Tsar Nicholas I, who had succeeded Alexander in late 1825, remained intensely suspicious of her. When Witt took her to Warsaw, the tsar wrote to Paskevich, the Russian commander-in-chief, that Sobańska should not be allowed to stay in the city and that Witt's career would be blighted if he made the mistake of marrying her. 'She is the greatest and most dexterous of schemers, and a Pole to boot, who can use her blandishments and cunning to entrap anyone in her net . . . ' In another letter, Nicholas crudely described her as 'this piece of skirt who is about as faithful to Russia as she is to Witt'.

Sobańska was ordered to leave Warsaw at the end of the year. Outraged, she wrote a long letter in French to Benckendorff, the supreme commander of the tsar's political police. This letter remained hidden in the secret files for more than a century until it was published in the Soviet Union in 1935, in a series of unedited and largely unknown documents concerned with Alexander Pushkin and his milieu. For the Polish literary world, it came as a horrible and humiliating shock.

> My General, [she wrote] the prince marshal has just delivered to me the order given by His Majesty the Emperor about my departure from Warsaw; I submit to it with total resignation, as I would to the decree of Providence itself.
>
> But may I be permitted, my General, to open my heart to you on this occasion and to tell you how overwhelmed by pain I feel, less by the decree which it has pleased His Majesty to issue against me than by the fearful idea that my principles, my character and my love for my master have been so cruelly judged and so unworthily distorted. I appeal to you yourself, my General, to you to whom I have spoken so openly, to whom I have written so frankly before and during the horrors which have disturbed this country. Only deign to cast your eyes over the past, which should already furnish enough to justify me! I dare to assert that there was never a woman who could display more

devotion, more zeal, more activity in the service of her Sovereign than I have, often at the risk of my own destruction . . .

The opinions which my family has always professed, the dangers which my mother incurred during the insurrection in the Kiev province, the conduct of my brothers, the bond which has united me for thirteen years with a man whose dearest interests were concentrated upon those of his Sovereign, the profound contempt which I feel for the nation to which I have the misfortune to belong; all, I dare to believe, should have set me above the suspicions of which I have now become the victim.

The letter goes on to detail some of her achievements: the penetration of the exiled insurrectionary command at Dresden, and her task of contacting and if possible turning leading Poles disillusioned by the failure of the November Rising. 'Polish by name, I was naturally the object here [in Warsaw] of those who, criminal in their intentions and cowardly in character, wanted to save their necks without actually renouncing their opinions or betraying those who had shared them.' The whole text reeks not only of ultra-conservative views (she refers to the Polish rebels as 'Jacobins'), but of an extraordinary loathing for her own fellow-countrymen.

I had to meet Poles; I even received some who were repugnant to my own character. But I could not bring myself to approach those whose very contact gave me the sensation of being licked by a rabid dog; I was never able to conquer this revulsion and, I admit, I may have missed some important discoveries because I would not submit myself to meeting creatures who filled me with horror . . .

Until 1935, the Poles had been able to take seriously the Mickiewicz version: that Sobańska had been working as a double agent whose ultimate loyalty was to Poland. But this letter struck all her apologists dumb. It seemed, finally, that there had been no fascinating Romantic dualism, no mirror-play of double identities about Sobańska at all. She had been just a Russian spy.

If this was the ultimate truth about Karolina Sobańska, Mickiewicz did not know it when they met in his apartment in Odessa to make love, and it is clear that he died without knowing it.

155

But he came to the Black Sea with his own secrets, and how many of them he shared with her it is impossible to know. He was young and a Romantic, but he already had some hard political experience; he knew the difference between student unrest and serious clandestine work, and he also knew what should not be written down. Soon after his arrival in Odessa there had been a fuss about a playful 'Map of the Black Sea', with which he had illustrated a letter to Malewski's sister Zosia in Vilnius; the letter was opened by Russian censors who thought the map was a coded military plan, and the file went all the way to St Petersburg and back to Vorontsov before it was reclassified as harmless. But Mickiewicz's discretion makes it difficult to know what he may really have been up to during his stay on the Black Sea. Some Polish historians give all his movements a conspiratorial significance. Others suggest more plausibly that, during these months before the catastrophic Decembrist rising in St Petersburg at the end of the year, Mickiewicz remained little more than a well-informed spectator.

There were certainly secret contacts. He and the two other Polish exiles had met almost all the leading Decembrist plotters in St Petersburg, and the Decembrist leaders Ryleyev and Bestuzhev gave them a letter of recommendation to take to their comrade the poet Tumansky in Odessa: 'They are wonderful, brave boys! In their feelings and thoughts, they have been our friends for a long time. And Mickiewicz is a poet and darling of his country.' Tumansky was at the centre of the conspiracy's southern wing, which at the time seemed the more promising. In the spring of 1825, when Mickiewicz reached Odessa, the plotters were developing a plan to stab Alexander I to death when he visited Taganrog on the Sea of Azov.

There were Polish conspirators already in Odessa, like Count Piotr Moszyński, a young nobleman who was a link between the Polish underground groups and the Decembrists. Mickiewicz met him, and must have discussed revolutionary politics, but nothing is known about what was said. Odessa was in any case full of foreign exiles with secret plans and dreams. The tsar had complained the year before to Vorontsov that 'people are arriving in Odessa from every direction, including the Polish province . . . who deliberately and purposefully, or through their own thoughtlessness, employ themselves in spreading baseless and alarming rumours, which could have a harmful impact on feeble minds . . . ' This was an enduring aspect of Odessa. Before Mickiewicz came, French émigrés there had plotted the overthrow of Napoleon. In 1814, the Odessa Greeks had founded the *Philike Hetaireia* (Society of Friends) in order to achieve the 'Great Idea': the defeat of the Ottomans and the restoration of the Byzantine Empire. Long afterwards, Odessa gave the world Vladimir Jabotinsky, founder of militant 'revisionist' Zionism, and Leon Bronstein, alias Trotsky.

Jan Witt knew about the plot for daggers at Taganrog. How much he knew is not clear, but it is not hard to guess who told him about it. He decided to make a visit of inspection to Crimea, in order to check on police readiness and political tensions, and being both sociable and shrewd, he turned the visit into a holiday house-party which would include some people he wished to know a little more about. In the middle of August 1825, there assembled on the Odessa landing-stage, complete with parasols, wine, easels, albums and telescopes, a truly improbable group of people. There was Mickiewicz, and Witt himself. There was Karolina with her husband Hieronym, whom she was about to divorce. Her brother Henryk came; and a jolly, brainless fellow called Kalusowski who was a tenant on the Sobański estates; and a gaunt, bespectacled Russian called Boshniak who said that he was an entomologist. With them travelled an assortment of servants, most of them Cossacks or Tatars.

Kalusowski had meant only to see them off, but he was unable to resist an offer of lunch on board the steamer and by the time he had finished he found that they were at sea. The first day was hot and calm; the second day brought a violent storm which Mickiewicz enjoyed on deck, strapped to the mast for safety, while the others lay below in agonies of sea-sickness. Finally they arrived at Sevastopol, and made their way by carriage to Evpatoria where Witt had rented a house. They were to stay in Crimea for nearly two months.

For most of the time, Witt and Karolina remained at Evpatoria and ostensibly did little but bathe and enjoy the sun. Mickiewicz roamed all over the southern mountains of the peninsula, some-times riding on his own with a guide, sometimes in the company of Henryk Rzewuski. The silent Boshniak came too, whenever he could. In the various accounts of this Crimean journey the dates are hopelessly muddled, so that it is not possible to make out exactly where Mickiewicz went and whom he met. He certainly visited the inland city of Simferopol, and he went to see the palace of the Crimean Tatar khans at Bakhchiserai and the rock dwellings of the Karaim in the fortress-mountain of Chufut Kale nearby. He climbed the heights of Shatir Dagh, and slept in Tatar cottages. But there are signs that he did more than tourism. One version asserts that in Simferopol he met the Russian dramatist and diplomat Alexander Griboyedov, who had just completed his masterpiece *Woe from Wit*; Griboyedov was connected with the Decembrists, and he may have arranged a conspiratorial contact for Mickiewicz with the Polish writer Gustaw Olizar.

This meeting, in Olizar's house on the Crimean sea-cliffs, certainly took place. Mickiewicz appears to have stayed for a week or so with Olizar, sleeping in a hut on the beach, talking to Tatar villagers and borrowing books from Princess Golitsyn who had settled in her own solitude a few miles along the coast. He would certainly have talked politics in the evenings with his host, for Gustaw Olizar was yet another typically ambiguous poet-conspirator. He had fallen in love with Maria Rayevskaya, daughter of a Russian general and a young woman who had also caught the fancy of Pushkin. When her father refused to consider him as a suitor because he was a Pole and a Catholic, Olizar had taken Romantic flight from a cruel world. He had bought a piece of land at Gurzuf, on the flanks of the Ayu Dagh promontory over the Black Sea, and built himself a comfortable hermitage in which to enjoy his loneliness. He named the house 'Cardiatricon' (Heart's Remedy), and devoted himself to the composition of melancholy verses and memoirs about lost love. Near the shore, Olizar set about constructing a 'Temple of Pain', surrounded by cypresses and dedicated to Woman.

It was never completed. Olizar, in spite of his apparent unworld-liness, was also closely involved with the Decembrists. In 1826, after the terrible fiasco of the Decembrist rising in St Petersburg and the failure of the southern wing of the plot to capture Kiev, he was arrested and his property was seized. From Romantic exile, Olizar graduated to the real thing. 'Cardiatricon' was bought cheap by the Golitsyn family, who knocked it down and built a luxurious villa, and today the site is covered by a half-abandoned sanatorium which used to belong to the Soviet Ministry of Defence.

Every so often, Mickiewicz would return to base at Evpatoria and rest for a day or so with Witt and the remainder of the house-party.

But Sobańska found him reluctant to talk about his experiences. She gave him one of her own notebooks, and warned him that if he did not write down his more interesting meetings and conversations and impressions, he would forget them. In return for the gift, he was to show her what he had written when he returned. He did so, but she found that he had put little on the pages but sketches of the landscape and Tatar costumes. Kalusowski told her later that Mickiewicz kept what looked like a set of blank cards in his pocket, and sometimes sat down and scribbled vigorously on them. But she never managed to read those cards.

And yet in a way she did eventually read them. They carried the notes, allusions and literary ideas which came to Adam Mickiewicz as he rode or climbed over the Crimean mountains, and which he developed that winter and the following year into the *Crimean Sonnets*.

There are eighteen of them, first published in 1826. In Poland, they are still widely known, quoted and taught. They are 'easy', compared to other, denser short poems which he was composing at the same time, and some of them are popular simply because they carry a charge of patriotic emotion. They are very direct and yet curiously restless poems, constantly changing focus or tone of address, often rebelling against the confinement of the sonnet form. One device of restlessness is memory; 'the poet', surveying some exotic scene, will be stabbed by recollection of another landscape (northern and lost), by the sound of a Polish voice, even by sheer otherness and distance. 'The Akerman Steppe', the first of the Crimean Sonnets and in some ways the best, is not about Crimea at all, but about travelling across the plains inland from the Dniester estuary, near the colossal fortress of Akerman. Mickiewicz evokes the oceanic silence of the steppe, in which he can hear a butterfly trembling on a blade of grass:

> Caressing herbs, the belly of a serpent crawls.
> In such a quietness, I cock my ear so sharp
> I'd hear a voice from Lithuania. – Drive on, none calls!

In these poems, for the first time, there appears the Mickiewiczian image of the poet as pilgrim. In some of them, the pilgrim is a Moslem guided across Crimean mountains and dales by a holy *Mirza*; in others, the journey is openly the poet's exile from 'the dear land from which I am cut off'. A few years later, Mickiewicz was to write the *Book of the Polish Nation and of the Polish Pilgrims*, addressed to the emigration which settled abroad after the failure of the November Rising in 1831. In this strange work done in the Biblical manner, which became a rod and staff of comfort for the Polish exiles through the worst times of despair, the pilgrimage is more than merely a metaphor of the physical wandering of the Poles in alien lands. It becomes a Way of the Cross, by which God's chosen nation, crucified and put down into the tomb, would find its path through suffering to resurrection and the redemption of all nations in liberty. 'When on your pilgrimage ye shall arrive in a city, bless it, saying: our Liberty be with you! If they receive and listen to you, then shall they be free, but if they despise you, are deaf to you and drive you away, then shall your blessing return to be with you . . . '

In the same book, Mickiewicz wrote that

the Polish nation is not dead: its body lies in the tomb but its soul has descended into limbo . . . to the life of all peoples enduring servitude in their own countries and outside them, so that Poland might be witness to their sufferings.

But on the third day the soul shall return to the body; the Nation shall arise again and deliver from servitude all the peoples of Europe.

And three days have already passed; the first ending with the first fall of Warsaw; the second day with the second fall of Warsaw; and the third day cometh but it shall have no end.

As at the resurrection of Christ the sacrifice of blood ceased upon the earth, so at the resurrection of the Polish Nation shall war cease among Christendom.

This was the extraordinary doctrine of Messianism, the identification of the Polish nation as the collective reincarnation of Christ. Messianism steadily gained strength over the next century-and-a-half. History saw to that.

Almighty God! The children of a warrior nation raise their disarmed hands to you from every quarter of the world. They cry to you from the bottom of Siberian mines and the snows of Kamchatka, from the plains of Algeria and the foreign soil of

France . . . By the blood of all our soldiers fallen in the war for faith and liberty, deliver us O Lord! By the wounds, tears and sufferings of all the prisoners, exiles and Polish pilgrims, deliver us O Lord!

That was written in 1832. It could equally well have been written in 1944, in the aftermath of the Warsaw Rising.

Messianism was not the only idea that Mickiewicz developed on the Black Sea coast. Like almost every writer in the generation of Goethe and Byron, he acquired 'Orientalism'. It was a universal fashion, and the impact of Crimea and its peoples on a young man who had never seen a mountain before, let alone an Islamic culture, was lasting. But his Orientalism was free of the patronising discourse of Western superiority, 'civilisation' contrasted to Eastern 'decadence', which became common elsewhere in Europe. He saw in the Crimean Tatars and in the relics of their khanate at Bakhchiserai not only a humanity and delicacy which was lacking in Slav Christendom, but a brother-people which had shared with Poland the fate of conquest and humiliation at the hands of Catherine and Russian power. Mickiewicz was able to assimilate this respect for Islam to his own Catholic enthusiasm, and in later years he found no difficulty in collaborating with the Ottoman Empire in the cause of Polish independence.

And it seems to have been in Crimea that Mickiewicz completed the mental structure of his own highly personal reverence for Judaism and the Jewish people. He already knew the Jewish communities of Lithuania: the Hassidic traditions of intellectual mysticism which had centred upon Vilnius, the *shtetl* life of small towns and villages and, probably, the Karaite colony at Trakai between Vilnius and Kaunas. But Evpatoria in Crimea was still then the 'capital' of the Karaim, and in Evpatoria Mickiewicz made a point of studying their customs and beliefs. Later, in his French exile, Mickiewicz was to insist on the seniority of the Jews to all other nations, as the first people to receive the divine revelation; and he was to argue – often to the irritation of the political leaders of the Polish emigration – that Jews should play a leading part in the struggle for independence. He considered, at a practical level, that Polish and Lithuanian Jews would make good soldiers, and that the peasantry would be more easily drawn into another insurrection if the Jews had already joined it; they had, he argued, great respect for Jewish realism.

These views were not so eccentric or unusual as they later came to seem. They were a voice from the lost, more tolerant world of the old commonwealth, in which Polishness had been a matter of political loyalty rather than of race or religion. It had seemed normal, for example, that a regiment of Jewish light cavalry should have fought to defend Warsaw against the Russians and Prussians during the 1794 Rising against the Partitions. Catholic anti-Semitism – though widespread enough in the commonwealth – did not yet pretend to represent some patriotic interest. It was only in the second half of the nineteenth century that the 'modern' nationalism of Roman Dmowski and his National Democrats began to preach that a 'true Pole' was a Polish-speaking Catholic Slav, and that the other communities who had co-existed under the Royal Commonwealth – the Jews above all – were obstacles to the realisation of the 'national interest'.

By the time of his Crimean journey, Mickiewicz knew that he would soon be leaving Odessa again. Within weeks of his arrival, the authorities in St Petersburg began to feel uneasy about what company the three Poles might be keeping in New Russia, and long, gentlemanly exchanges began about his next destination. Mickiewicz wanted the Caucasus, St Petersburg would not agree, and in the end he had to consent to a post in Moscow. He returned to Odessa from Crimea in mid-October. A month later, he and Jezowski boarded the Moscow coach. A vigorous, ice-cold poem, 'Thoughts on the Day of Departure', presents a last walk through his empty and silent apartment, an impatience to be gone, a shrug at the absence of any tearful cheek or eye in this 'sad, alien city'.

He and Sobańska had already broken up, apparently over another man and her dislike of 'exclusivity'. Without her, it became harder to be casual about Jan Witt's professional activity. Then, not long before his departure, there took place a small, grisly event which Mickiewicz never forgot.

Some two weeks after the party's return from Crimea, he went to dinner at Witt's. As the guests arrived, a tall, thin officer in uniform stalked into the dining-room, epaulettes on his shoulders, his chest heavy with medals. Because the man was no longer wearing spectacles, it took Mickiewicz a few seconds to recognise Boshniak, the 'entomologist', but when he did so he was, for perhaps the first time in Odessa, seriously frightened. After the meal, he took Witt aside and asked, as lightly as he could: '*Mais qui est donc ce monsieur?* I thought his only job was catching flies.' Witt answered meaningly: 'Oh, he catches all kinds of flies for us!'

Next day, the three male Poles who had been on the Crimean excursion sat down to an anxious conversation in which they tried to work out exactly what Boshniak might have overheard or seen, or read in letters left in bedrooms. But they had to wait some months, until the trials of the Decembrists, before they could be finally certain about his identity. Alexander Karlovich Boshniak, it turned out, had been a major in the Ministry of the Interior when he set out on the Crimean journey, but had been promoted to colonel by the time of the trials, in which he was mentioned as a distinguished investigator.

He was in fact Witt's senior counter-intelligence officer, just possibly a man who reported to St Petersburg on Witt himself, and during the spring and summer of 1825 he had been leading the unit assembled to penetrate the assassination plot against Alexander I. A daring, rather imaginative man who wrote travel books and novels, Boshniak had developed a simple technique: he would call upon a conspirator, disclose that he was a police agent and then, declaring revolutionary convictions, beg to be allowed to join the plot. These were trustful, amateurish times. Boshniak had several successes with this approach in Odessa. One legend says that he managed to arrange a meeting with three of the most important Decembrists in St Petersburg, and told them that General Witt was secretly disaffected and wished to be assigned a role in their plans. Pavel Ivanovich Pestel, the leading figure in the conspiracy, was tempted to take Boshniak's offer seriously until his colleagues took him aside and talked sense into him.

Adam Mickiewicz must now have realised that the whole Crimean trip had been a cover devised by Witt for an operation by Boshniak. That realisation in turn pointed to questions about Karolina Sobańska which even he must have found difficult to ignore.

But his obstinacy about her inner 'goodness' persisted. In his play *The Confederates of Bar*, Boshniak appears as 'The Doctor', a sinister interrogator and spy who advises the bluff Russian general in charge of the city of Kraków. He implores the general to let him take over and run the countess, the general's Polish mistress, who would be an invaluable agent if she could be persuaded to collect intelligence from all her contacts. But the doctor also warns his chief that the countess is politically unreliable. In her youth, she loved Józef Pułaski, the leader of the Polish anti-Russian conspiracy, and he strongly suspects that she or at least members of her 'numerous family' may still be in contact with him.

Before the manuscript infuriatingly breaks off, on a situation of cliff-hanging suspense at the end of Act Two, it has turned out that the countess is still in love with Pułaski, and that her father is joining him in the hills to prepare an attack on the city's Russian garrison. Meanwhile the general, with the countess in tow, has set off on a journey of reconnaissance into the same hills and is about to burst into the very clearing where the plotters have gathered. Her father, though he has discovered that his own daughter is with the approaching Russians, is standing by his order to kill every man of them – and every woman.

The rest of *The Confederates of Bar* is lost. But melodrama has its own rules. Enough survives to point towards a climax in which the countess is revealed to be a patriot (possibly at the cost of her own martyrdom, even dying in Pułaski's arms?), while the doctor will almost certainly slink off frustrated, snarling that he will do better next time.

The journey from Odessa to Moscow was a slow one. By the time that Mickiewicz arrived it was mid-December, and Russian history had been made while he was on the road.

Alexander I had died. He had gone to Taganrog, but the plot against him had been broken up by Witt and Boshniak and he perished not by the dagger but in his bed of a fever. A few weeks later, after an ill-concealed family struggle, he was succeeded by his brother Nicholas. Two days after that, the conspirators in St Petersburg struck.

All through a day of terrible frost, their troops stood drawn up on Senate Square, penned in by regiments loyal to the new tsar. Nicholas I stood and watched as the conspirators turned down one offer of negotiation after another. Finally, as a greenish-black dust settled over the snow, he ordered the artillery to open fire with grapeshot at point-blank range. That was the end of the Decembrist uprising, and the beginning of a reign of police terror which was to last, with few intermissions, for thirty years. The arrests spread all over the land. Several of Mickiewicz's friends, including Ryleyev, were hanged. Many more ended their lives in Siberia.

Adam Mickiewicz left Russia three years later, hiding below decks in a British steamer bound for Germany. He never returned. His ardent support for the Polish national uprising in 1830 condemned him to a lifetime of exile; this, as it turned out, was the 'sea tempest' which blew the hawk far from land and left its fate to the tolerance of strangers. Almost the whole intellectual class of Poland, as well as the military and political leadership, went abroad, and the 'Great Emigration', which settled principally in Paris, contrived to maintain not only the cause of independence but the integrity and even the fertility of the national culture. The classic age of Polish literature is the early and middle nineteenth century, and almost all of it was written in exile. The central figure of that literature was Mickiewicz himself.

The same gale soon blew Karolina Sobańska away as well. She had made Pushkin's acquaintance in Odessa, and on a visit to St Petersburg shortly after the departure of Mickiewicz she met him again and added herself to the list of his brief, desperate conquests. Some love letters to her survive, and a portrait-sketch, and a poem or two, but the letters are mere drafts and may never have been sent (Pushkin, characteristically, toiled over their wording and every apparently dashed-off phrase – 'I was born both to love and to pursue you!' – turns out to be the product of a mess of crossings-out and discarded bits of vocabulary). In 1836, well after the Polish uprising and her crisis with Benckendorff, Witt finally threw Karolina out, and in the same year she married his old adjutant, Stefan Cherkovitz, a Serbian officer in Russian service who had been responsible for some of the worst butchery during the recapture of Warsaw.

When Cherkovitz died, Karolina moved to Paris. She married Jules Lacroix, translator of Shakespeare and author of fourteen novels, brother of the more famous and even more fecund writer Paul Lacroix. In 1850 she was joined by her sister Ewa (Evelina), who had finally married the dying Balzac in the church at Berdichev, near her Ukrainian estate, and brought him back to Paris. For the rest of her life, which turned out to be a very long one, Karolina Sobańska lived in calm and comfort, playing cards, going to the theatre and taking no interest whatever in politics.

It is possible that she met Mickiewicz once more. The biography of the poet by Mieczysław Jastruń describes an ambitious dinner party which Karolina and Jules gave in Paris, at which Honoré de Balzac was placed next to the guest of honour, 'the greatest Polish poet'. The evening is supposed to have turned out badly. Mickiewicz detested the new fashion of Balzacian realism, and said rudely that nothing would be lost if two-thirds of the books published in Paris were burned like the Library of Alexandria. Balzac, talking offence, retorted that poetic narrative, the favourite form of both Pushkin and Mickiewicz, was as dead as a doornail.

The problem with this story is its dating. It was in 1847 that Mickiewicz wrote to Margaret Fuller remarking that he 'hoped' to meet Karolina in Paris one day. The dinner must therefore have happened in the three years before Balzac's death in August 1850. But the novelist had spent almost the whole of the previous two years on Ewa's Ukrainian estate at Wierzchownia, and in the three months between their return to Paris and his death he was far too ill to go to smart dinner-parties. It is true that Balzac was back in France between January and September 1848, but for almost all that time Mickiewicz was in Italy raising Polish legions for the revolution. Perhaps they did meet, in one of the few weeks when it was possible. At all events, the divergence of spirit was a real one. Mickiewicz did not appreciate Balzac's gigantic energy and humanity, and thought him vulgar. Balzac, although he knew a great deal about Poland through his 'Evelina', could only dismiss Mickiewicz as a dinosaur left over from the epoch of Romantic delusions.

After Balzac's death, Karolina for a time kept her widowed sister company as she confronted the task of paying off Balzac's debts – her Ukrainian estate had to be sold – and arranging for new editions of his work. The awful Balzac family, in spite of Ewa's patience and kindness, spread the word that she was a gold-digger and tart who had only married Honoré for his money. They hated Karolina too, mostly because she talked Polish to her sister while playing whist with them. Karolina outlived them all. But if she ever did meet Adam Mickiewicz again, there is no reliable record of it.

The Turkish policeman, in his brown uniform, holds out the tray on which a pair of scissors has been laid on a scarf of Polish embroidery. Mr Jastrzębski, Prefect of the Province of Warsaw, steps forward and performs a ceremonial snip. The covering slips from the memorial plaque, and the small crowd of Turkish and Polish dignitaries claps. Then they move in to peer at the inscription.

'Here in the Polish village anciently known as Adampol, Poles lived and are living.' The words are repeated in Polish and Turkish: on the plaque, the crowned White Eagle of Poland and the Star and Crescent of Turkey are engraved side by side.

A few miles inland from the Bosporus and the Black Sea, in the hills of the Asian shore, lies the village of Polonezköy or Adampol. It was founded a hundred and fifty years ago, with the permission of the Ottoman sultans, as a settlement for Polish soldiers and their families, veterans of the long struggle against Russia who had enlisted in the Ottoman armies on the principle that 'my enemy's enemy is my friend'. Twenty-five Polish families still live here; another ten, now living in Istanbul, come back to their cottages for the holiday season.

The place was named Adampol after Prince Adam Czartoryski, the uncrowned king of the Great Emigration, who came from his headquarters in the Hotel Lambert in Paris to rent the land from the sultan in 1842. The first settlers were officers and men who had retreated into the Ottoman Empire after the failure of the 1830 Rising. In 1858, after the end of the Crimean War, they were joined by the demobilised troops of the 'Ottoman Cossacks', the legion raised from emigrants and Polish prisoners of war in the vain hope that Allied victory over Russia would bring the liberation of their country. The last big influx came with the defeat of the January Rising in 1863.

Polonezköy still feels like a colony. The neat little houses, with their walls, barns and orchards, resemble a village in western Poland. The school is closed now, but the Catholic church, dedicated to the Black Madonna of Częstochowa, is still full every Sunday. Visitors are taken to the house of 'Aunt Zosia', the matriarch of the Ryzy family, where seven different icons of the Madonna hang in the dim wooden bedroom and the front room is decorated with portraits of Czartoryski, Marshal Piłsudski and General Sikorski. On one wall is a large, lurid poster showing the defence of Lwów (now Lvov, in western Ukraine) by Polish schoolchildren and cadets in 1919. Near the front door, tactfully, the picture of Mustafa Kemal Ataturk is put beside the inevitable photograph of Karol Wojtyła, Pope John Paul II.

167

When Polonezköy was founded, the Ottoman Empire was a multi-national realm – not unlike the old Polish Commonwealth. Military loyalty and civil obedience were required from the subjects, rather than ethnic, linguistic or religious conformity. Greeks (the large and ancient population known as Pontic Greeks) still dominated the southern shore of the Black Sea; Armenians and Jews ran the bureaucracy and the economy. It did not seem at all unnatural to the sultan to ally with Catholic Poles against Russia; it was the Poles, although they needed the alliance most, who at first found it hard to swallow. Their national self-image as the eastward bastion (*przedmurze*) of Christendom had been formed mostly in war against the Ottoman Empire and the Tatars, and in 1683 King John Sobieski, by saving Vienna from the Turks, had brought to an end the threat of Moslem expansion into Central Europe. But the partitions of Poland in the eighteenth century and the loss of independence forced the Poles to reassess their view of the world. Russia, not Turkey, was now the great enemy. The flower of Eastern Catholic chivalry resolved to make an agonising compromise.

The sultans took a more pragmatic view. At receptions for the diplomatic corps in Istanbul, the marshal who called out each ambassador for presentation continued to announce 'His Excellency from Lechistan' (Poland). The awkward silence which then followed was a source of fury for one Russian envoy to the Supreme Porte after another.

For the first few Adampol generations, the colony was effectively run from Paris without Turkish objections. The church and the school flourished, and weekly reports on the settlement were drawn up by the *wójt* (the governor of the little colony) and sent back to the Hotel Lambert. Then, after 1863, the climate began to change. The collapse of the last great insurrection brought about a profound national disillusion; at Adampol, it was no longer possible to regard the settlement as a military colony in which new legionaries were being bred for the next uprising. Insensibly, the Poles there began to come to terms with Turkish society about them. When Poland regained independence in 1918, the warriors' great-grandchildren no longer felt like going home. The new Kemalist republic, which had succeeded the Ottoman Empire, left the Poles in peace, in spite of its fanatical insistence on ethnic homogeneity and 'Turkey for the Turks'. The settlers decided that they would continue to be Polish, but in Turkey.

Today, the colony is beginning to dissolve. New roads, and the huge motorway bridges across the Bosporus, have brought Polonezköyu within half an hour's drive of Istanbul. New laws have undermined the colony's structure. In 1968, the settlers were granted the right to sell their land and houses, and the strict control of the *wójt* over the colony's territory broke down. In recent years, the Istanbul middle class has begun to move in, buying up farmland for holiday bungalows or private clinics. Most of the families whose names are on the gravestones in the village cemetery, the Ochockis and Wilkoszewskis and Nowickis, have turned their houses into thriving 'pensions' with restaurants, popular with well-off Turks looking for a discreet place to take a girl for the weekend. Real estate and the hotel trade have replaced farming as the main sources of income.

The current *wójt*, Frederic Nowicki, sits under the arbour of his hotel garden and offers guests glasses of tea and *naleszniki* pancakes. In fluent Polish, he points out what is taking place on a map of Polonezköy spread out on the table. Prince Adam's island, the patch of Slav fields radiating from the village street, is slowly submerging; the state forests are lapping over one corner, the sanatorium builders and country-club developers over another.

For one more generation, Polish will be spoken in the street here, and Mass will be celebrated in the church with 'Under Thy Protection, We Take Refuge' written across its chancel arch. But the colony itself, as a self-governing outpost of Poland, is over. Mr Nowicki is still a young man. It seems likely that he will be the last *wójt* of Adampol.

When the last Polish-speaker is laid in the ground at Polonezköy, the monuments will remain. One of them, outside the church door, is a bronze slab with a bas-relief portrait: 'To Our Bard: Adam Mickiewicz, on the anniversary of his death'. Another, the most magnificent tomb in the village cemetery, consists of an altar surmounted by broken classical columns. On the tallest column is carved the crowned White Eagle; on the side of the altar is the *Pogoń* – the charging horseman with raised sword who is the crest of the Grand Duchy of Lithuania. Here lies Ludwika Sadyk, born Śniadecka, 'daughter of Jendrzej and niece of Jan, wife of the general commanding the Ottoman Cossack Dragoons; died in February 1866 at Dzehangir in Constantinople, buried in Polish soil at Adampol'.

169

Mickiewicz had once written about how, as death approaches, first things return to mingle with last things. In 1855, when he came to Istanbul in the last months of his life, he found there a woman whom he had known as a young girl in the Lithuanian countryside. For the Vilnius students, Ludwika Śniadecka had been a pretty, black-eyed young woman who had been famous for her alarming opinions about women's rights as a programme for the next revolution. Her father was professor of chemistry at the university of Vilnius and her uncle was the university's Rector; 'Ludwisia' was afraid of nobody, and when the young poet Juliusz Słowacki fell in love with her, she told him firmly that he could expect friendship but nothing more. As an exile in Paris, he was still dreaming vividly about her nearly twenty years later.

In Istanbul, Ludwika treated the middle-aged Mickiewicz not only as a bard but as an old friend. Experienced in problems of poverty, pride and emigration, she realised at once that his health was bad and that he was concealing the fact that he was too poor to eat properly. She tried in vain to lure him into comfortable lodgings: to a hotel in the Pera district, or to her own tall wooden house above the Bosporus at Beşiktaş. But Mickiewicz preferred to remain in what she called his 'holes'; a damp, dim cell in the Lazarist monastery at Galata, and then later a single unfurnished room in Pera. One visitor said, hauntingly, that it was 'the sort of half-empty room you might find at the back of an inn, on some Ukrainian country road, in autumn.'

Ludwika Śniadecka had married one of the wildest of all Romantic exiles. Michał Czaykowski, another well-born Eastern Pole, had led partisans in the forests of western Ukraine during the November Rising of 1830. Escaping to Paris, he wrote lively historical novels about Cossacks and gypsies and, at the same time, managed to persuade the French intelligence services that he was not only a trained conspirator but an expert on Near Eastern politics. Despatched to Istanbul in 1851 with Ludwika, he staggered his French employers by converting to Islam and joining the Turkish Army. Michał Czaykowski became General Sadyk Pasha.

Ludwika, it seems, thought this would be a wise move. She turned out to be right. Within a few years, the Crimean War had broken out, the very conflict between Russia and the Western Powers allied with Turkey for which the Poles had been praying. Prince Adam Czartoryski in Paris urged all Poles to support Turkey, and at

Burgas, between Istanbul and the Danube mouths, Sadyk Pasha began to raise an army. It was supposed to be a Polish legion. Many Poles came from France and Britain to join it. But it also recruited in the Allied prisoner-of-war camps for anyone willing to change uniform and fight against the tsar. The force under Sadyk Pasha came to include large numbers of Ukrainians, Cossacks and Jews. These 'Ottoman Cossacks', although blazing with enthusiasm, were a mixed bag.

During the Crimean War, Ludwika became the most important political figure of the Polish emigration in Turkey. Among other functions, she acted as liaison officer between the commanders of the Polish forces training in their base at Burgas, on the Black Sea coast, and political visitors from Paris concerned with how to use the 'Ottoman Cossacks' as a bargaining counter to influence the Allied war aims. This woman – whose tomb so typically describes her as a man's daughter, a man's niece and a man's wife – spent much of her life giving men orders and seeing that they carried them out. In return they charged her with 'bossiness', which she ignored, and complained that she was 'hard', which she was not.

Adam Mickiewicz arrived in the autumn of 1855, on the steamer *Mont Thabor* from Marseille. His cover-story was a research trip to study education in the Balkans, but he paid little attention to Ottoman schooling. He felt happy, for the first time in years. The war in Crimea seemed to be going well, and he was back in the Islamic world again for the first time since his journey to Crimea. Going ashore at Smyrna on the way, he did not bother with the conventional sights. 'I found something else worthy of my attention,' he wrote in a letter. 'I saw mounds of dung and garbage, bits of bone and crockery, the sole of an old slipper, some loose feathers. That really appealed to me. I stood there staring for a long time; it was what one used to see in front of a Polish country inn.'

He liked living hard. He was genuinely short of money in Istanbul, but he may also have wanted to show himself that at fifty-seven he could still exist like a nomad, a soldier or a student. In the Lazarist monastery, Mickiewicz slept under his greatcoat and used his trunk as table and bookcase. He had brought his favourite stick, a 'pilgrim staff', and he followed his own favourite morning routine: a glass of Turkish coffee topped with thick cream and laced with cognac, followed by vigorous pipe-smoking. Up at Burgas, he was happy too. Back in 1848, at another moment when the iron landscape of European autocracy seemed to be falling apart, he had raised his own Polish legion in Rome and marched with it through Milan to challenge the might of the Habsburg Empire. Now, in the company of Sadyk Pasha, Ludwika's husband, he slept under canvas again and rode about watching the Polish forces, the Ottoman Cossacks, at their training. He went hunting in the hills, and listened to soldiers' songs round the camp-fire.

The optimism did not last long. Mickiewicz fell out with Sadyk. A political crisis was building up between Burgas and Paris; Sadyk wanted supreme command of an independent Polish force under the sultan, while Czartoryski preferred a British plan for dividing up the Poles between several foreign commands and accused Sadyk of hankering after dictatorship. But this did not bother Mickiewicz. Sadyk was the sort of impulsive eastern Pole he liked, and he shared his instinct for a free Polish army fighting as a recognised, distinct member of the anti-Russian coalition. His difficulty with Sadyk was about the Jews.

Mickiewicz had travelled a long intellectual journey in his reflections about Jewish destiny. There is a possibility that his own mother came from a 'Frankist' family, from the eighteenth-century Ukrainian sect led by the magnificent charlatan Jakub Frank (Jankiel Lejbowicz) which defected from Judaism and sought conversion to the Catholic faith. His wife Celina was of Frankist descent, and Mickiewicz's sense of a providential relationship between the two nations, Poles and Jews, became steadily stronger as he grew older. The cause of 'Israel, our elder brother' and the cause of Polish independence could not, he decided, be separately solved.

He always believed in full equality and civil rights for Jews. But for a long time, especially during the years when his mind was dominated by the mystic Towiański (a much dingier charlatan than Frank), he assumed that the self-realisation of Jewry would be through conversion to Christianity. Later, he was able to shake off this notion of convergence, and look forward to a free Poland in which Jews and Poles would help one another to follow parallel destinies. 'Without the emancipation of the Jews, and the development of their spirit, Poland cannot rise. Should she rise without the emancipation of the Jews, which I do not believe, she certainly will not be able to maintain herself'.

When he reached the camp at Burgas, he found that the troops included hundreds of Polish, Ukrainian and Russian Jews. As far away as Plymouth, where prisoners of war were kept in the Mill Bay gaol, Polish emissaries had already been recruiting anti-tsarist Jews to serve against Russia. Now Mickiewicz conceived a new vision. He would form the Jews into a separate legion within the Ottoman Cossack division: the 'Hussars of Israel'.

This plan took up the remaining weeks of the poet's life. The Polish exiles had long ago decided that the first step to the liberation of their country – the token to the oppressed millions at home that a free Poland already lived and fought – was the establishment of a Polish army abroad: the 'legionary idea'. Mickiewicz now applied this thought to the Jews. The Hussars of Israel would be a Jewish legion. His friend Armand Lévy, an assimilated French Jew who had travelled with him to Turkey, told Turkish officials that 'we want to elevate ourselves as a race, and we believe that the best means . . . is the submission of proof that we are not only as intelligent but also as brave as the others'.

The creation of the Hussars and their victories in battle would not only announce to the world that the Jewish nation had broken away from the ancient Gentile caricature of egotism and servility; it would also electrify and transform the Jewish masses throughout the Russian Empire. And, as Mickiewicz put it, the Christian peasantry would follow the Jewish example. 'We shall spread like lava with our continually growing legion, from synagogue to synagogue, village to village, into the very depths of Poland and Lithuania.'

For a time, the Hussars of Israel seemed to be possible. Sadyk Pasha agreed to a proposal from Mickiewicz that a synagogue should be opened in the camp, and that Jewish soldiers should have Saturdays off during training. Lieutenant Michał Horenstein designed a fine uniform for the Hussars and wore it about Burgas, to the delight of Mickiewicz. But, behind the poet's back, Sadyk grew satirical. He had no doubts about the fighting qualities of Jewish troops; at the capture of Bucharest the year before, Jewish soldiers had done well and later – after the death of Mickiewicz – they fought bravely under his command outside Sevastopol. He also calculated that the project would help to raise money for the Polish cause from the Jewish financial world, and he wrote letters and reports criticising 'the ridiculous yet factually existing prejudice against a Jewish army'. But he could foresee what Turkish objections would arise, above all the fear that a Jewish legion might turn its energies away from Russia and towards Palestine, still an Ottoman province. And Sadyk himself was not free of racial and religious prejudice.

In the end, they quarrelled. Sadyk told Mickiewicz that 'an army with separate Jewish and Ukrainian units under the leadership of a Polish nobleman is unthinkable. It would be a freak.' Mickiewicz went angrily back to Istanbul and his dank room in Pera at the end of October 1855, and tried to revive the Hussars of Israel at meetings with Turkish officials, Jewish dignitaries and foreign diplomats. He continued to see Ludwika but even she, in spite of all her affection for him, found it hard to take his plans seriously. Unwisely, she read to him a letter from her husband at Burgas in which he referred casually to 'scurvy Jews'. The poet was appalled. After his death, she wrote to Sadyk: 'Perhaps Mickiewicz's origin, or that of his family or wife, was [Jewish], for where did such love for Israel come from? I never thought about it until I read him your letter and came to the "scurvy Jew" bit; how he trembled, how excited he was! I don't know whether it is possible to love strange things so much, but perhaps he was in love with his own idea, wishes and thoughts.'

In Istanbul, it began to rain. Among the sick and wounded of the Allied armies, who crowded the streets or lay in hospital, cholera broke out. On the Asian side of the Bosporus, Florence Nightingale struggled to hold back the epidemic in the wards at Scutari. On the European side, one morning in late November, Adam Mickiewicz felt suddenly sick and giddy. He drank coffee and smoked a pipe, and felt a little better. Horenstein and a friend came to see him, in their sleek grey Hussars of Israel tunics, and talked about the war news and the gossip from Burgas. Then, when they had gone, the first violent stomach cramps began.

He was dead by the following night. There was no effective treatment, and he and his friends knew it. Colonel Kuczyński, a friend from Paris, called during the last evening and bent over his bed. Mickiewicz managed a smile, and began to say something: 'Kuczyński . . . the Ottoman Cossacks . . . ' Then he lost consciousness. It was six, and growing dark. Just before nine, he died.

The war went on. The Ottoman Cossacks, with Sadyk at their head, went off to Crimea and fought 'for your freedom and ours': the Jews served in their ranks, and nothing more was heard of the

Hussars of Israel. Nothing more was heard about Polish independence either, once the war was over. When the Allies and Russia sat down in Paris to make peace the following year, they agreed to overlook the Polish question. That was the price already agreed for keeping Austria and Prussia, the two other partitioning powers, in the alliance against Russia. The French and the British, who had deliberately raised the hopes of the Poles, now abandoned them. The Russian ambassador at the Peace Conference reported with relief that the word 'Poland' had not been so much as mentioned.

Seven years later, in January 1863, the last and most terrible of the Polish nineteenth-century insurrections broke out. Men and women chanted the poems of Mickiewicz and Słowacki as they marched through the forests or lay waiting in the trenches, hoping that they would live up to the prophecies of 'the nation as Christ' or 'resurrection through sacrifice'. When the January Rising failed, most Europeans thought that the age of Romantic nationalism had closed for ever. The future must surely belong to great supranational blocks of power, to the empires.

The corpse of Adam Mickiewicz was taken back to France by steamer, and buried in Paris. Many years later, in 1890, it was dug up again and brought to the Wawel Cathedral in Kraków, where Mickiewicz was laid among the Polish kings. Then the world changed once more, in a quite unexpected direction. The First World War ended with the collapse of four empires: Ottoman, Hohenzollern, Habsburg and Romanov. All along a line drawn between Galway and Georgia, all round the Black Sea and across the triangle between the Baltic, the Black Sea and the Adriatic, the graves opened and the forgotten nations emerged to claim sovereign statehood. One of them was Poland. From Partition to Resurrection had taken 124 years.

Ludwika stayed in her grave by the Black Sea, where the first and last passions of Adam Mickiewicz were enacted. The phrase 'in Polish soil' written on her tomb is not about politics or territory. It is about a sort of transubstantiation, held to take place wherever Polish blood falls or bones are buried – much what Rupert Brooke meant by the 'corner of a foreign field / Which is for ever England'. In the Sikorski Museum in London, there is an urn containing earth mixed with blood, taken by a Polish soldier from the slope at Monte Cassino on which his dead comrade lay. This substance is *polska ziemia* – Polish soil.

Chapter Seven

Home,
A sort of honour, not a building site,
Wherever we are, when, if we chose, we might
Be somewhere else, but trust that we have chosen right.

W. H. Auden, 'In Wartime' (1942)

THE BUS JOURNEY from Ankara to Trabzon, which used to be Trebizond, takes thirteen hours. The road begins in the steppe of central Anatolia and then winds down through the forests and passes of the coastal mountains to the Black Sea. This is the route that Xenophon and his Ten Thousand took in 400 BC, on their march home from Persia. But where exactly they were when the soldiers saw the blue band on the horizon ahead of them, and cried out '*Thalassa*! The sea!', cannot be known.

Some think that it was near the port of Ordu, about a hundred miles west of Trebizond, others that they filed down from the mountains a little further east. The point is that when the soldiers shouted '*Thalassa*!', the local people understood them. They were Greeks too. Trebizond, which was their 'Trapezos', was only one of the chain of colony-cities which lined that shore, in touch with all the other Greek settlements ringing the Black Sea. They had been there for three hundred years already when Xenophon and the survivors of his army came out of the wilderness. The Pontic Greeks, as these settlers came to be called, remained on that coast and in its green, foggy valleys running up to the snowline for almost two and a half thousand more years. They were ruled by the Romans, then by the Byzantine emperors, then – briefly – by the Grand Comnenoi, emperors of Trebizond. After that, the Turks came. That too the Pontic Greeks survived, negotiating and

176

conceding a little, converting to Islam a little. The end came only in 1923, with the event known in diplomatic language as 'The Exchange' and in undiplomatic Greek as the *Katastrofē*.

Greece, in a wild imperial venture supported by Britain, had invaded western Anatolia, hoping to make itself an Aegean 'great power' and to construct a 'greater Greece' out of the ruins of the Ottoman Empire. But the invasion ended not simply in Greece's defeat at the battle of Dumlupinar in 1922, but in a calamitous rout and slaughter which drove not only the Greek armies but much of the Greek civilian population of Anatolia into the sea. The Treaty of Lausanne, in 1923, settled the frontiers of the new Turkey under the leadership of Mustafa Kemal Ataturk. The universal caliphate – a sprawling, multi-ethnic and multi-religious empire – now imploded like a dead star, metamorphosing itself into a compact, homogenous modern state of Moslem religion and Turkish speech. At the same time, Greece and Turkey agreed to exchange minorities. Nearly half a million Moslems (many of whom were Greeks in all but religion) were forced to leave Greece, while more than a million Christians (some of whom were culturally Turks) were expelled from Turkey. Most of the Christians were Pontic Greeks, who abandoned their monasteries and farms, their town houses and banks and schools, and fled with what they could carry down to the docks.

People on Turkish buses are either going home or leaving home. I never met anyone who admitted to travelling on business or on state duty. Before each passenger climbing into the Trabzon coach floated the picture of a house. For some, it was an urban apartment doorway, crowded with women and children weeping or waving farewell. For others, it was a red-roofed house above the Black Sea, an expectant house in which the family have finished preparations for the welcome and are telling each other to go to bed and not wait up. Everyone on the coach was a little tremulous, anxious to be consoled or distracted.

A beautiful woman, tall and narrow-eyed as a Kazakh, had flown back from her job with an oil company in Japan to see her family in Giresun – the town which the Greeks named Kerasos and which gave its name to a fruit which the Romans found there and planted all over their world: the cherry. A well-wrapped family, with a married daughter in a heavy Islamic cowl, talked to each other in scathing Brooklyn English; they were heading home from New York to the port of Samsun. A peasant woman was helped by the other passengers to settle her handicapped daughter, paralysed and lolling, into a front seat; she arranged a white scarf about the girl's head and then, twisting her hands, made a speech about the family's misfortune. Beside me, a young woman studying media sciences in Holland talked to me about her mother waiting for her at Ünye, about her experiences as a trainee in Dutch television. As night fell and a misshapen, waxing moon blazed over the bare hills, she told me that snow had fallen that day in the high Pontic Alps.

This was a swift, strong Ulusoy bus, from the long-distance road fleet which binds the Turkish continent together. Every hour or so, the conductor came down the aisle with a glass carboy of cologne. Cupped hands were held out and filled; faces and necks were laved and massaged. The conversations fell away, and the passengers slept. On my other side, by the window, a bearded man remained silent. Once he turned to me, opening his black eyes wide, and said, 'I am a Turk!' He regarded me for a long moment, then turned back to the window.

I half-woke at Samsun, and then again at Ünye where the girl from Holland got off. Now the Black Sea was present, no more than an oppressive darkness on one side of the highway. When I woke again, at first light, a shrill voice was shouting and wailing. At first I thought it belonged to an eighteen-month-old boy, being tossed up and down and comforted by his parents a few rows ahead of me. Then I realised it was coming from further forward, where the handicapped girl had been placed with her mother. The sound strengthened into a sort of chant, a loud, protesting crying. Some of the men had gathered round the seat from which the noise was coming. The crying was not from the girl, it seemed, but from her mother. Low voices muttered in Turkish around me, and I saw that two women sitting across the aisle from me were silently wiping away tears with their scarfs.

Two men came down the aisle, carrying with great difficulty the handicapped child wrapped in a blanket from head to foot, and laid the bundle across one of the rear seat rows, near the door. I understood then that the girl was dead, that she must have died some time back in the darkness as the coach made its way down through the hills towards the sea. The mother came past and sat down by her daughter's body. Her cries became a rhythm, and then

178

a song, a Pontic dirge of mourning in which the same musical phrase rose and fell in verse after verse.

Ahead of us, to the east, a huge red glare was rising from behind the next cape as if the city of Trabzon were burning. The sea was visible now, still black, with viscous dark-blue gleams. As the sun rose, the bearded man next to me began to pray, sitting upright and moving his lips. When he was done, he made the Moslem gesture of reverence, passing his hands gently down his face as if awakening from a dream.

The coach stopped by a mosque already lit for dawn prayers. A taxi was waiting. Several of the male passengers carried the girl's body down the steps of the bus and laid it in the back of the taxi. Somebody opened the taxi boot and gestured to the mother; her face twisted, and she flung her handbag into the boot and turned away. Presently she was persuaded to get in. Two men from the bus squeezed into the rear seat, beside the bundle, and the cab set off ahead of us towards Trabzon. The driver and the bearded man walked across to the mosque. I could see their outlines against the lit windows as they prostrated themselves, then rose again.

They returned, and the Ulusoy coach moved off for the last twenty miles to Trabzon. The conductor came round for the last time with the cologne bottle. The two women across the aisle continued to weep small tears in silence. The red sun rose into heavy clouds, which grew thin and then burned away. As the coach swung into the Taksim Meydane, the main square, it was six in the morning and already a hot, clear day.

Trabzon is built upon ridges, between deep ravines which run down to the sea. On one of these ridges stands the ruined citadel of Trebizond, the palace and fortress of the Great Comnenoi. The town itself is full of Byzantine churches which are now mosques: St Eugenius, St Anne, St Andrew, St Michael, St Philip, the cave church of St Savas, the church of Panaghia Chrysocephalos. On a headland in the western part of the city, cool in the wind from the sea, is the cathedral of Aghia Sofia, now a museum, its Byzantine frescoes restored by David Talbot-Rice and Edinburgh University.

There is something of Edinburgh in the commercial centre of Trabzon, tall classical buildings of grey volcanic stone built in the nineteenth century by Greek bankers, Greek shipping lines, Greek benefactors who endowed schools and hospitals. But to walk those streets today is to be constantly impeded by Turkish kindness and curiosity. Men call to you from the terrace of tea-houses, and tell you the story of their lives over glasses of smoky tea grown on the slopes above Rize, on the Black Sea. In the restaurants, the cook comes to lead you by the hand into the kitchen and make you choose from the hissing pans. The waiter gently pulls the book from your hand to see what you are reading. The cobbler who mended the leather strap of my bag fetched me a glass of cold, fresh lemon juice from the café while I was waiting, and then tried hard to refuse payment for both lemon juice and strap. The man in the camera shop (who turned out to have replaced my exposed film, so that two entire rolls were wrecked) gave me a long lecture about how an English professor had gone to Erzerum to investigate the mass grave of a 'so-called Armenian massacre' and found that all the skulls were perfect examples of Turkish heads, not an Armenian among them.

The Comnenian Empire began here in 1204, after the Crusaders had stormed and sacked Constantinople; Alexis Comnenos, son of the Byzantine emperor, escaped to Trebizond and made it his capital. A stroke of commercial luck ensured that the Comnenian state would survive and flourish even after the Greek emperors had regained the throne at Constantinople. In the mid-thirteenth century, the Mongol conquest of Persia opened a new, southern branch of the 'Silk Routes' which began at Tabriz and ended, after crossing the Pontic Mountains, at Trebizond.

Professor Anthony Bryer, who in our own times is the historiographer-imperial of the Comnenoi, lays emphasis on the compactness of this Pontos which was governed from Trebizond, 'hemmed like the Lebanon and south Caspian by its Alps . . . select by climate and geography'. Coastal agriculture, once oil, wine and grain but now nuts, tea and tobacco, is fringed with temperate rain forests 'which give way to summer pastures, overlooking the dry highlands of Armenia, upon which the Pontos turns its back to face the Black Sea'.

From the beginning, the Greek settlement here was unlike those on the other Black Sea coasts. It was a settlement in depth, reaching up into the wooded valleys of the interior. Behind the usual city-colonies along the shore, 'Greek-speaking settlement extended inland to the watershed'. In the time of the Comnenoi, the relatively tiny city of Trebizond enjoyed a turbulent urban and political life, but the mass of the population lived in the hills behind, growing crops and driving their beasts up to high pastures in summer. Most of these Christian peasants were the tenantry of a chain of opulently endowed monasteries which perched along the steep flanks of the valleys; as Bryer says, 'a monastic economy of almost Tibetan proportions'.

Apart from the cities, this rural Pontic society amounted to far the greatest concentration of Greek-speaking population in the Hellenic or Byzantine worlds – much more numerous than that of the Peloponnese. Constantinople finally fell to Mehmet the Conqueror in 1453, and Trebizond was captured by the Turks in 1461 after a siege of forty-two days. But the Pontic Greeks remained in their valleys and villages, and the monasteries clung to their wealth and most of their estates for many more centuries. Many people, including some of the great families of Trebizond, converted in a superficial way to Islam, but continued to speak Pontic Greek – a language which over the millennia had steadily diverged from the tongue spoken in the Aegean or in the capital of the Byzantine Empire.

Who did they think they were, in this pre-nationalist age? In the first place, they did not think of themselves as 'Greek' or as a people in some way rooted in the peninsula and islands we now call 'Greece'. Sophisticates in Trebizond might address one another in the fifteenth century as 'Hellenes', but this was a cultural fancy rather than an ethnic description. Outsiders, whether Turks or northern Europeans, referred to them and to all the inhabitants of the Byzantine Empire as 'Rom' or 'Rum' people, or as 'Romanians' – citizens of the Roman Empire, in other words, who were also distinguished by their Orthodox Christian faith. Struggling with these categories, a Pontic Turk whose village had once been Greek told Anthony Bryer: 'This is Roman (Rum) country; they spoke Christian here . . . '

The people of the Pontic valleys and cities themselves seemed to find identity in three things: in belonging to a place or *patris* which could be as small as a village, in not being Western (Roman Catholic) Christians, and in feeling themselves to be members of a polity which was so ancient, so sacred and superior to all others that it scarcely required a name. We call this community, weakly enough, 'the Eastern Empire', or 'Byzantium'. That cannot convey the almost Chinese degree of significance which the 'Rom' people attached to the Empire even long after it had been overthrown, as if it were the eternal essence of all political community in comparison to which other states and realms were only transient realities.

We call the imperial capital Constantinople or Byzantium; the Vikings called it Micklegard; the Turks called it Istanbul, which is no more than the three Greek words *eis tin polin* – 'into the City'. And for its citizens, whether they lived within its walls or in Pontus or Georgia or Crimea or at the Danube mouths, that was its name: 'The City'. There was no other. Nor was it possible that this city could come to an end except in a purely phenomenal way. The essence was indestructible. Inevitably, its earthly manifestation would return.

This is a Pontic folk-song composed five hundred years ago, when the news of the fall of Constantinople reached Trebizond:

> A bird, a good bird, left the City,
> it settled neither in vineyards nor in orchards,
> it came to settle on the castle of the Sun.
> It shook one wing, drenched in blood,
> it shook the other wing, it had a written paper.
> Now it reads, now it cries, now it beats its breast.
> 'Woe is us, woe is us, Romania is taken.'
> The churches lament, the monasteries weep,
> and St John Chrysostom weeps, he beats his breast.
> Weep not, weep not, St John, and beat not your breast.
> Romania has passed away, Romania is taken.
> Even if Romania has passed away, it will flower
>   and bear fruit again.

To visit the monastery at Sumela, you have to go to the Taksim Meydane at Trabzon and find the old man with the Bel-Air Chevrolet. Then it is a matter of sitting on a low wall in the sun until the old man has found enough fellow-travellers to fill the car. The Bel-Air, whose engine drinks a fuel tank the size of a small Byzantine cistern every day, is expensive to run.

The car heads inland, up the main road which leads to Gümüshane (Argyropolis), the silver-mine city at the head of the valley. After a few miles, the Bel-Air turns off and follows a long forest ravine with a noisy river. Cowled, mediaeval figures urge heifers over bridges made of logs, or scythe hay on the verges. Thirty miles from Trabzon, the car stops. The ravine has become a gorge of naked rock soaring above pine forest. The river makes echoes. The sky is a blue slit overhead.

Far above, something broken is clinging to a cliff-face. It resembles the remains of a swallow's nest, after a fierce broom has swept the eaves. This is Sumela, the 'Holy, Imperial, Patriarchal and Stavropegic Monastery of the All-Holy Mother of God on Mount Mela', endowed by at least five of the Grand Comnenian emperors of Trebizond, once owner of the entire valley and all its villages.

A path, sometimes a staircase, goes zigzagging up the cliff from the river below, and it takes a strenuous half-hour's climb through the black pines and azaleas to reach the monastery. The place was built on a ledge, only a few hundred feet from the top, which reaches back into the mountain in a broad, shallow cave. Everywhere there are ruins. But these are hate-ruins, rather than time-ruins: the gutted walls of the hostel leaning out over the gulf, the blackened holes where timber buildings and galleries stood, the scarred doors of stone chapels whose interiors have been vandalised. The inmost shrine, a cave-shelter constructed against the living rock, was plastered and then covered with frescoes. Now the plaster is sagging off, hanging away from the rock in dark scabs painted in dim colours. Vast heads of the Madonna and the Pantocrator look down, and a Comnenian emperor with his court is visible in the half-light. Everything within reach is defaced with graffiti, names and dates, mostly Turkish but often – curiously enough – Greek, from the years before the *Katastrofé*. Here and there, square holes in the ceiling-plaster and long vertical scars on the walls show where professional art thieves have used power tools, cutting out sections of fresco destined for the auction houses of London and New York.

Outside, in the brilliant sunlight on the ledge, water is falling from a spring a hundred feet overhead, at the tip of the cliff's overhang. Each gout of water separates into glittering drops as it floats down through the air, finally hitting the ledge with a shrill crash. A muddy pool has formed there, under a signpost inscribed in Turkish and English: 'Sacred Water'. Nearby, there are builders' fences and scaffolding and men wheeling cement bags down planks. Restoration is under way. But it is difficult to imagine how Sumela looked in the eighteenth century when the Abbot Christoforos and his twenty-three Elders received delegations bringing tributes of gold coin from as far away as Moldavia, or when Victorian scholars from Europe snuffled and squinted over manuscripts in the monastery's library – now no more than a painted sign on a wall leading to a thousand feet of empty air; or when Sumela was abandoned for ever in 1923.

When a cult began on this ledge, nobody knows. A fourteenth-century inscription says that the monastery was founded 'by the Emperor, Master of Orient and Occident', but there must have been a shrine here long before then. The old myth of Sumela says that St Luke painted an icon of the Madonna which was taken to Athens, but that the Madonna, growing tired of the sinful city, persuaded several angels to arrange her escape. She flew across the Aegean and the Black Sea, and then swooped down to hide in the cavern under the cliff. Here she was finally rediscovered by two detective monks sent from Athens, Barnabas and Sophronios, who decided not to extradite her back to Greece but to build a new monastery around her icon on the mountain.

Sumela's first period of glory was in the time of the Comnenians of Trebizond. Alexis III (1349–90) was a special patron. Saved from a tempest by the intercession of the Madonna's icon, he paid for the reconstruction of the monastery and, in 1361, climbed up there to watch an eclipse of the sun. The second prosperity arrived in the eighteenth century, long after the Turkish conquest, when the Gümüshane silver mines were opened up. The archbishops of Chaldia, the region around Gümüshane, took Sumela under their wing and paid for more building, more wall-paintings and the restoration of the mediaeval frescoes. They could afford to: most of them came from the Phytianos clan, the family which held the silver-mining contracts from the sultan.

The Turkish guide-books on sale in the Taksim Meydane offer this account of the 1923 *Katastrofē*: 'After the proclamation of the Republic, the Greeks who lived in the region returned to their own country, and the monastery of Sumela was evacuated and abandoned.' Their own country? Returned? They had lived in the Pontos for nearly three thousand years. Their Pontic dialect was not understandable to twentieth-century Athenians. Their world was the Black Sea littoral, and their family connections abroad, by the twentieth century, were with the enormous Pontic Greek

184

emigration which had already settled in the Russian Empire: in the Caucasus, Crimea and the lands around the Sea of Azov.

Yet the guide-books are not entirely wrong. All through the nineteenth century, two historical forces worked on the antique community of the Pontic Greeks with growing intensity: an ideology and a practicality. One was Greek nationalism, radiating from Constantinople and then from Athens, at once modernising and romantic. The other was the rise of Russian power around the Black Sea, and the successive wars which advanced Russia into the Balkans in the West and down into the coastal regions of the Caucasus in the East. Each war, increasing the tensions between Christians and the Ottoman authorities in Anatolia, led to an outflow of Greeks into the welcoming Russian Empire and to an inflow of Moslem refugees, mostly from the Caucasus, into the Pontos. After the Russian-Turkish war of 1828–9, some 42,000 Greeks, almost a fifth of the Pontic population, followed the withdrawing Russian armies. More Greeks left after the Crimean War, settling mainly in Georgia and Crimea, and another emigration took place after the 1877–8 war between Russia and Turkey, until by about 1880 nearly 100,000 Greeks had taken refuge under the Christian protection of the tsar. The last of these movements took place during the First World War. Russian troops advancing along the south coast of the Black Sea occupied Trebizond for two years, between 1916 and 1918, and when they withdrew another 80,000 Greeks departed with them, fearing reprisals.

The 'Pontic Renaissance', by contrast, came from the West. All round the Black Sea, the Greek communities flung themselves into the huge commercial opportunities of the nineteenth century, into shipping, banking, tobacco-growing and manufacturing industry. They used their prosperity not only for investment but for enlightenment and culture. George Maraslis, for example, whose family came from Plovdiv in modern Bulgaria, was mayor of Odessa from 1897 to 1907; with his personal wealth, he founded schools, libraries, publishing houses and teacher-training colleges not only in Odessa but in Thrace, Plovdiv ('Phillipopolis'), Salonica, Corfu and Athens.

Trebizond shared this property, especially during the decades when the port served as the western terminal of the overland route from India through Persia (the boom ceased abruptly when the Suez Canal was opened in 1869). There were European consulates in the city, and half a dozen Greek banks. The whole Pontos benefited from a surge of school-foundation, and with modern education came an entirely new, lay generation of teachers trained in Constantinople or Athens for whom the Greek language was not Pontic but classical.

For the first time, intellectuals set out to give the Pontians an ethnic national consciousness. That required 'origins' and 'roots'. Anthony Bryer relates how 'Triantaphyllides, a Chaldian school-master ... christened his son Pericles and sent him to Athens, whence he returned after 1842 to teach Xenophon and classical Greek at the Trebizond Phrontisterion ... By 1846, schoolmasters had renamed Gümüshane a fancy "Argyropolis".' In a typical example of cultural nation-invention, the teachers proceeded to graft the Pontos onto the stock not just of Byzantium but of Periclean Athens itself. All round the Greek world of the Black Sea, the same process was going on. The teachers and the school curricula came from Athens, bringing with them a new concept of Greekness which linked the Greek-Orthodox communities of the Black Sea and the 'nation' of Greece.

This was in no way a 'Little Greece' nationalism restricted to the arid peninsula in the Aegean Sea. A speaker in the Greek parliament in 1844 expounded this newly designed identity: 'The Kingdom of Greece is not Greece. It constitutes only one part, the smallest and the poorest ... A Greek is not only a man who lives within the Kingdom, but also one who lives in Yoannina, Serrai, Adrianople, Constantinople, Smyrna, Trebizond, Crete and in any land asso-ciated with Greek history and the Greek Race ... There are two main centres of Hellenism: Athens, the capital of the Greek Kingdom, and the City, the dream and hope of all Greeks.' Here was 'The Great Idea', the vision of a restored 'Romania' with its capital in the City, reaching from Athens to the borders of Georgia and Ukraine. But 'The Great Idea' had now acquired a far more impressive myth of origin, which led back to the Parthenon and the stoa and the battle of Marathon.

This is why, in 1923, it was possible for Chrysanthos, last Metropolitan of Trebizond, to lead 164,000 Pontic Greeks 'home' to Greece – a country alien to them physically, climatically, politically and linguistically. By then, admittedly, there was nowhere else for them to go. The Russian Empire had become the Soviet Union, suspicious of Greeks ever since a disastrous occupation of Odessa and Sevastopol by the Greek Army in 1919. Georgia, where hundreds of thousands of Pontic Greeks had settled, had become an independent state after the Russian Revolution but had been reconquered by the Bolsheviks. Attempts at the Versailles Peace Conference to gain international support for an independent 'Pontic republic', or for an Armenian state in Asia Minor which would include Trebizond and give the Pontic Greeks internal autonomy, had come to nothing.

The Greek invasion of Anatolia, egged on by Lloyd George, was smashed by Kemal Ataturk in 1922. The following year brought the Treaty of Lausanne, and the 'exchange' of Moslem and Christian minorities. The Greeks of Istanbul and the Aegean islands west of the Dardanelles were allowed to remain for another half-century, until most of the surviving Greeks left during the Greco-Turkish confrontation over Cyprus after 1974. 'The Great Idea' was extinct at last.

But the Pontic Greeks were not extinct at all. From being a motherland with widely scattered children, the Pontos had become a diaspora. One part of the diaspora now made its life in Greece, remaining for other Greek citizens a puzzling, inward-looking nation-within-the-nation. The other part vanished behind the fortress walls of the Soviet Union and the outside world, including most Greeks, forgot about them. But they, it turned out, did not forget about Pontos or Greece.

Most Greeks in the new Soviet Union lived around the Black Sea. Settlers who concentrated around the north shores of the Sea of Azov (the 'Mariupol Greeks') had a dialect and culture of their own; they were the descendants of an older farming community in Crimea which Catherine the Great had moved into southern Russia. But the majority was of Pontic origin. The Greeks lived in the port cities, especially Odessa, Rostov and Sevastopol, in the fertile Kuban steppes, in the coastal towns and villages of Georgia and Abkhazia and in the hills of central Georgia.

The first Soviet years were tolerable, even encouraging. The Greeks rapidly recovered from the devastations of the Civil War. They kept most of their farms, and there was a vigorous cultural revival: a reform of the Greek alphabet; a wealth of bold and interesting Greek books, journals and newspapers in the kiosks; a state-assisted network of Greek-language education. On the Kuban coast and in some districts of Ukraine, Greek autonomous regions were established.

But with the collectivisation of farming after 1928, and Stalin's usurpation of supreme power, the Greeks were transformed almost overnight from beneficiaries of the Revolution to victims. Everything about them was now construed as counter-revolutionary: their tradition of free enterprise, their links with the 'imperialist' world outside and especially with Athens (many of them held Greek passports), their independent culture. The Greeks in south Russia and Ukraine strongly resisted the loss of their farms, and thousands were arrested. As the 'Great Purges' developed in the 1930s, their cultural and political leaders were charged with treachery or Trotskyism and murdered. The Greek schools were closed and Greek literature destroyed. In south Russia, political persecution rapidly turned into ethnic pogroms; entire Greek communities were arrested and deported. Dr Effie Voutira, who has done much research among the Pontic Greeks in the ex-Soviet Union, estimates that as many as 170,000 Greeks were expelled to Siberia and Central Asia after 1936.

But this had been only a prelude. The full impact of state terror was turned against the Greeks in the aftermath of the Second World War. Like the Crimean Tatars, the Chechens and the Volga Germans, the Greeks of the Soviet Union became a condemned nationality and were banished.

The 70,000 Crimean Greeks, almost all Pontic by descent, went first. Then came the Greeks of Kuban and south Russia. Finally, on the night of 14/15 June 1949, a single immense operation planned in secret for many months rounded up almost the entire Greek population of the Caucasus. The settlements in Abkhazia and along the Georgian coast down to the Turkish frontier were the principal target. About 100,000 people were seized. Their villages were surrounded in darkness by NKVD special troops, and they were given only a few hours to pack. Many of them perished on the sealed trains, and when they arrived at their destinations – usually weeks later – they were deliberately dispersed: scattered among small Moslem communities and *kolkhoz* cotton farms across the Central Asian plains.

Why was this done? There is no clear answer, even today. Stalin's fear of war in the Black Sea, his memories of the 1919 Intervention, Georgian intrigue and envy or the possession of Greek passports by so many Pontic Greeks — all these have been put forward as explanations. Perhaps the real provocation was that the Greeks were a family. Their human links were stronger than the artificial bonds of totalitarian politics. They were residents of the Soviet Union, but their crime was to be 'cosmopolitan'; to be members of a wider world of trade, gossip, marriages and family funerals which carried on its activities across and beyond the Soviet frontiers.

But Black Sea life without Greeks — the local politicians and factory owners, the grocers and café proprietors, the journalists and bank-clerks and grain-dealers and ship's captains — was a thin shadow of what it had once been. The Greeks had been envied by their neighbours. Now they were painfully missed.

Fazil Iskander is the great man of twentieth-century Abkhazian poetry and fiction. In his novel *Sandro of Chegem*, there is a scene in which Sandro, an Abkhaz hero of opportunism, is tempted to buy the house of a Greek family. The husband and wife have been deported to Siberia; their abandoned children taken for adoption by relations in Russia. It is a pretty little house, well looked after, surrounded by flowers and fruit trees. But then Sandro's father, a village patriarch from the hills, gradually realises why the house is empty, and why the city soviet is selling the house to his son for the price of two pigs.

'My son,' he began in a quiet and terrible voice, 'before, if a blood avenger killed his enemy, he touched not a button on his clothes. He took the body to the enemy's house, laid it on the ground, and called to his family to come out and take in their dead man clean, undefiled by the touch of an animal. That's the way it was. These men, now, kill innocent people and tear their clothes off them to sell cheap to their lackeys. You can buy this house, but I will never set foot in it, nor will you ever cross the threshold of my house!'

Like the Crimean Tatars whose exile they shared, the Pontic Greeks in the Soviet Union did not merely sit down and weep by the waters of Babylon. They tried, illegally and in secret, to teach Pontian Greek to their children, who at school were being indoctrinated into a monoglot Russian-Soviet culture. In the dusty *kolkhoz* villages of Kazakhstan and Uzbekistan, parents managed

189

to transmit at least fragments of their culture – music and cookery, especially. At the same time, their sense of identity slowly changed and hardened during the decades in Central Asia. Although they had now lost contact not only with Athens but with the remnants of the old Greek diaspora around the Black Sea many thousands of miles away to the West, their sense of 'Greekness' tightened into a belief in their own Greek political identity.

Most of the Pontic Greeks who went into exile had retained Greek passports. After the First World War, the government in Athens had distributed national identity papers throughout the diaspora, a gesture which paid respect to the dying, irredentist 'Great Idea'. At the same time, it was in line with a new current in post-1918 nationalism: the notion that nation-states had a right and even a duty to extend some degree of membership to their own ethnic compatriots abroad. Cultural affinity was to be developed into political affiliation. This idea was taken up principally by nations with a tradition of emigration and a recognisable diaspora. Germany, Ireland and finally Israel were among the nation-states which constructed versions of a 'right to return', the right to citizenship based on ethnic criteria which could be biological, religious, cultural or a mixture of all of them. Poland, before and after the Second World War, experimented with several versions of 'Polonia', a category which was intended above all to tap the wealth of the huge Polish diaspora in the United States.

What did this call to identification with a 'motherland' really mean? The contemporary states of Greece, Ireland, Israel, Hungary and Poland are all modern restorations of lost polities. As restorations, they are all highly inaccurate; none of them has the frontiers of its 'original'. But those originals all had in common the fact that they were obliterated from the political atlas by imperial violence. Accordingly, those who left the old national territory as emigrants – mostly in the nineteenth century – retained and passed down some sense that their departure from their native countries had been a matter of coercion rather than of free choice.

The resurrection of these countries as independent nation-states was therefore at once touching and reassuring to a diaspora. It was emotionally touching because independence did not merely avenge the trauma of emigration but also legitimated it. In a country like the United States, the appearance of Ireland or Poland on the world stage as a fully fledged, passport-issuing, conference-attending state raised the self-esteem of the Boston Irish or the Chicago Poles. The whole rhetoric of triumphant national liberation ascribed the tragedies of the past to foreign imperial oppression. 'We did not run away from our country in its hour of need. We were driven overseas by English landlords, or Prussian gendarmes, or tsarist Cossacks.'

And it was reassuring to the diaspora because it demanded little of the emigrant. There could of course be strong moral pressure to 'return' – intense in the case of Zionism, perfunctory in the cases of Ireland or Poland. But for the most part the emigrant could both have his cake and eat it. He or she could remain in the relative comforts of Chicago, New York or Melbourne with the extra sentimental empowerment of a second passport and a flag to carry on the old country's independence day parade.*

At the same time, the cultural gap between diaspora and 'homeland' could widen very rapidly indeed. Less than two centuries have been enough to make the average Illinois Pole into a foreigner in Warsaw, where, if he speaks Polish at all, he usually baffles his listeners with remnants of extinct peasant dialect. In Budapest, the Szekelyi women from Transylvania, wearing peasant costume and selling embroidered linens in the underpasses, are not exactly emigrants – their country left them, when Hungary lost Transylvania to Romania, rather than the other way round – but their culture is now remote from that of late twentieth-century Magyars. The German *Einsiedler*, now arriving in the Federal Republic after hundreds of years of village life in Eastern Europe, Ukraine, Russia and Siberia, often speak little or no German and bring with them an idea of Germany – pious, servile to authority, repressive – which was already obsolete when Bismarck was chancellor.

Two different processes operate here, apparently contradictory but actually complementary. As the cultural gap widens, so the subjective importance of national identity – in the narrow sense of nation-state membership – intensifies. This new diaspora patriotism may remain little more than a luxury of the imagination, but

* Scotland forms a curious exception. Although there are large and well-organised Scottish diasporas in North America and Australasia, the Scottish National Party's plan for an independent Scotland would restrict citizenship to those resident in Scotland (whatever their ethnicity) or born there, and their children. This determination to avoid ethnic nationalism seems admirable, but it enraged the late Scottish Conservative MP Sir Nicholas Fairbairn, who protested that any 'Greek, Tasmanian or the bastard child of an American serviceman' would have more rights in Scotland than an emigrant of pure Scots descent.

there are times when, suddenly and desperately, these cheques on the Bank of Symbolism are presented for payment. We have been living through such times for fifty years. Twentieth-century anti-Semitism in Europe, followed by the rise of Arab nationalism, brought the Jews of Europe and the Middle East to Israel. As the Soviet dictatorship weakened, the Volga Germans (also deported by Stalin to Central Asia) set out for Germany announcing that they were 'returning home'.

The Pontic Greeks were doing the same thing. Perhaps 300,000 are left in the territories of the old Soviet Union, more than half of them in Kazakhstan and Uzbekistan. Most now intend to 'return home', and nearly 200,000 have already done so in the last few years. And by 'home', they mean modern Greece.

Even Zionist Jews cannot match the extravagance of this statement, as a remark about history. It is nearly three thousand years since the first Greek colonists passed through the Bosporus and set up trading-posts around the Black Sea. Most of them originated from the Ionian cities, on the Aegean coast of what is now Turkey, rather than from the Peloponnese. Since then, their culture and language have steadily diverged from those of the peninsula we call 'Greece'. And yet now their descendants head for Athens or Salonica as if it were the most natural thing in the world.

After Stalin's death in 1953, the deported Greeks who had acquired Soviet nationality were allowed to return from Central Asia. (Most went back to Georgia, although their houses and farms had been sold off or confiscated after 1949.) The rest, those who held Greek papers issued by a country which they had never seen, remained in exile. At this stage, it seems, their concept of their status and of their relationship to Greece began to change. They had accepted their first great uprooting, the flight from the Turks in Pontos, as an emigration, a move to new shores on the same sea. But Stalin's banishment turned the Pontic Greeks, in their own estimation, into refugees.

Dr Effie Voutira has pointed out that the modern use of the word 'refugee' – especially in English – predicates the existence of a nation-state. By the mid-twentieth century, everyone was assumed to be a member of a national community. Everyone was at home somewhere, each with his or her passport. The great and growing number of human beings who had become internationally 'homeless' – the refugees – were therefore people whose primary plight was that they had been separated from their rightful nation-state. This is why we almost always add a national adjective to the term, as in 'Bosnian/Polish/Zairean refugee'. The refugee is somebody who once had a nation, but lost it.

This is an odd, inadequate way of designating the millions of displaced individuals and families carried back and forth on the tides of the world, but the displaced themselves are increasingly inclined to adopt it – precisely because 'refugee' implies membership of a state community. This was not always so. The Gaelic-speaking Highlanders who were removed from their townships and transported to Canada considered themselves emigrants, rather than refugees, although their departure (the 'Highland Clearances') was not usually voluntary. The Pontic Greeks who fled from Trebizond to run beach cafés at Sukhum, or print newspapers in Odessa, or plant vineyards in Georgia, grieved for their lost homes but prepared to put down fresh roots. But when Stalin snatched them away from the Black Sea and dumped them in the steppes of Central Asia, threatening their whole community with physical and cultural extinction, they could no longer consider themselves emigrants. This time, they had been not merely transplanted but condemned.

In Central Asia, the Pontic Greeks faced two extreme alternatives. One was to assimilate to Soviet society, and to seek to climb the Party ladder – which many Greeks did. The other was to reject the whole new environment. In the end, the choice was effaced. The Communist Party and then the Soviet Union capsized and sank, leaving climbers and rejectors together in the same leaky boat: all were now non-Kazakh or non-Uzbek 'colonialists' in newly independent Moslem states. The 'natives', who under-standably drew no distinctions between outsiders who had arrived in their land as conquerors, imperial settlers or banished victims, contemplated the farms and bureaucratic posts occupied by Russians, Ukrainians, Crimean Tatars, Greeks, Volga Germans, Chechens and Meshketian Turks, and began to close in. By 1990, ethnic rioting between locals and incomers was spreading across the Central Asian republics. Now, with fresh desperation, the Pontic Greeks appealed to 'their nation': Greece.

In the first years after the Russian Revolution there had been some outflow to Greece, and more Greeks contrived to escape in 1938–9, after the Great Purges. But then the Soviet external frontiers closed tightly. They did not open again for almost fifty years, when Mikhail Gorbachev began to lift the ban on mass emigration.

At that time, in the mid-1980s, probably around 500,000 Greeks were living in the Soviet Union, almost all of them of Pontic origin. By the end of the decade, they were arriving in Greece at the rate of 20,000 a year, and by the mid-1990s, the Greek villages in Central Asia were practically empty. Some, a minority, went back to the Black Sea coasts in south Russia or Georgia. There was even some optimistic talk of reviving the old idea of a Greek autonomous region in the Kuban; a congress of Greek delegates was held at Gelendzhik, near Novorossisk, in 1991, and a Greek-language newspaper (*Pontos*) appeared in the little port of Anapa. But the Caucasus grew much less attractive for Greek exiles in the next few years. Civil war in Georgia was followed by an even more violent struggle as Abkhazia, historically one of the centres of Greek settlement, fought Georgia for its own independence. Most Pontic Greeks headed 'home' – to Athens or Salonica.

Travelling westwards from Central Asia by train and then by ship, they brought with them enormous wooden packing-cases, crammed not only with their own possessions but with every kind of cheap Soviet household goods they could buy before they set off. Arriving at a Greek port, the new immigrants levered open the cases and sold their contents on the stalls of suburban flea-markets. Finally, when the trade goods had gone, the packing-cases were recycled as shacks for Pontic families to live in.

They had come 'home' to a poor country, which had forgotten that they existed. Greece opened to them its door but not always its heart. Less than a third of these immigrants spoke any kind of Greek which their neighbours could understand, while their Soviet qualifications and educational certificates were meaningless. Work and housing were and remain hard to find. And although there has been a large Pontic Greek minority in Greece since 1923, when Metropolitan Chrysanthos of Trebizond led his followers out of Anatolia, prejudice against Pontics endures. Right-wing Greeks often regard them as 'Russian' and therefore politically suspect. The Left, in turn, resents their nightmarish (and perfectly true) tales of persecution, poverty and corruption in the old Soviet Union. But the real problem, in a country which regards ethnic uniformity as the badge of Greekness, has been the Pontic insistence on maintaining their distinct cultural identity.

As Anthony Bryer writes: 'Pontic Greeks . . . will not lie down. They are perhaps the most astonishing of all survivors. But some seek a history, some seek a homeland, and some both.' It is not surprising that modern Greeks often feel baffled by the contradictions of Pontic attitudes. On the one hand, they have opted for Greece as 'home', but then – as soon as they have disembarked in the promised land – they begin to weave together a wonderful, exotic bower of special tradition and private destiny which suggests that their home is, after all, entirely elsewhere. Their emblem is the Pontic eagle or the Byzantine peacock, perhaps the 'good bird' which flew from the City to proclaim that 'Romania is taken'. Their slogan is the last line of that song: the proclamation that dead Romania will 'flower and bear fruit again'. Their ceremonies are an intimate mixture of religious and cultural revivalism. The old icon of the Madonna from Sumela was lost after 1923, but every August, on the feast of the Dormition of the Virgin, there takes place at Panayia Sumela in northern Greece a great procession of Pontic Greeks in traditional costume who carry down the street the icon of the 'refugee' Madonna of Sumela. At the core of this cultural revival is the Pontic Theatre. The scholar Patricia Fann describes it as a semi-religious ritual; the community itself considers it a baptismal font, a 'Pool of Siloam' whose holy waters open the blind eyes of actors and spectators alike to the true faith of Pontic identity.

The good bird mourns and prophesies again, but what will be the flowers and fruit? Once this tree of Romania, felled but rising magically from death to blossom once more, seemed to be a version of 'The Great Idea': the restoration of the City's imperium over all the lands and coasts of Byzantine Christianity. But now 'Romania' seems to have retreated into itself, contracting – rather like the modern Turkish state – from a universal realm into an ethnic defensiveness concerned with a single tradition and a single language. 'Romania' seems to have become less a kingdom of this world than the secret garden of those who keep faith with the past.

The bird sings that, one day, the glory and pre-eminence of the Pontic Greeks will be recognised wherever Greek is spoken. When that day of justification comes, the two-and-a-half millennia of *Anabasis* will at last be over. The theatre of transformations which made this people first colonists, then strangers in their own land, then emigrants, then exiles and then refugees will lower its curtain. The journey which led from the Ionian shore to Pontos, from

Pontos to Crimea and Kuban and the Caucasus, from the Black Sea to the nomad steppes of Central Asia and finally from Kazakhstan to Greece, will be complete.

To reach the country of the Lazi, you have to drive about fifty miles eastwards from Trabzon. It is a fast, dangerous road, a new coastal highway along the entire southern shore of the Black Sea which cuts off every town and village from the sea with a barrier of concrete. Every few miles, you pass the fresh, crumpled wrecks of cars and trucks, often brown with dried blood.

In the opposite direction come caravans of old red Ikarusz buses. They list to port or starboard and gush black smoke, like paddle steamers. They are heading for Trabzon, from the old Soviet frontier at Sarp which is now the border between Turkey and the independent Republic of Georgia. Their passengers – Russians, Ukrainians and people from every nationality in the Caucasus – bring with them anything they can pack and carry – tea-sets and busts of Stalin, toy tanks and lavatory seats, cutlery and clocks, garden furniture and surgical instruments – to sell in the new 'Russian market' which stretches its stalls along half a mile of pavement beside the harbour at Trabzon. Many of the sellers have travelled for days and nights from as far away as Kiev or St Petersburg, paying bribes and protection money at one frontier after another, keeping a special wad of banknotes to sweeten the Caucasian mafiosi who allocate the stalls at Trabzon.

This is a trade route. It is part of the network of markets and caravans of travelling merchants which reappeared from antiquity in the late 1980s, spreading all over Eastern Europe and western Eurasia as the Soviet Empire began to fall apart. Like most trade routes, it is dangerous. The danger is worst on the journey home, as the merchants return across the frontier with bales of Turkish leather jackets and cheap computers and bundles of greasy Western banknotes. Near Kabuleti, a few miles into Georgia, bands of armed robbers in military uniform ambush the bus convoys and strip the passengers of their treasure.

To the east of Trabzon, the green mountains grow steeper and press towards the sea. Tea-bushes cover the slopes. The road passes through the port of Rize, where the tea is packed, and then comes to a bridge just before the town of Ardeşen. Here I turned off. This is the outfall of the river Firtina, blue-green and ice-cold, which has run clashing and foaming over its stones all the way from the summit of the Pontic Alps, from the comb of bare stone peaks at the watershed which is called the Kaçkar Dagh.

It is not a Turkish place-name. But the Lazi and their neighbours the Hemşinli are not Turks. Tucked into the north-eastern corner of Turkey, between Georgia and the Black Sea, these two peoples form a small precinct of different and more ancient ethnicity. They have their own spoken languages, which are non-Turkic. They have their own myths and customs and ways of dressing, and their own magic (although both peoples are now Moslem). Until now, they have kept these differences to themselves, like some ancestral wedding dress which is of no interest to anyone outside the family. Given the paranoia of the Turkish state about differences, this has been prudent.

Kemalism, as an ideology, drew on some of the more extreme concepts of 'modern' nationalism which were current in late-nineteenth- and early-twentieth-century Europe. Homogeneity – one language, one religion, one *Volk* – was considered to be the prerequisite of a strong and independent state. It followed that nothing could be more offensive to this scientific spirit, with its blind drive to categorise and segregate, than the multi-ethnic, decentralised and in certain ways tolerant Ottoman Empire.

The scholar Effie Voutira has put this very prettily. For her, the unreformed Ottoman state 'looked like a Kokoschka painting where the plurality and diversity of the different points of colour is such that there is no clearly discernible pattern, though the picture as a whole does have one . . . ' The different groups within the Ottoman Empire were roughly identified by religion – Orthodox, Christian, Armenian, Jewish – but even that criterion was made highly elastic by the option for any Ottoman subject to become a Moslem (as many Pontic Greeks did). 'By contrast, the modern world map looks more like a Modigliani painting, where all shapes and colours have clearly circumscribed boundaries and well-defined surfaces with no ambiguity or overlap . . . ' In Voutira's sense, the Turkish revolutions of the early twentieth century were therefore the overthrow of Kokoschka in the name of Modigliani. The reformers, and Mustafa Kemal Ataturk above all, lusted after those single, well-circumscribed blocks of primary colour, and their 'Turkey for the Turks' offered no security for minorities. The genocide of the Armenians during the First World War, followed by the expulsion of the Greeks and the other Orthodox Christians, were precedents for the bitter struggle against Kurdish nationalism which flamed up again in the 1980s and 1990s.

Smaller minorities, watching these horrors, learned how to avoid the fatal Kemalist accusation of 'separatism'. The Lazi, numbering perhaps 250,000, have been infinitely discreet and unprovocative about their own identity. The tiny Hemşinli group, a mere 20,000 strong, has especially compelling reasons to keep its head down; its members are the descendants of Armenians who converted to Islam in the distant past and who – though they still speak old Armenian – escaped the massacre of the main Christian-Armenian community eighty years ago.

Both groups have been loyal Turkish subjects. They have taken an unobtrusive part in society as tea-farmers and fishermen or – in the case of the Hemşinli – as talented pastry-cooks. They have their own little diasporas in Istanbul and western Anatolia, and they take a cheerful interest in the fortunes of Istanbul football teams. Until now, they have made no claims for themselves as communities. Most Turks do not even have a clear understanding that they exist. They confuse them with the popular term 'Laz', which means no more than the provincial Turkish-speaking culture of the whole south-eastern Black Sea coast as far west as Samsun.

The valley of the Firtina became a gorge, winding up between forests cobwebbed with mist until the tarmac stopped and the road degenerated into a stony mule-track. When I could drive no further, I parked the car under trees and walked on. Far above me, on either side, I could see black-painted wooden houses built into the mountain slopes, each perched over a grassy clearing like an Alpine meadow. Long cables ran down the hillside to the bank of the river, attached to travelling boxes in which goods could be winched up to the farms overhead.

Presently two haycocks with human legs appeared, staggering down the track towards a stone-built barn. A young man laid down his burden to show me how I could cross the river – by squatting in another large box, suspended from wires and drawn slowly and shakily across the Firtina torrent by a boy winding a handle.

Across the river, there was bracken, brambles, long meadow grass and a scent of Scotland. In the woods, among wild strawberries and stinging nettles, the dew began to condense on my hands as I walked; the whole valley is heavy with the vapour of river-spray and with skeins of mist which rise as the sun stabs down into the wet forest.

In a clearing, a Hemşinli family were making hay with wooden forks and rakes. The women were wearing the black and yellow, leopardspot scarves which identify Hemşinli people outside their own country. Some people think that these scarves first reached the Pontos from India in the fourteenth century, when the Trebizond branch of the Silk Route opened up. Ruined towers standing above the track as it mounts towards the Kaçkar Dagh passes suggest that the route was sometimes diverted down the Firtina valley, in times when the usual road through Gümüshane was blocked. At the little town of Çamlihemşin, where these scarves can be bought in the grocery store, they say that they are made in Iraq and traded up to the Pontos through Kurdistan or, when the Kurdish war is too intense, across the Turkish border with Syria.

The huge 'temperate rain-forest' which still covers the mountains of the eastern Pontos has wild animals: boar, bears and deer. The Lazi, or perhaps only the older Lazi in their more remote villages, think that it also contains monsters. The Germakoci, for instance, is a giant creature, human in form but covered with fur, which sometimes approaches hunters in the high forest. Slow-witted, the Germakoci reacts to human beings with curiosity rather than aggression, and likes to imitate whatever they do; the way to be rid of him is to set fire to a twig and wave it around, so that the giant, seizing the burning brand, sets light to his own fur. Roaring with alarm, he plunges downhill and runs until he reaches the Black Sea and leaps into it. A more dreadful monster, ancient and female, is the Didamangisa, who lives closer to human settlements. In the season when cucumbers are ripe, she crawls over the earth like a ground-mist, shapeless and sack-like, armed with a long iron hook with which she snatches children picking cucumbers and drags them away to her underground lair.

To ask 'Who are the Lazi?' is to be at once lost in the chaotic building-site of nationalist definitions. European linguists and social anthropologists have been fascinated by this little people for more than a hundred years, and they provide their own type of answer. The language, Lazuri, is a survival from a previous, almost lost deposit of human speech. A pre-Indo-European tongue, it belongs to the Kartvelian language-family of the Caucasus whose other members are Georgian (much the largest), Mingrelian and

Svanetian. Mingrelian is the closest to Lazuri, and it would appear that both peoples were living as neighbours along the eastern shore of the Black Sea as long ago as 1000 BC. This coastal region around the river Phasis, near the modern Georgian ports of Poti and Batumi, was the land which the Greeks called Colchis, in mythology the home of Medea and the destination of the Argonauts who stole the Golden Fleece from its Colchian shrine. But it is unlikely that a single Colchian nation ever really existed. It was said that more than seventy different languages could be heard in the market at Dioscurias, the Greek colony on the site of Sukhum in modern Abkhazia, and 'Colchian' – like 'Scythian' or 'Celt' – was probably one of those generic Greek terms for peoples of broadly similar culture living in a particular region of the world.

At some point, a large part of the Lazi abandoned their country. They left 'Colchis' and the Caucasus, and moved round the south-eastern corner of the Black Sea to their present territory in what is now Turkey. The Mingrelians, in contrast, stayed much where they were; most of them retained their Christian religion, like the Georgians, while the Lazi and the much larger Abkhazian language group living further north along the Caucasian coast converted to Islam in the fifteenth century. Why and when this migration took place is not known for certain, but it seems to have happened about a thousand years ago, in the middle Byzantine period, and the Lazi may have been displaced by an Arab invasion of the Caucasus.

In 1864, the Russian armies finally broke tribal resistance in the north-west Caucasus. Much of the Moslem population of Abkhazia and coastal Georgia fled or was expelled into the Ottoman Empire, and many Lazi were swept along in the disaster. A small number still remain in Georgia. But their distinctiveness – like that of the Mingrelians – is resented by Georgian politicians and intellectuals who insist, inaccurately, that Georgian is their 'mother-tongue' and that Mingrelian, Lazuri and Svanetian are mere 'dialects'. Arguments to the contrary, and attempts to provide these languages with a written literature and grammar, are shouted down as tokens of Russian cultural subversion, designed to undermine and divide Georgian culture and independence.

But the 'Who are they?' question is not properly answered by scholarly research into the origins of a language. Who do the Lazi think they are?

Until very recently, this question did not seem important to the

Lazi. Some accepted, out of a mixture of prudence and indifference, the Turkish fiction that they were a Central Asian nomad people who entered Anatolia with the Turks themselves. Most Lazi are aware that their language is not Turkic but Caucasian, and close to that of the Mingrelians across the border. At the same time, they are remarkably vague about 'where we came from', and some trace their origins not from the Caucasus but from further west along the Anatolian coast, which is plainly wrong.

This is the portrait of something now rare in the world: a pre-nationalist nation. The Lazi, with their distinct language and folk-culture, are perfectly aware of their distinctiveness. But they have been content with the statement 'We are', rather than being drawn on towards the question 'Who are we?' They have felt no imperative to discover 'roots', or to externalise their collective identity by researching or inventing a history of the Lazi people. Nor, until the last few years, have they been concerned with the very European idea that the disappearance of their language would lead to the disappearance of their Lazi identity, and that these two processes would amount to a bad development which ought to be resisted.

The pre-nationalist attitude to the national language can, in fact, be quite hostile – especially in the case of small ethnic groups. Professor Chris Hann of the University of Kent, who has worked as a social anthropologist in the eastern Pontos, recalls that 'our very limited attempts to learn Lazuri were often greeted with amusement and mild ridicule: it made sense to learn a foreign language such as English or Russian, which could help you to communicate in the outside world, but Lazuri was "no use" anywhere outside the area of the Lazi.'

In this view, there are two different categories of language. There is 'our' tongue, which is spoken at home and which is not appropriate for formal learning or teaching. In contrast, the language of the wider society in which 'we' participate requires not only to be taught and learned but also to be written. It follows that any demand for 'our' language to become a taught and written one is a serious misunderstanding. In practical terms, it could actually hinder 'our' participation in that wider society, and be harmful to the whole community.

A good many of the older Lazi generation think in this way. But far more spectacular examples of this approach can be found in the

Caucasus. The row about Mingrelian and Georgian – whether Mingrelian should be taught in schools, and if so in what script, and whether it is a 'language' at all or just a peasant argot of Georgian – has been raging for a century. It is fairly easy to understand (if not to accept) Georgian cultural imperialism and Georgian paranoia about separatist movements within Georgia which are deliberately fomented from distant Moscow. What is much more startling is the furious involvement of Mingrelian intellectuals and politicians in the fight to prevent the upgrading of their own tongue to a literary language, from the pre-Revolutionary scholar Tedo Zhordania to Zviad Gamzakhurdia himself, that sputtering meteorite who became first President of independent Georgia in 1991, and died a rebel and fugitive three years later. Both men were frantic Georgian patriots, for whom anything short of total assimilation was treachery to the joint Kartvelian destiny.

Lavrenti Beria, head of the Communist Party in Georgia in the 1930s and then Stalin's last and most terrible head of the secret police, was the most famous Mingrelian of them all. He exterminated the flower of Georgia's intellectuals, taking care to destroy their families as well. But he showed no favour to his own people. Quite the opposite: in Beria's time, the forcible integration of Mingrelian culture with Georgian was hurried forward.

In the pre-nationalist age, there were leading figures in the Gaelic-speaking communities of Ireland and Scotland, as there were Czech-speakers in Bohemia, who believed that their languages should remain in the kitchen and the byre in case they became obstacles to the full participation of their peoples in the progress of the English- or German-speaking empires in which they lived. A tiny example from the Caucasus is the pathetic fate of the Ubykh people, a Moslem group related to the Abkhazians, who were driven into the Ottoman Empire by the Russians in 1864. Their leaders took a deliberate decision that their followers should adapt to other languages, Turkish and Circassian above all, and the last Ubykh-speaker, an old man named Tevfik Esenc, died in 1992.

The Lazi were spared these open conflicts and tragic decisions. Safely settled in their remote corner of Turkey, they behaved as if the private language of home and the public language of schools and jobs could remain indefinitely in equilibrium. But then, in the late twentieth century, the balance began to tip. The coming of television and the huge expansion of the Turkish economy during the last twenty years have served the Lazi notice that a choice is becoming inevitable. The past suggested that they would choose passive assimilation, allowing the language and the culture to fade away into the general pattern of Turkish provincialism. They would regret this, but their sense of loss would be a private mourning. And yet, although this at first occurred to only a very few young men and women with experience of the world outside Turkey, there was another option.

In the Black Forest, in the pretty village of Schopfloch, lives a German scholar called Wolfgang Feurstein. He inhabits an old wooden house on the village's main street, a house filled with fair-haired children, books, papers and envelopes with foreign stamps. Feurstein, who has a yellow beard and very candid blue eyes, is not a rich man. He does not teach at any university and, unusually for a German intellectual approaching middle-age, he is not a Herr Professor or even a Herr Doktor. But he is a very busy man. In the wooden house at Schopfloch, he is creating a nation.

Feurstein first went to the Lazi country in the 1960s, travelling around the villages and learning to speak and understand Lazuri. He found an elaborate oral culture, music and songs, fairy tales and rituals and a spoken tongue which had fascinated linguists before him. But he also found a community with no written language save Turkish, with no knowledge of their origins, with no memory that they had been Christians until the final Turkish conquest of the Pontos in the fifteenth century. Feurstein saw, too, that the tides of mass communication and social change were beginning to reach these distant Pontic valleys, and that, if nothing was done, the Lazi identity would be washed away within a few decades.

What came over this mild young man then was something like a religious revelation. It came to him that the Lazi were a *Volk* – an authentic national community, whose survival and growth and flowering was one of the precious components of humanity's inheritance. If nothing was done, this tiny people – defenceless, still at an almost foetal stage in its development – would be lost for ever. Feurstein resolved to save it.

He was soon in trouble. News of his interests and movements came to the Turkish authorities. Framed by the security police for 'illegally entering a frontier district', he was arrested, beaten up, threatened with death and then, after a brief imprisonment, expelled. Since then, for some fifteen years, Feurstein has carried on his life's mission from Germany. He and the small group of Lazi expatriates who form the 'Kachkar Cultural Circle' set about the task of building a written national culture for the Lazi.

First came an alphabet. That had to be the start. Then came little text-books in Lazuri for primary schools, which went out from Schopfloch towards Turkey through many clandestine channels. For a time, it seemed that nothing was happening. Possibly they were not reaching their destination. More probably, Lazi families who found the whole enterprise baffling and dangerous, as many did, were suppressing them. But then, gradually, the first echoes began to come back to Germany. The text-books were being photocopied, page by page. There were reports that they were being used discreetly among Lazi pupils in unofficial lessons after school. Here and there, a few young teachers were adopting this new idea and were prepared to take a risk for it. It was still very small, but it had begun.

The first Lazuri dictionary is now being prepared at Schopfloch. So are the first volumes of what will be – not a history, for it is too early for that, but a source-book and bibliography of the Lazi past. In periodicals which are now finding their way to the valleys, folk-tales and traditional poetry are edited and written down. These are the basic raw materials with which the first Lazi 'national intelligentsia' can begin its work and go on to compose a national literature. And already, something is starting to flow back, through the post or in the bags of migrant Lazi workers returning to Germany. Feurstein says reverently, 'With every poem, there come new, unknown Lazuri words!'

To bring an alphabet to a people who have never written down their speech . . . that is something given to few human beings. In myth, it is gods who bring letters down from heaven. When I held in my hand Feurstein's Lazuri alphabet, done in Turkish Latin script for clarity, with Georgian characters opposite, I felt a sense of awe, as if I were holding something like a seed but also like a bomb. With an alphabet, a people – even a tiny one – sets out upon a journey. Ahead lie printed novels and poems, newspapers and concert programmes, handwritten family letters and love letters, angry polemics and posters, the proceedings of assemblies, the scripts of Shakespeare translations for a theatre and of soap-operas for television, the timetables of ferries, the announcements of births and deaths. Perhaps, one day, laws. But perhaps, too, leaflets with a last speech from the condemned cell. This is a long journey, and it may be a dangerous one.

What is at once astounding and touching about Wolfgang Feurstein's work for the Lazi is that he seems, at first glance, to have walked straight out of the European past. He is repeating, step by step, the process of creating 'modern nations' out of folk-cultures which was first outlined by Johann Herder in the 1770s, and which was to form the political project of most Central and Eastern European revolutions for the next century-and-a-half.

Herder, in his *Essay on the Origin of Language* (1772), suggested a dialectical philosophy of social development in which language – the medium in which natural 'feeling' and human 'reflection' could be reconciled – was the most powerful dynamic. Societies passed through growth-phases analogous to the ages of human individuals. Language was supremely important in the 'childhood' phase, above all in the form of epic and 'uncivilised' poetry: Homer, the Edda, Ossian. 'What a treasure language is when kinship groups grow into tribes and nations! Even the smallest of nations . . . cherishes in and through its language the history, the poetry and songs about the great deeds of its forefathers.' And Herder went further, casting the leading actor for the tragedies and comedies that were to be acted out on the barricades of the nineteenth century: 'A poet is the creator of the nation around him; he gives them a world to see and has their souls in his hand to lead them to that world.'

In these writings about the nation (*Volk*), Herder prefigured at least three elements of Romantic nationalism. The first was the idea of a *Volk* as something dynamic rather than static, a living organism subject to 'natural' laws of development. The second was the central importance of language in this development – which led Herder away from the universalism of the Enlightenment towards a celebration of national differences and particularity. The third was the supreme role to be played in this process by the intellectual, as literary creator but also as national historian and as lexicographer – and, often enough, as insurrectionary leader on the barricades.

Popularised, elaborated and often vulgarised, Herder's ideas flowed into the mainstream of European radical thought after the end of the French Revolution. Above all, they helped to form the political programme of nationalism. European intellectuals had no doubt about where this journey with an alphabet should end. A

Volk which became literate and culturally self-aware was headed for 'nationhood', which was held to culminate in the establishment of independent nation-states. It was in that spirit that František Palacky standardised the Czech language and reconstructed a Czech history, that Vuk Karadzić plunged his hands into treasure-chests of words to select a single 'Serbo-Croat' language, and that – at the end of the nineteenth century – Douglas Hyde founded the Gaelic League to 'de-Anglicise' Ireland.

These intellectuals were the forgers of nations, often in more than one sense of the word. Using peasant speech and oral tradition as a foundation, they set out to build what were, in fact, entirely new models of political community designed to fit into a modern world of nation-states. The patriotic need to discover lost Homeric epics (which, in Herderian terms, would justify the whole national project) was sometimes stronger than probity. James Macpherson, the real author of Ossian, was the first deceiver. Palacky himself was fooled by Vaclav Hanka, librarian of the new National Museum in Prague, who faked a succession of 'ancient' manuscripts (*The Song of Vyšehrad* and *The Love Song of King Wenceslas*) to bolster the Czech claim to authentic nationhood. From Finland to Wales, Romantic nationalism still has many literary skeletons in its cupboards.

Since then, the intellectual world has changed almost out of recognition. Nationalism still thrives, whether in the open-hearted, modernising form of the 1989 revolutions or in the genocidal land-grabs in Bosnia and Croatia. But the old Herderian underpinning has been discredited. The sovereign nation-state is beginning to grow obsolete, while Herder's comparison of a nation to a living organism which must develop and change according to laws of nature is dismissed as empty metaphysic. The concept of ethnicity is still a dangerous minefield, fifty years after European Fascism was overthrown. Most students of nationalism play safe by suggesting that what they evasively term an 'ethnie' exists only as a subjective conviction: an imagined sense of community in which a shared language or a religion or a belief in some common biological descent are usually present, but in widely varying proportions.

If there were no more to be said, then Wolfgang Feurstein would be no more than an anachronism. He would be the last Herderian, the last European intellectual to invent a nation. He would be another Lord Jim, who took 'the leap that landed him into the life of

Patusan, into the trust, the love, the confidence of the people' (except that Patusan already existed and Jim was required only to save it, not to devise it). But there is a great deal more to be said.

Feurstein does not believe that the Lazi *Volk* is merely subjective. 'This is not something invented in a European head! In every village, I saw this lighting-up of faces and eyes when they understood that I valued their culture. Call them a nation, a folk, an ethnicity – I don't care.' Knowing only too well the problems of non-conformity in Turkey, he is careful not to explore political perspectives; the centre at Schopfloch is only a *Kulturkreis* – a cultural working group. But the journey has begun, all the same, and its first years of travel are already heading in a very familiar direction.

To his critics, who include some Western academics, what Feurstein is doing is morally and scientifically wrong. Their crudest argument is that nationalism is in all circumstances evil, and that to encourage it is therefore unpardonable. The second, more formidable line of objection is that any student of another society has an obligation to do no more than study. It may be inevitable that the very presence of a foreign researcher will to some extent contaminate and modify the behaviour under examination, but to take sides in that society's disputes, still more to set out to change its attitudes irrevocably, is a monstrous intrusion and a violation of scientific responsibility.

Feurstein, however, believes that events have already justified him. The alphabet which was sent from the Black Forest to the Black Sea is alive and walking now, out of his hands, precious to a small but growing band of young Lazi who discover fresh ways to use it every day. He is impatient with those who say that he should have stood by, recorded and remained silent as one more human language made its exit from history. He says, 'I did not wish to write about a people, but for a people. In that sense, my own personality was only a means to an end.'

This is a dilemma as old as the social sciences – which are not very old, but already battle-scarred. It sounds like a dispute over professional ethics, but it is really an argument about cognition. One side defends the idea that 'facts speak', and that the scholar must therefore listen to them in impartial silence. The other side retorts that facts say almost anything the investigator wants, and that what he hears in the silence is no more than the mutter of his own unacknowledged prejudices. The student is part of the study, acting inside the situation rather than peering at it through some imaginary window, and to admit that fact is the precondition of knowledge.

In that spirit, Feurstein's interventionism has found backers. Dr George Hewitt, Reader in Caucasian Languages at London University, shares his feelings about another imperilled culture: Mingrelian.

Those who seek to reprimand Feurstein and myself for meddling in others' affairs and not being satisfied with letting the Mingrelians (and the Svans) decide for themselves conveniently forget what happens to those Mingrelians who do dare to raise their heads above the parapet in order to try to initiate a debate – [their heads are] metaphorically, and in the conditions currently prevailing in Mingrelia perhaps not merely metaphorically, shot off . . . Is it not reasonable for interested and concerned Western linguists to suggest to colleagues . . . that untaught, non-literary languages are in danger of ultimate extinction in the conditions prevailing at the end of the twentieth century, and to try to encourage a calm and rational debate as to how their viability can be best safeguarded?

Hewitt knew the last speaker of Ubykh.

I regard myself as immensely privileged to have met and worked with Tevfik Esenc, in 1974, and ever since I have not deviated from the belief that it behoves all of us with an interest in the languages of the Caucasus to do all we can to prevent any of the rest suffering the same fate as Ubykh, whether by language-death through accidental or deliberate neglect or by the threat of physical annihilation . . .

This is the real answer to the last charge made against Feurstein – that by encouraging the Lazi to defend their language and culture, he is actually reducing their freedom. At present, this critique goes, the Lazi have the option of multiple identities: they are full members of the wider Turkish community, with all its possibilities, and at the same time they can enjoy a private Lazi existence at home. But if Lazi nationalism develops, rejecting assimilation, these two identities will become incompatible, and the Lazi will be forced to choose between them. To this, Feurstein and his supporters retort that dual culture is no longer an option. Unwritten, the Lazuri language is dying as surely as the Ubykh, and with it the heart of a small but unique human group will cease to beat.

What Feurstein has done is not to narrow choice but to enlarge it. For him, as for Hewitt, a scientist is not a camera, and the scientist's duty to a vanishing culture is not only to record but to offer wisdom and to say: 'This end is not inevitable. There is a way to survive, and I can point you towards it.'

Where does this journey end? Common sense, wringing her hands, cries desperately that one thing does not have to lead to another. A decision to write a school-primer in a certain language does not have to lead to demonstrations, broken heads, sedition trials, petitions to the United Nations, the bombing of cafés, the mediation of powers, the funeral of martyrs, the hoisting of a flag. All the Lazi enthusiasts want is to stabilise their memories, to take charge of their own culture. That is not much, no provocation. Logically, the journey should stop there – a short, peaceful journey to a more comfortable place within the Turkish state.

But the rougher the journey, the further it goes. In 1992 Feurstein's alphabet was seen for the first time on student placards, in an Istanbul demonstration. Early in 1994, a journal named *Ogni*, written in Turkish and Lazuri, was published in Istanbul by a group of young Lazi. The editor was arrested after the first number, and now faces charges of 'separatism'. A second issue of the journal appeared a few weeks later. It called, more clearly than before, for an end to the assimilation of Lazi culture. One of the publishers said: 'A new age has dawned!'

Cadmus, first king of Thebes, brought the alphabet to Greece. But he also planted dragons' teeth, which sprouted into a crop of armed men.

Chapter Eight

The deputies do business there [in the Polish parliament] with sword in hand, like the old Sarmatians from whom they are descended, and sometimes, too, in a state of intoxication, a vice to which the Sarmatae were strangers.

Voltaire, *History of Charles XII* (1731)

FOR MORE THAN a thousand years, between the eighth century BC and the fourth century AD, the Pontic Steppe and much of south-eastern Europe were controlled by 'Iranians' – speakers of the Indo-Iranian family of languages. The peoples whom the Greeks named 'Scythians' emerged from Central Asia and reached the Black Sea in the eighth and seventh centuries BC. Four hundred years later, when the Scythians had come to dominate the whole northern shore of the Black Sea and its fringe of Greek colonies, another race of Iranian-speaking nomads began to appear with its covered wagons and herds of horses, moving out of the steppes around the Caspian Sea and the outfall of the Volga and pushing into the regions round the lower Don.

The Scythians and the Greeks both considered the newcomers to be non-Scythian, although their way of life was similar and their speech – so modern linguists say – was closely related. They called them 'Sarmatians', another vague generic term which was draped over one tribal group after another as it reached the Black Sea in the next few centuries. The Sarmatians gradually occupied Scythian territory, pushing the Scythians themselves westwards towards the Danube delta. They remained in the Pontic Steppe for some five hundred years, until the onslaught first of the Goths and finally of the Huns in the fourth century AD drove them in turn towards the West.

Because of Herodotus, the Scythians are much better known than the Sarmatians. They feature as the original 'barbarians', strange, fierce and free. Because it is more enticing to write about horse-bowmen and the royal death-ritual and the wagon fleets voyaging across the grassland, their enormously successful adaptation to settled agriculture and to the opportunities of the Hellenic Empire is usually ignored.

Only one novelist resisted that temptation to 're-invent the barbarian'. Naomi Mitchison's astonishing historical novel *The Corn King and the Spring Queen* is concerned not with 'otherness' but with multiple identity – with culture-switching. She introduces an élite of semi-Grecianised Scythians, living in the third century BC in a Black Sea village rather like a small version of Olbia. They still take the lead in the fertility rites which their tribe requires (the ritual death of the king, mass copulation in the fresh-sown furrows . . . Mitchison, as she admits, was much under the spell of Frazer's *The Golden Bough* when she wrote the book), but they also venture confidently into the Greek world. The two main characters, a Scythian princess with shamanistic powers and her brother, travel back and forth on Greek trading ships between the coast of what is now Ukraine and the Peloponnese. There they become involved in the politics of Hellenic ruling families. In Sparta, they are intro-duced to King Cleomenes III by his tutor, the Stoic philosopher Sphaeros (a historical figure who spent some years at Olbia). Informally adopted into the family of Cleomenes, they witness his doomed attempt to construct a communist utopia and to defend it against the Achaean League.

There are some problems of historical detail in Mitchison's novel. Given the tale of Scyles, for instance, it seems unlikely that Scythian chiefs and shamans could have moved between the two worlds with such immunity. But what she got right, by the sheer force of her imperious, empathetic imagination, was the adaptability of these Iranian peoples and their talent for assimilating to a different culture without any sense of surrender to 'civilisation'.

The Sarmatians – in many ways closer to Mitchison's characters than the Scythians – were especially creative with this talent. In the Bosporan Kingdom, Sarmatians became the guiding caste of a brilliant, wealthy, culturally hybrid empire which at its widest reached from the Dnieper estuary round to Colchis, in the south-eastern corner of the Black Sea. Many centuries later, when the

Sarmatians were driven out of the Pontic Steppe and when their separated nations found their way into central and western Europe, they used this innovative gift again. They entered the agrarian societies on the fringes of the disintegrating Roman Empire and grafted into their consciousness a new image of social leadership: the mounted knight in armour.

Nothing remains of the Scythians but their tombs and the memory of their nomad 'otherness', indelibly written into European consciousness by Herodotus and his successors. The Sarmatians, by contrast, survive unrecognised. This is something that scholarship has only recently begun to investigate: a fable which is turning out to contain elements of fact. Physically, there is one place where the Sarmatians are still present; the Ossetians of the Caucasus, descendants of the Alan group of Sarmatian tribes, have kept their Indo-Iranian speech and traditions. And culturally the Sarmatians survive in much of what we know about or have inherited from the Middle Ages of Western Europe. They hide in the decorative style which is misleadingly called 'Gothic'. They ride in disguise as the class of mailed horsemen who hold land and whose manner of living is called 'chivalrous'. To the extent that we have not yet completely escaped from that notion of aristocracy, the Sarmatians are among us.

We are on our way to the Bosporan Kingdom, by car to Panticapaeum. As a car-load, we resemble some overcomplicated ethnic joke. I sit in the back, the middle-aged Brit. Beside me is Lara, a young Russian expert on Caucasian ceramics, who believes in culture and science. In the passenger seat, resting his suppurating leg in bandages, is Sasha, a Cossack truck-driver who was injured in a road crash and is practising to be a tourism entrepreneur. The wheel is held by Omyk, who owns the car: a Lada. He is a Rostov taxi-driver, an Armenian for whom nothing is surprising and nobody is immune to persuasion. When we find a petrol queue, Omyk goes straight to the front of it and shows the 'administrator' his card as a Veteran of the Great Patriotic War. Omyk was not even born when the Great Patriotic War ended; this is his father-in-law's card, with his own youthful photograph glued into it. But it always works. We get served first; the other waiting drivers look at us with silent hatred. Why does it always work?

We have been to some queer places on this journey. We started in

Rostov and headed south across the Kuban steppe to reach the Black Sea at Anapa. On the other side of Krasnodar (Ekaterinodar), a hundred heavy biplanes stood drawn up in ranks in a field, grass growing round their wheels. At Abinsk, in the middle of an oilfield, rusty oil pumps were nodding up and down in the backyard of the bus station. Here we found an open shop, its tiled floor brown with autumn mud, selling what seemed to be long rectangular blocks of horse paté. 'Chocolate butter!' cried Lara. 'It's back! I haven't seen it since I was a child.' We bought two kilos at once, wrapped in porous grey paper, and used a Cossack dagger to spread it on slabs of bread. It was marvellous, a five-year-old's design for bliss.

At the port of Novorossisk, in the art gallery on Sovetov Street, there was a show of horrible paintings by Anatoly Zubtsov devoted to the private life of Lavrenti Beria, last and worst master of Stalin's terror. Here was Beria tearing with his nails at the skin of screaming adolescent girls. Here, climax of the exhibition, was the great Mingrelian clawing lustfully at the groin of Stalin's corpse – a fantasy first imagined, I think, in the mind of Alexander Solzhenitsyn but now disseminated into folk-history. It was a relief to emerge into the Black Sea sunlight and walk a little further along the street to the Museum of History. There I found a photograph of General Denikin boarding *Emperor of India* in 1920. By the saluting Admiral Culme-Seymour stood the figure of a junior officer, perhaps a midshipman – but the face was in shadow.

We drove out to Myskhako, the tip of the Malaya Zemlya peninsula whose heroid defence against the Germans during the Great Patriotic War is supposed to have been organised by the young Leonid Brezhnev. A Greek port-colony once stood here. Now there is nothing to see but a weedy melon-patch and the Black Sea knocking gently against low, yellow-white cliffs. As Lara and I looked for bits of pottery, an old lady in spectacles and headscarf appeared pushing a trolley made out of a wooden box and pram wheels. She visited two cows tethered on what had been the Greek cemetery, talked to them briefly and then began to cut leaves for rabbit-food, tossing them into an enamel pail on the trolley.

Behind her, a few hundred yards inland, was the war-memorial to the Malaya Zemlya defenders: a parade ground, laid out around a metal sculpture which represents a bomb bursting into splinters. It seemed neglected, the ground dusty and the metal tarnished. In and around Novorossisk, there are more and larger war memorials –

213

torpedo-boats mounted on plinths, concrete Kalashnikovs two stories high – than I have ever seen in one place. They are all fairly new, demonstrating the truth of the rule that the remoter the war, the bigger the monument. They were mostly put up in the 1970s, the later years of the Brezhnevian 'period of stagnation', suggesting that the sculpture patrons of this Hero City were mostly concerned to heroise Leonid Ilyich.

We spent the night at Abrau-Dyurso, a few miles along the coast from Novorossisk. This camp of pine-board chalets hidden under a witchy wood used to belong to the Soviet Navy but has been taken over by the University of Rostov. Dropping our luggage, we went down to the sea and swam off a stony beach equipped with the usual Russian bathing-furniture: wooden slat-beds and iron *Vespasienne* modesty-shelters, like old Paris *pissoirs*, in which to change.

Sasha unwound the dirty bandages from his leg. He discovered a repulsive, inflamed wound eating into his shin and dribbling as it ate. His spirits rose instantly. Stumbling to his feet, he faced in the direction of Istanbul and shouted, 'Turks! Drink and get poisoned!' He waded in, and thrashed his gangrenous leg about in the Black Sea. We all dived and splashed and played, and then dried off in the sunset with the help of Sasha's vodka and my cognac. When it began to grow cold, Omyk and I played ducks and drakes. He ran up and down the edge of the water, yelling with glee as the flat stones skipped and skittered.

That night, the Rostov academicians gathered in the mess-hall to watch a video of *Terminator II*, dubbed in Russian. Most found it positive – even very positive. A neighbour explained to me that life itself, and even *Terminator II*, taught that altruism and solidarity would always triumph over the mechanistic context. I went to bed in our chalet, where three of us slept in one room and Omyk snored.

To reach the site of Panticapaeum, the modern port of Kerch, we had to cross the sea into another country. The city was built on the western, Crimean side of the Cimmerian Bosporus, the Kerch Straits which connect the Black Sea to the Sea of Azov, and as Crimea is now part of the independent state of Ukraine, the ferry crosses an international frontier. None of us had proper identity papers, let alone the $20 Ukrainian visa required for foreigners. But it turned out not to matter. The customs-shed on the Kerch side was deserted.

We had breakfasted at Anapa: a resourceful, Russian occasion. After much banging of dented iron trays and screaming in the scullery, the hotel restaurant had produced thick, fluted glasses of café-au-lait, and for the rest, we made a picnic. I had put the chocolate butter and some frankfurters in the hotel fridge overnight, from which they emerged frozen like lumps of scrap-iron. Sasha, unperturbed, stood the sausages in his hot coffee until they relented. Omyk and Lara brought out some pieces of fried carp saved from a previous meal at Tanais, and bread and cheese.

At the tip of the Taman peninsula, a queue of vehicles was waiting for the ferry. The sun was hot, and there was a scent of herbs and seaweed. In the reedy mud-flats by the Taman Gulf, thousands of terns were feeding while herons, egrets and bitterns waded in the shallow sea. Wild olives were ripe on bushes by the side of the road: tiny, white and delicious to chew.

By the jetty, peasants squatted beside tables heaped with jars of sprats, strips of sturgeon with yellow-barred skin and packets of foreign cigarettes. A young heifer strolled unhindered between the stalls, splattering the turf with dung. Truck-drivers dozed in the shade of abandoned railway tanker-wagons which had rusted to their rails, while an old man fished for Azov herring off the sea-wall. It was peaceful. Leaning back against the hot metal of the Lada and chewing a wild olive, I fell asleep for a few minutes as the ferry laboured towards us, seeming to make no progress, drifting sideways in the mid-stream current. Then, opening my eyes, I saw her suddenly quite close, with a yellow-and-blue Ukrainian ensign at her stern. The ramp rumbled against the slip. Engines were switched on, passengers climbed back into their cars and lorries, and we bumped on board for the crossing from Asia to Europe. It is a twenty-minute voyage from the flat Taman shore, heading towards the tall grey downs of Crimea and the lighthouse which stands above the old Turkish fortress at Yenikale.

In winter, the Straits freeze over. Long ago, when winters were even harder here, Strabo wrote that 'bronze water-jars burst, and their contents freeze solid . . . the waterway from Panticapaeum across to Phanagoria [Taman] is traversed by wagons, so that it is both ice and roadway. And fish that became caught in the ice are obtained by digging with an implement called the "gangame" and particularly the *anticaei* [sturgeon] which are about the size of dolphins.'

Leaning over the rail, I pulled out some pages from the 1920 *Admiralty Pilot*, pages which my father must have read anxiously in the gunroom before going on watch. Luckily for him, the Straits were too shallow for a serious warship to penetrate, let alone a battleship like *Emperor of India*. Even the weird, disc-shaped ironclads which the Russians once designed for the Sea of Azov could get into trouble here. This passage between shoals was much too dangerous to be attempted without a pilot.

The naval directions are a severe poetry:

Vessels . . . having given Cape Takil a berth of about 3 miles, should haul up for Kamuish burnu until Pavlovski leading light-towers are in line bearing 357' true, which being steered for will lead through the first or Pavlovski section of the dredged channel between the black spar buoys on the starboard hand and the red spar buoys on the port hand, until the Kamuish burnu leading lights are coming on, when these kept in line astern, bearing 217' true, will lead through the second, or Burunski section, midway between the buoys on either side; from thence alter course in good time to bring Churubash and Kamuish light-towers in line astern, bearing 247' true . . .

Fathers cannot always, or easily, be present to take their sons through danger. They die, and we go forward alone. To starboard, the end of the Taman spit was opening wider and wider upon the Sea of Azov; the Cape Yenikale light to port was closing across the safe channel which leads through to the Kerch roads. Reading the *Pilot* again, I saw that these were not neutral instructions, not the sort of data that one might access or retrieve from a computer. This was a human voice, speaking pauselessly and patiently in flowing speech which does not abandon the listener even for the space of a full stop. Its archaic, Latinate grammar, with its ablative-absolutes and passive past-participles, is in fact deliberately selected in order to convey continuity, reassurance. This voice, transmitting the compiled knowledge of hundreds of generations of seamen, was now talking quietly into the ear of a young and very nervous officer on the bridge, so that, altering course in time on a true bearing, he would come through to safety.

Laurence Oliphant, a twenty-five-year-old Scotsman, came

to Kerch the long way in 1852. He took a sailing-ship from Taganrog southwards across the Sea of Azov, a Prussian brig ('arrant tub') bound for Cork with a cargo of wool, and it was slow going. 'For four days we went edging on through the thick pea-soupy substance of which the water seems composed, literally ploughing our way through scum and passing over every conceivable shade of green and yellow – for the Sea of Azov can never be accused of being blue.' Oliphant smoked cigars and ate caviar spread on ship's biscuit; the ship's pig ate his handkerchiefs and socks off the washing-line.

It might have been, for another passenger, very restful. But Oliphant was a young Scot in a hurry. His admiration for Crimean Tatar culture was matched by his self-important fury at Russian sloth and corruption. Here he was, drifting across the pea-soup with his notebooks full of economic and military information eagerly awaited at home, and when he finally did reach Kerch at six one morning ('crumbling village'), the chief customs officer had the impertinence to let him know that it was a bit early to get up and clear his baggage. Oliphant took it out on the officer's servant. 'Finding that our entreaties were useless, and that the man was becoming insolent, I suddenly beat a double rap with my cane which would have done honour to a London footman, upon which his face assumed a persuasive expression, and he said something by which I understood him to mean that he would wake his master for a rouble . . . '

Oliphant was probably a spy as well as a gentleman traveller. He had taken a lot of trouble to get into Sevastopol, even then a closed city, getting a good look at the extension to the naval base and dockyard and trying to estimate the numbers and types of the warships moored in the creeks or alongside. Less than two years later, the Crimean War broke out. Oliphant's book about Russia was snatched up by readers and went into revised editions. His career took off. He was dragged in to advise generals, then hired by the *Daily News* to report the war, and finally despatched by the British government to lead a secret mission to the north-east Caucasus; there, Oliphant tried but failed to make contact with Shamyl, the fundamentalist Imam from Daghestan who was leading armed resistance to Russia in the mountains. After the war, as a protégé of Lord Elgin, Oliphant became an adventurous diplomat, a novelist on social problems (*Piccadilly: A Fragment of*

Contemporary Biography) and finally a Liberal member of Parliament.

Mount Mithridates looks down on Kerch, and out over the misty horizon of the Sea of Azov – known to Greeks and Romans as the 'Maeotian Marsh'. From a crumbling village, Kerch has become a city of dignified yellow-and-white imperial buildings, quiet boulevards, suburbs of little white houses with green board fences. Everything in Kerch lies open to the view of anybody standing on Mount Mithridates. In the naval base, the day I was there, a few small frigates flying the Russian flag were alongside, and a blue welder's spark glittered in the dry-dock. There were old tiled roofs, and the green dome of an Orthodox cathedral.

For most of the last fifty years, Kerch has been closed to foreigners. The naval base, used by Soviet coastal submarines, was sensitive and too visible from the hill, although for the last decade of the Soviet Union each parked car and each rifle carried by a shore patrol has been recorded by the cameras of American satellites. But when Ukraine became independent in 1992, naval ports in Crimea like Balaklava and Kerch simply ceased to bother about who entered the town or strolled along the waterfront. Only Sevastopol, headquarters of the Black Sea Fleet and still effectively under Russian control, kept up its check-points across the highways leading into town.

Kerch is another 'Hero City', but its war memorials are discreet compared to those of Novorossisk, although terrible things happened here. The Germans – Ohlendorf's *Einsatzgruppe D* again – murdered the entire Jewish population of the town and anyone with a remote connection to the Soviet bureaucracy. Partisan resistance continued all through the three years of Nazi occupation, carried on by guerrilla soldiers hiding in a labyrinth of tunnels under Mount Mithridates. In 1944, Kerch was shelled and bombed to ruins when the Red Army launched an assault landing across the Straits to begin the recapture of Crimea.

Little of this suffering shows now, except for a partisan memorial – obelisk and eternal flame – on the mountain summit. Kerch, resigned to the idea that its position at the eastern tip of Crimea has always made it a target for bombardment and piracy, takes an ironic, southern view of politics. Most of the inhabitants I met were Russians; they were satirical about their sudden Ukrainian citizenship, but equally indifferent to the 'Crimea for Russia' campaign banging its drum far away at the provincial capital of Simferopol.

When I was there, the main exhibition in the Kerch museum was entitled 'Presents for Brezhnev'. This touring show of some of the gifts laid at the feet of Leonid Ilyich by the toadies of the world catered in a distinctly un-Russian way to visitors assumed to have taste and humour. From the man-sized china vases with his portrait to the black boxes of lacquered Feduskino papier-mâché showing Brezhnev's war deeds in the manner of Andrei Rublov, from the statuary groups of Leonid Ilyich solving problems for wondering foremen and scientists to the Vietnamese portrait with real medals and a suit of real cloth glued to the canvas, to the rugs from Central Asia embroidered with disgusting, servile inscriptions, the six-foot pencils from the Karl Liebknecht Pencil Factory, the models of machinery with love from the working people of Krasnodar . . . not one single object was desirable. Everything was hideous. We all agreed – the Russian, the Armenian, the Cossack and the 'British guest' – that even if we were begged to take away anything we fancied, we would take nothing. We left the museum with a new respect for ourselves.

Panticapaeum, capital of the Bosporan Kingdom, stood on the broad, flat summit of Mount Mithridates. Half-excavated ruins and foundations still cover the plateau, and most of the old houses at the top of Kerch are made of square stones looted from Hellenistic buildings. I clambered over a temple of Aphrodite and sat on the hot stone paving of the Palace of the Basileus. A green praying-mantis made its way along the footings of a wall, and a fritillary sunned itself on the palace threshold. Lara, poking about in the grass, found the handle and rim of a Scythian cooking pot.

To reach the hill-top from the town, you climb a marble staircase, a hundred steps whose landings are decorated with griffins. Once this led up to a fake temple, the 'Theseum', which held the main Kerch museum with all the finds from the excavations which had not been taken off for permanent exhibition in St Petersburg. Now there is nothing at the top of the stairs but thin air. During the Crimean War, the museum was broken open and looted by Allied troops, some of them British, and the contents – statuary, glass and pottery – were never seen again. When shaken scholars protested after the war, it was pointed out that Mrs Cattley, the British consul's wife, had bought a quantity of Greek jewellery, coins and architectural fragments from local dealers during her stay, and that when war broke out she had shipped her collection back to London and presented it to the British Museum. What more could anyone ask for?

Panticapaeum began in the usual way, as a Milesian-Greek colony established in the sixth century BC. But then, around 480 BC, trouble with the Scythians drove about thirty Greek colonies to combine for their own safety. Back in Greece, such a provisional 'league' would have been no more than an alliance of independent city-states, ready to dissolve again when the emergency was over, intending no permanent central government. But out here, in the colonies, city-state sovereignty seemed less important. The Greek expatriates set up a 'Bosporan' state (named for the Cimmerian Bosporus), and made Panticapaeum its capital.

This was already an un-Greek thing to do. This was not the normal pattern of small city-states, each set in its *chora* or hinterland. Instead, it resembled the Greek idea of a 'barbarian' kingdom, in which a single magical ruler and his tribe occupied a whole extended territory. Soon the resemblance grew closer. In 438 BC, a certain Spartocos, probably a Thracian mercenary officer, carried out a putsch and emerged as sole ruler. The Bosporan state began to expand; the rulers hired an army of Greek and Thracian infantry, with Scythian and Sarmatian cavalry, and soon controlled the shore of the Sea of Azov up as far as Tanais on the Don and down the other side to the Kuban and the Taman peninsula, bringing into their dominions most of the Maeotian and Sindi peoples on the eastern shore. Around 400 BC, the descendants of Spartocos declared themselves kings or 'tyrants', and Satyrus I and his son Leuco inaugurated the 'Spartocid' dynasty which ruled the Bosporan Kingdom from Panticapaeum for more than three hundred years.

The kingdom grew into an empire, an early Byzantium of the north whose merchants, shipping magnates and urban governors were Greek but whose rulers and soldiers were Thracian, Scythian and, increasingly, Sarmatian. In its first years, the Kingdom had been a satellite of Athens, an outpost of the short-lived maritime empire established by Pericles, and its importance was as a source of food. Half the wheat sold and distributed in Athens came from the

Bosporan Kingdom, and until the power of Athens was crippled by defeat in the Peloponnesian War in 404 BC, all grain exports to Greece from the Black Sea had to be shipped to the Athenian market. After 404 BC, the kings at Panticapaeum were free to sell to anyone they pleased, and the kingdom entered an enormous wealth boom which lasted for almost a century.

When Olbia weakened and grew beleaguered, as the Sarmatian advance spread unrest and instability across the Dnieper steppes, Panticapaeum took over its markets. Wheat remained the great export commodity. Grown in eastern Crimea or the plains round the Sea of Azov, on huge estates leased from Scythian or Sarmatian rulers and worked by slave labour, the production costs were minimal and the profits enormous. But fish from the Sea of Azov was almost as important, and near Panticapaeum the ruins of a fish-processing factory with twenty-four tanks for salting Azov herring have been found. Caviar from Black Sea sturgeon was exported to the Mediterranean, with furs and slaves brought from the forest zone far to the north.

The grain trade transformed the lives of the Scythian and Sarmatian steppe lords, and of the settled peoples in the plains east of the Sea of Azov. The cash economy burst over them like a flood. Even after the grain dealers and shippers in the port-cities had taken their cut, the profits were colossal. They could afford to buy anything which the ancient world had to sell. But what did they really want? They already had all the slaves and livestock they could use. This is a familiar colonial problem, and it was solved in a way which was to become equally familiar. The Greeks invented new needs for them. They supplied the up-country chieftains with luxuries: above all, with the most magnificent goldwork and jewellery ever produced in the classical world.

At first, the gold and silver articles seem to have been produced in Greece itself or in the Ionian cities of Asia Minor, although the gold itself came mostly from Transylvania, from Colchis or from as far east as the Altai Mountains in southern Siberia. The form of the bowls of vases and their decoration were Greek, and made no allowance for alien tastes or habits.

Then a change set in. New craftsmen in gold and silver opened up workshops in Panticapaeum, next to their clients and markets, and the product itself started to alter. An example of that change was the gold-covered wooden *gorytus* (that very Scythian article which was a combined bow-case and quiver) found under one of the Five Brother *kurgans* near Rostov – under the very mound which I had discovered to be still in use as a modern Russian graveyard. This *gorytus* had been made by Greek or Greek-trained goldsmiths in the fourth century BC, probably in Panticapaeum. The repoussé scenes on it were impeccably Greek, but the object itself, the main item of a steppe horseman's armoury, was an entirely Iranian form.

Soon the Bosporan goldsmiths and silversmiths took another step. They began to produce custom-made work for rich Scythians, whose decoration showed Iranian rituals and celebrations rather than Homeric myths. At the same time, the style remained absolutely non-Iranian: the human figures and animals are naturalistic and physically detailed in the Greek manner, and owe nothing to the magical stylisation – the 'animal style' – which the nomads had brought with them out of Central Asia.

The result, for us, is what Rostovtzeff called 'illustrations to Herodotus': scenes from Scythian life. The globular electrum bottle from the tomb of a prince at Kul-Oba, just outside Kerch, shows bearded warriors in trousers apparently after a battle: talking, stringing bows, bandaging a leg wound, even extracting a tooth. The Gaymanova Mogila bowl, of gold-plated silver, has two pairs of fat, expansive little chieftains in flapped tunics exchanging stories, while servants creep towards them with a skinbag of *kumis* (fermented mare's milk) and a live goose. On a huge gold pectoral from the Tolstoya Mogila barrow near the Dnieper, Scythians are milking sheep and shaping a fleece into a coat, while a silver amphora from Chertomlyk is decorated with scenes of men with horses: a bald old servant hobbling a saddled horse for grazing, a young cavalry trooper with a *gorytus* training a recalcitrant pony to lift its forelegs.

The Panticapaeum goldsmiths not only represented daily life. They were trusted with Iranian religious subjects as well, like the mounted god giving a 'communion' drink to a mounted king on a drinking-horn from Karagodeuashkh, or the strange ceremony shown on a huge gold tiara-plate from the 'queen's grave' in the same complex, where an enthroned goddess holds the sacred cup and an androgynous figure –probably one of those gender-crossing, transvestite 'Enareis' shamans – prepares to serve her from his bottle. (Most of these treasures can be seen in the Hermitage at St

Petersburg, and nobody has seriously challenged Rostovtzeff's attribution of them to the craftsmen of the Bosporan Kingdom.)

This symbiosis of Greek (or Greek-trained) artists and Iranian nomad patronage is an extraordinary moment. Nothing quite like it has happened before or since. As Timothy Taylor writes: 'uniquely in the ancient world, and perhaps within the history of art in general, literate, urban colonisers produced their greatest art-works to the order of a nomad élite . . . It is somewhat as if Velázquez had heroised native Mexicans in his major commissions.'

Rostovtzeff, seventy years earlier, had made the same point, but he related it to a profound change in the Greek world-view which was setting in even before the imperial conquests of Alexander of Macedon. 'This is the dawn of Hellenistic art . . . which was influenced by the interest taken by science and literature in the hitherto barbarian peoples who were now entering into the great family of civilised, that is, Hellenised nations . . . an art which was glad to place itself at the disposal of foreign nations.'

The trade continued with new customers, after the Sarmatians had begun to displace the Scythians in the third century BC. But the relationship of Greeks to Sarmatians was very different. In spite of the common Iranian source of their languages, the Sarmatians were in many ways unlike the Scythians. As warriors, they were not lightly equipped horse-bowmen but heavy cavalry, wearing metal helmets and iron coats of mail and carrying long lances. This armament, much later to become the battle outfit of mediaeval chivalry, was quite unknown to Europe and the Eurasian fringe, and was for a time irresistible. A few centuries later, after the Sarmatian Alans had charged and slaughtered a Roman legionary army at Adrianople in 375 AD, the Roman Empire changed its whole mode of warfare and raised heavy cavalry units of its own.

The Sarmatians were in some respects closer to their Central Asian cultural roots than the Scythians. They brought with them a new decorative tradition, adding to the Central Asian 'animal style' a taste for heavy, ornate forms and for metalwork encrusted with coloured enamel and semi-precious stones – the style which in the nineteenth century was misleadingly called 'Gothic'. While Sarmatian nobles bought or commissioned ornaments and luxury articles from the Hellenistic world, as the Scythians had done, they also kept in contact with other, developed Iranian cultures far to the east. The great golden collar of Volodya Guguev's princess, buried by the Don, probably came from some sacred treasury in Bactria.

Above all, the Sarmatians were more intrusive. It may be wise to think of them as a number of small military élites, or warrior clans, who conquered and then assimilated to the peoples they encountered. The Scythians had by and large stayed outside the walls of the Greek cities. The Sarmatians entered, not necessarily by siege or cavalry charge but more often as powerful settlers whose request to be let in could not easily be denied. They intermarried with Greeks, and took a growing part not only in government but in trade and manufacturing. At Panticapaeum this assimilation was not difficult; the ruling Spartocid dynasty had never been Greek but had Thracian or Scythian ancestry, and by the Roman period the Bosporan Kingdom was thoroughly Iranianised. Greek was still its official language, but most people probably spoke Sarmatian or Thracian, and the gods they worshipped were the Mother Goddess, or heroes of Persian solar cults like Mithras, rather than the Greek pantheon.

Up on its acropolis above the Kerch Straits, the city of Panticapaeum flourished. Its coins showed a rampant griffin, symbol of gold, grasping an ear of wheat in its claws. On each side of the main gate stood a relief of the Mixoparthenos, the snake-legged Mother of the Scythians. Its kings were honoured and flattered all over the Greek world, and the annual Athenian festival, the Panathenaia, presented them with wreaths of oak or olive leaves fashioned from beaten gold. But then, in the first century BC, a tortuous political crisis began.

A new Scythian-Crimean kingdom, established by princes driven out of their old capital on the Dnieper by the Sarmatians, attacked Chersonesus and the other Greek coastal cities. Unable to dislodge the Scythians, the Spartocid king, Peirisades the Last, took the fatal step of appealing to Mithridates Eupator, king of Pontus.

This was the equivalent of inviting a cat to chase a mouse out of a fish shop. Mithridates ('the Great') was a brilliant, erratic imperialist whose dream was to expand his Anatolian kingdom into a pan-Iranian empire and to conquer the rising power of Rome by an offensive from the east. His generals subdued the Crimean Scythians, but then provoked a Sarmatian riot within Panticapaeum in order to overthrow the Spartocids and seize their throne. Mithridates conquered the whole eastern shore of the Black Sea and dragged the Bosporan Kingdom into his twenty-five-year war with Rome. After his defeat by Pompey and his death at Panticapaeum in 63 BC, more upheavals finally produced a new royal dynasty, again of mixed Indo-Iranian descent, which accepted Roman sovereignty and ruled the kingdom until it was occupied by the invading Goths in the fourth century AD.

The director of the Kerch archaeological museum drove us out in her own car to the Tsarski Kurgan. Beyond the last allotments and gardens, where the grassland begins, it rises like a hill; a fifty-foot turf mound covering one of the royal tombs of the Spartocids.

In front of the tumulus is a little wooden cottage with a garden and fruit-trees. The director stood at the fence and shouted, 'Maria Andreyevna! Maria Andreyevna!' Presently a very old lady in a headcloth, grinning through gold teeth, appeared and picked her way towards us through a confusion of geese, kittens and broken white enamel buckets. She was, explained the director, the hereditary *storozh* (guardian) of the *kurgan*. When the great Ashik, first director of antiquities at Kerch, had completed his excavations here in 1837, he appointed one of his men as *storozh* and ordered him to remain on the site, and – in the absence of any instructions to the contrary – his descendants have lived here and kept the keys ever since. Maria Andreyevna, great-great-granddaughter of the first guardian, hobbled over to an iron gate and unlocked it.

What we saw is one of the architectural wonders of the world. A deep, V-shaped cutting, lined with masonry, leads into the centre of the hill. At the end of this tapering slit is a portal of darkness, a crack framed in corbelled freestone, the door to the underworld. It is like the crevice of darkness which leads into the Sibyl's cave at Cuma, near Naples. It is also, inescapably, the mouth of the Mother Goddess's womb. A deliberate trick of perspective, done by a subtle narrowing of the slabs in the cutting, makes the distance to the portal seem less than it really is, so that each step forward seems to rush you towards the blackness at the end.

Inside the hill is a square stone chamber supporting a cupola. There is nothing else there, for when Ashik cleared the approach-cutting of the earth and rubble which had filled it and reached the chamber, he found that it had been robbed, probably only a few centuries after it had been constructed. But when you look back down the empty passage, you see that it has been carefully aligned. Far away in the sunlight glitters Mount Mithridates, acropolis of the Bosporan Kingdom, outlined for dead eyes at every dawn by the rising sun.

In the Tsarski Kurgan, Iranian and Greek senses of holiness have fused. The tomb dates from the early fourth century BC, but it is not known for whom it was built. Possibly it was Peirisades I, but it seems more likely that it was the grave of Leuco, son of Satyrus I, who reigned in Panticapaeum from 389 to 349 BC. This was a king renowned for political and economic cunning, who spent much of his reign successfully manipulating the Greek business community into subsidising his budget for war and internal security. Leuco, in fact, managed to defy the laws of orthodox economics: he financed the budget by increasing money supply, without precipitating inflation. In his *Stratagems of War*, Polyaenus relates that Leuco,

> when his treasury was very low, issued a proclamation for a new coinage, and directed everyone to carry in his money and to receive the same in value struck in a new die. A new die was accordingly struck, and every piece of money bore a value double to that it possessed before. One half he kept for himself, and every individual received the same current value he gave in.

Leuco was almost the first Bosporan monarch to strike coins. The last were minted at Panticapaeum in 332 AD, and the last ruler, King Rheskuporis IV, died in about 360 AD. The Bosporan Kingdom, in other words, survived as the centre of power, wealth and industry in the north-eastern corner of the Black Sea for no less than seven hundred years.

There were two reasons for this survival. The first was economic. For even the most aggressive nomad leaders (until the arrival of the Huns in the fourth century AD), the advantages of finding a way to live with the Bosporan Kingdom rather than conquering and looting it were obvious. Wheat and fish from Crimea, slaves, furs and Chinese textiles from further inland, went to the Mediterranean markets, and in return for their assistance the chieftains and their families grew magnificent in Panticapaean goldwork and silverwork, clothing and weaponry.

The second reason for Bosporan survival was pragmatism. The kingdom was a state, but not what we would now call a nation.

All the strongest powers in the region could share in its political control through dynasties whose origins were a mélange of Scythian, Thracian, Sarmatian and Maeotian. At the same time, trade and industry was carried on by a literate citizenry who were Graeco-Iranian in their speech, clothes and religions, and as diverse as the royal family in their descent. On the whole, the court and the business community respected one another. They were mutually dependent, as the Leuco story suggests. This was a show which had to be kept on the road, and there was no place for imperial aggression, or for defending 'national independence' to the last drop of blood. In the Bosporan Kingdom, there was plenty of intrigue but no Quixotry. If Mithridates the Great or the Romans wanted to impose a protectorate, then there was no reason to risk the destruction of Panticapaeum for the sake of an abstract like sovereignty. The kingdom, like a chameleon, took on the colouring of its strongest neighbours. It was Grecianised, and then Iranianised itself and then adapted to the Roman Empire. Politically, it was unprovocative. Unlike Constantinople-Byzantium, its capture did not promise to change the history of the world or even to make its conqueror a hero.

This capacity to seem unthreatening made possible the final achievement of the Bosporan Kingdom: the taming of the Goths. This Germanic migration had fought its way down from the Baltic and arrived on the Black Sea in about 200 AD. The Goths had sacked both Olbia and Tanais in the early years, but in contact with the Bosporan Kingdom they soon softened and allowed themselves to be transformed into neighbours and customers. Panticapaeum studied their tastes and made some adjustments to the old Sarmatian-Bosporan jewellery designs which had been so successful. Willingly enough, the Goths let the Bosporans enrich their decorative tradition into something distinctly Sarmatian. Under the Goths, who gradually assembled an 'Ostrogothic' state in Crimea and the Pontic Steppe, the Bosporan Kingdom won another century of existence. But then came the Huns. They were not open to taming.

By the fourth century AD, for reasons still not understood with any certainty, the arrivals of successive waves of mounted intruders from Central Asia were not only taking place at shorter and shorter intervals, but were often accompanied by a new degree of savagery and destructiveness. As far as we know, the Huns were the first major nomad group to enter the Black Sea region as a plundering expedition pure and simple, apparently lacking all interest in settlement or trade. They destroyed Tanais and Panticapaeum for ever. The citizens fled or were murdered, and grass grew over both sites. When the next city was built on the Cimmerian Bosporus, in Byzantine times, it was on the slopes of Mount Mithridates rather than among the ruins on the summit.

As Mikhail Rostovtzeff wrote: 'How curious, this semi-Greek tyranny which lasted for centuries and gradually changed into a Hellenistic monarchy! . . . How interesting, the mixed religion which slowly developed in the Cimmerian Bosporus! How singular, this prolific art, working mainly for export to Scythian dynasts and the Scythian aristocracy! . . . ' Since then there have been nearly two thousand years of contact between literate and preliterate cultures, between wealth-creating cities and tribal empires of the interior. But nothing like the symbiosis of the Bosporan Kingdom has ever reappeared.

Chapter Nine

Sarmatia is an imaginary country – which does not change the fact that it is the fatherland of us all . . .

We live like spies, with a foreign biography in our own country. We enter in a forged register: 'place of birth, Sarmatia.' And we are fond of this forgery. A numismatist valuing two old coins will take more interest in the forged one, because it is not just – like the original – a token of value but also a token of aspiration. After a while, the forgery will be more valuable than the original. The scale of values is reversed, and that is why Sarmatia Felix, our fatherland, still lives within us.

Marek Karpiński, 'Jacek Kaczmarski – Aneks do wniosku o awans', in *PULS*, Nos 64/5, Sept–Dec 1993

I am back, and I remain as much of a barbarian as my forefathers!

The Squire in Mickiewicz's *The Confederates of Bar*, who has just returned from a tour of Western Europe

DEBATES ABOUT NATIONALISM tend to revolve around the concept of the nation as 'imagined community'. The phrase comes from Benedict Anderson's short and brilliant book of that title, and there is much to be said for it. Early modern nationalism, he argued, arose from an imaginative leap: the assumption by individuals that thousands or millions of people whom they would never meet shared their particular culture, language and outlook. In the time before mass communications or easy travel, this assumption about solidarity was fostered by what Anderson called 'the print revolution', the circulation of printed literature written in the vernacular, but it remained an act of faith.

Later, in the eighteenth and nineteenth centuries, Europe experienced a widespread 'invention of nations'. Intellectuals assembled ballads and oral traditions into 'national literatures', synthesised standard written languages out of dialects, and composed histories of the nation from chronicles and folk-epics. From every capital city, a legion of Wolfgang Feursteins set out for the villages with notebook and pencil. They worked to a teleology: the belief that a reawakened national community would set out on the journey towards supreme self-realisation as an independent nation-state.

Yet the nation, as imagined or even forged community, is far older than the nation-state. It existed before the political mobilisation made possible by the print revolution. It will, in fresh mutations, exist when the nation-state has passed into history. Indeed, the practice of inventing history to legitimise some aspiring social group is also older than modern Romantic nationalism. John Dee, the Welsh wizard and con-man, seduced Elizabeth I of England with his argument that, as the Tudor descendant of Welsh kings, she had re-established the Celtic realm of Arthur not only over all 'Britain' but over the mythical Arthurian empire beyond the ocean: the Americas, announced Dee, were the rightful inheritance of this 'Great Britain'. But no sleight of history is stranger, or more laced with ironies, than the resurrection of Sarmatia.

At the end of the twentieth century, we think of Poland as a country of the Baltic shore. Polish origins seem to us to lie among proto-Slav farmers, settled along the river Vistula as it flows north to reach the Baltic in the Bay of Gdańsk. But there was a time when Poland looked towards the Black Sea as its native coast, and when Poles claimed ancestry in a race of Indo-Iranian pastoral nomads – the Sarmatians.

In the sixteenth century, Polish writers began to assert that Poles were the descendants of the Sarmatians. At first, this claim did not seem grotesque. It was no more than a Polish response to a European fashion. In the Renaissance, the flattering of dynasties through genealogies dug out of classical learning had become a literary convention – driven forward, indeed, by the print revolution which made Greek and Roman histories available to courtiers. If Elizabeth of England was the heiress of the pre-Saxon Britons, if the Swedish kings were descendants of the Goths, the French kings sprung from Gaulish loins and the Muscovite tsars (in a particularly weird conceit) related through Rurik to the emperor Augustus, then it was not too eccentric for the Polish commonwealth to boast of origins in a race of Iranian 'barbarians' from the Black Sea.

But then, in the next hundred years, the Sarmatian myth took an extraordinary, freakish twist of its own. From being the official myth of a court, 'Sarmatism' became the mass faith of a class.

In the sixteenth and seventeenth centuries, the Polish nobility (*szlachta*) came to believe that it was they – not the Polish population at large – who were the exclusive descendants of the Sarmatians. They were not just a superior caste within Polish society, but a different race. Other classes, like burghers or peasants, must therefore have other, inferior racial origins. Soon, more pseudo-classical borrowing allowed scholars to refer to the lower orders as 'Getae' or 'Gepids' – lesser tribes of Thracian or Germanic origin, who were imagined to have migrated into east-central Europe as slaves of the noble Sarmatians.

The *szlachta* dominated the old Polish-Lithuanian commonwealth. This enormous social group came to number something like 10 per cent of the population. Its members ranged from princely families wealthier than many European kings to muddy-arsed squireens who dug and hoed their own patches of rye. Its obscure origins lay in a clan system, recruited by military allegiance and adoption as much as by hereditary connection: a pattern which resembled traditional society in the Scottish *Gaeltacht* rather than the feudal order of Western Europe.

This 'Sarmatian Ideology' had a clear legitimising function. In the commonwealth, or 'royal republic', the nobility had achieved almost total ascendancy over the state. They elected the king. They composed the *Sejm* (parliament) and enforced on it the rule of unanimity: the Liberum Veto, which allowed a single dissenting voice to block all proceedings. They established, step by step, their own immunity to any central interference with their own limitless privileges. The *szlachta* did not so much rule as prevent anyone from ruling. This gave rise to the curious proverb that '*Polska w nierządem stoi'* – roughly, that Poland is founded upon disorder (the word *nierząd* also has connotations of prostitution, like the French use of *bordel* to mean chaos or the English legal expression 'disorderly house', meaning a brothel). In this view, the *szlachta* alone constituted the true nation, and as Sarmatians its members were entitled to do as they pleased. That was the so-called Golden Freedom for which the *szlachta* repeatedly took up arms.

In the course of the seventeenth century, other elements were added to the ideology. One was xenophobia. Sarmatism was devoutly conservative, a hymn of thanksgiving addressed to the status quo. To the Sarmatian eye, Poland was perfect: Poland was the nobleman's paradise, the bravest, wisest and happiest *Terra Felix* on earth. It seemed to follow that any proposal for change was a threat of pollution by foreign influence. Royal initiatives to raise taxes or reform administration were attacked as the work of German or French advisers, poisoning the mind of the king in order to introduce absolutism and subvert Polish independence. The Reformation, especially for the middle and lower nobility, was perceived as another disruptive import from Bohemia and Germany, embraced by vulgar non-Sarmatians like urban merchants. A fanatical Counter-Reformation Catholicism became a component of Sarmatian patriotism.

Sarmatism also repositioned Poland's sense of geography – or of 'geopolitical destiny'. In spite of their Catholic enthusiasm, the neo-Sarmatians looked eastwards rather than westwards. For the 'descendants' of noble barbarians from the Pontic Steppe, the Black Sea coasts and the plains between the Danube and the Don seemed to be their ancestral home and heritage.

In this way, the Sarmatian idea was used to authenticate an aggressive foreign policy towards the East. The word 'Sarmatia' was restored as a description of all Slav populations and their territories. To the Polish nobility, convinced that they were the chosen race, this implied not only that the *szlachta* was the aristocracy of all Slavdom, but that Poland – in a period of almost continuous war against Russians, Tatars and Turks – had an historical claim to old Sarmatian realms in Russia itself, in the Cossack lands of Ukraine, in Moldavia and Bessarabia.

Sarmatism was also a style. It was a way of life: extravagant and ostentatious, sometimes wildly generous and at other times savagely violent and vengeful, based on rural life in wooden manor-houses and on a cult of the healthy, pious environment of the countryside. Hospitality, which mostly meant drinking and hunting, was a particular Sarmatian pride. Arcadia, however pure, could be boring, and some noble families posted small boys in trees to watch for the dust of an approaching carriage, which would then be virtually ambushed and the stranger dragged indoors to be entertained. His attempts to leave, often weeks later, were sometimes frustrated by removing his coach wheels.

The style was also, and famously, about dress and decoration. Here all the ironies of Sarmatism were concentrated. By the early eighteenth century, the Polish-Sarmatian noble was a startling, unmistakable figure. He shaved his skull, cultivated long, drooping moustaches (the Sarmatism of Lech Wałęsa's whiskers did wonders for Solidarity in 1980), and wore a long *kontusz* caftan held in over his paunch by a sash. His sword would be a curved scimitar, its hilt probably encrusted with gold and jewels. In short, he looked like a Turk – or possibly a Turkified Tatar.

Of course, this had nothing to do with what the historical Sarmatians had worn. Reliefs and wall-paintings of the Bosporan Kingdom show the men in trousers and belted tunics, bearded and long-haired. This neo-Sarmatian outfit was actually the clothing of Poland's enemies, the oriental gear of Turk and Tatar warriors appropriated by those who boasted that they were the bastion of Catholic and European Christianity against the pagans. The grandest Sarmatian hero of them all, King John Sobieski, is still honoured as the 'saviour of Christendom'; at the battle of Vienna in 1683, he relieved the siege of the city and inflicted on the Turkish armies a defeat so crushing that the Ottoman Empire never seriously threatened central Europe again. But at that battle the Polish troops looked so much like the enemy that they were obliged to wear a straw cockade, in case their Habsburg allies mistook them for Turks.

Poland today still insists on its 'European', Western allegiance, now based not only on the Catholic faith but on diligently Western institutions and tastes. On the surface, nothing of that orientalising style remains. And yet in subtle ways Poland is a much more oriental culture than Russia. While the Muscovites hid from the Mongols in their northern forests, the Poles were already open to influences from the Black Sea steppes. The Tatar *quriltai*, as I have suggested, helped to inspire the Polish decision to elect kings by a mass gathering of mounted nobles. The idea of a 'noble democracy' may have nomad origins, like the cloudy beginnings of the Polish *herby* (clans), and the relationship between Polish rulers and urban colonies of foreign merchants – Germans, Scots, Jews, Armenians – was an echo of the symbiosis of Iranians and Greeks by the Black Sea.

At the end of the eighteenth century, Sarmatism collapsed under the weight of its own stupidity. But in its fall, it also destroyed Poland itself, and the independence for which the nobility had fought so fiercely for so many centuries.

It had been obvious for many years that unless the decaying Commonwealth were reformed and modernised, Poland would disintegrate and be annexed by its neighbours. Russia, under Catherine II, already exercised a *de facto* protectorate over Poland, and a first Partition had taken place in 1772. The last Polish king, Stanisław August Poniatowski, was a sophisticated European who sought to build a modern state with a strong central authority; the 1791 'Constitution of the Third of May', composed on the most progressive Enlightenment principles, made the monarchy heredi- tary, reformed the administration and government, and abolished most of the ancient abuses which had allowed the *szlachta* to retain a stranglehold over change. But it was too late.

It is wrong to say that the nobility, as a class, opposed reform. By 1791, the American and French Revolutions had converted educated Poles to the reform cause, and a large part of the *szlachta*, realising that without radical change the nation was doomed, supported the king. The members of the *Sejm* who voted through the Constitution, abolishing noble privileges, were themselves aristocrats. But the great Sarmatian families remained blindfolded in their own arrogance. It was not Russia but reform, on 'foreign' and 'Jacobin' principles, which seemed to them to threaten the survival of Poland. If the *szlachta* lost its independence, then Polish independence was lost too – for the *szlachta* was the nation.

In 1792, a group of Sarmatian magnates – most of them from eastern Poland, in what is now Ukraine – appealed to Catherine II to intervene. They raised their standard against King Stanisław August in the rebellion known as the 'Confederation of Targowica', and nearly a hundred thousand Russian troops surged across the frontier. There followed the Second Partition; the desperate but unsuccessful rising of 1794 led by Tadeusz Kościuszko; and then the Third Partition which wiped Poland off the map of Europe for 123 years. Sarmatism, in short, achieved precisely what its ultra-conservative patriotism sought to prevent. It allowed foreigners to destroy Poland and abolish Polish independence.

But, to the end of their lives, many of these Targowican barons failed to understand what they had done. They kept their vast estates, travelling now to St Petersburg and Odessa rather than to Warsaw and Kraków. They had lost the political influence they had enjoyed in the old commonwealth, but to be appointed Marshal of Nobility in some Ukrainian county was not a bad substitute. It baffled and appalled them when some of their sons and daughters took up arms for Polish independence in the nineteenth-century insurrections, often to end up in a forest grave or a Siberian penal colony. But this, no doubt, was further proof that the terrible French germ of Jacobinism was still infectious. Meanwhile, the fact that they themselves were secure and prospering could only mean that all was well with Poland too.

One of those who signed the Confederation of Targowica was Seweryn Rzewuski. He was one of the patriarchs of a great family which was proud of its Targowican connection and which saw no reason for remorse in the years which followed. He was also the grandfather of Karolina Sobańska, born Rzewuska.

In the end, there is only one plausible track towards the mystery of her inmost feelings. This track leads through a hall of mirrors into a chapel with a self-portrait above the altar: the monstrous solipsism of conservative aristocracy. What was good for the Rzewuskis was good for Poland. What diminished the ancient liberties of the Rzewuskis was treachery to the liberty of Poland.

She saw, perhaps with genuine pity, the fate of those she betrayed. They walked Paris pavements, borrowing money to feed their children, or sat all day in Dresden cafés over a cup of coffee, or dug trenches in the Siberian permafrost under the eye of a sentry. They talked all the time about 'Poland', whatever they meant by it. Some of them had been to bed with her. Some of them were honest enough in their way. But they were not 'our sort of people'. The tradition in which she had been brought up taught her that they were another, lower species who shared her country, who might be owed some protection in return for loyal service, but who could not be expected to think as 'we' thought, or to understand what 'we' understood.

Karolina Sobańska was indeed a sort of patriot, although not in the sense which Mickiewicz hopefully invented for her. She was the last Sarmatian.

The village of Ribchester is in Lancashire, not far from Preston. Broad and shallow, the river Ribble flows round its margin, and on the spring day when I made my visit, there were children paddling in the river around boulders which had once been Roman masonry. Ribchester is built on the site of Bremetennacum Veteranorum, a Roman cavalry fortress on the road north to Hadrian's Wall. Most of its streets cover the native cantonments outside the ramparts, where Brigantian workers and discharged soldiers lived. Under the churchyard is the *principia* headquarters block with its pillared drill-hall for rainy days, and the underground *sacellum*, the strongroom where the regional military command kept its cash.

Here, towards the end of the second century AD, a large force of Sarmatian lancers arrived. They were Iazygians, the vanguard of the slow Sarmatian migration from the Black Sea steppe towards the west, who had crossed the Transylvanian mountains and entered the north-eastern Hungarian plains. From there, they began to raid the Roman frontier on the middle Danube until the emperor Marcus Aurelius led an army across the Danube and defeated them. He had intended, it seems, to have them massacred. But problems elsewhere in the Empire required his attention, and he offered them the option of enlistment instead. The Iazygians accepted, and were drafted to northern Britain. Some 5,500 cavalrymen, presumably accompanied by their horses and families, made the journey across a continent and a sea. They may have served initially on the Wall, where some of their horse-armour has been found, but within a few decades, in the early third century, they had been transferred to Ribchester, a powerful mobile reserve of cavalry watching the Ribble gap and the passes through the Pennines.

But the Sarmatians never went home. The Empire lost control of the plains north of the Danube, which meant that they could not be returned on discharge to found military colonies and form a Romanised cordon on the frontier. Instead, each generation was settled locally as it reached retiring age. For two hundred more years, until the final Roman evacuation of Britain in the fifth century, the descendants of Iranian-speaking nomads continued to multiply and to be found land in the lower Ribble valley, perhaps draining the marshes to provide farmland, possibly directed into horse-breeding. By the time of the first Anglian or Saxon settlement in the region, the Sarmatians must have formed a large and deeply rooted community in western Lancashire.

What happened to them in the end is unknown. Most probably, they lost their military, imperial character and simply merged into the general post-Roman population of Britain. The study of genetic history by the analysis of DNA traces is still a highly inexact science, treated with utmost caution by historians, and biology alone cannot answer the question of 'who people are'. But if one day it is established that there are distinctive Indo-Iranian genes, a DNA survey in the Preston hinterland might well reveal that the Sarmatians are in a sense still present.

History – the product, not the raw material – is a bottle with a label. For many years now, the emphasis of historical discussion has been laid upon the label (its iconography, its target-group of customers) and upon the interesting problems of manufacturing bottle-glass. The contents, on the other hand, are tasted in a knowing, perfunctory way and then spat out again. Only amateurs swallow them.

'Discourse' matters. In history, the priority now given to what a writer signified by the choice of language or matter, the function of his or her narrative, has amounted to a successful revolution. A new quality of intellectual freedom exists, and nobody can now read history without asking what end the text serves, and how. But truth matters too. Apart from their discourses, did the historians get their facts right? As I have argued about Herodotus, no discussion about his part in designing a Scythian 'mirror' for Greeks is complete without some judgment about whether he was an accurate reporter or made things up.

This applies to the Polish cult of Sarmatism too. Sarmatism was, blatantly, a discourse about superiority. Its political claims were so preposterous, its style so 'Turkish' and orientalising despite its Indo-Iranian title, its function as a class myth of origin so shameless, that few historians bothered to examine the myth's relationship to fact. Naturally, the Marxist approach which dominated Polish historiography for fifty years found Sarmatism easy meat. In the words of the *Wielka Encyclopaedia Powszechna* (*Great Popular*

Encyclopaedia), Sarmatism – as a theory of descent – 'was promoted by the oligarchy and the church in order to subjugate the masses of the pauperised petty *szlachta* . . . main elements of the ideology were limitless personal freedom for the nobility; xenophobia, self-glorification, national-class megalomania combined with a belief in historical mission, intolerance, bigotry and orientalisation of tastes and customs . . . '

The idea that there might be elements of fact in the myth itself – that the Poles and specifically Polish noble families might actually be the descendants of Sarmatian immigrants – has seemed to most modern historians too silly to be worth investigating. But Sarmatism has waited until now to deliver its last and most disconcerting irony. There may be 'something in it', after all.

The early history of the Slavs is bound up with the late history of the Sarmatians, and with their gradual arrival in central and Western Europe. The Iazygians, who ended up at Ribchester, were the first Sarmatian people to reach the Roman frontier on the middle Danube. The last group to follow that route was the huge tribal confederation known as the Alans. They were the rearguard of the Indo-Iranian migration into Europe, which had begun with the Scythians some eleven hundred years before. Behind the last Sarmatian groups – the Eastern Alans and the Antae – rode the Huns. They were not Iranians but Turkic-speakers, who reached the Black Sea around 355 AD and inaugurated over a thousand years of Turkic supremacy in the Pontic Steppe.

Early in the third century, a new ruling group, heavily armed and wealthy, entered what is now southern Poland. When they buried their dead, they equipped them with wheel-turned pottery made on the northern Black Sea coasts, Sarmatian brooches and lances with iron heads inlaid in silver. They were unmistakeably a Sarmatian people, possibly the Antae, and their material culture showed that they had been in long and close contact with the Bosporan Kingdom. But the surest evidence for that contact – and the key exhibit in the argument about the Sarmatian ancestry of the Poles – is the *tamga*.

Tamgas are a family of signs. A *tamga* resembles a graffito monogram, a simple Chinese character or even a cattle-brand (*tamgas* were in fact used until recently to mark domestic animals in the northern Caucasus). Each one appears to be individual, to stand alone. Rostovtzeff thought that groups of them formed complete texts, 'the first stages in the development of a Sarmatian style of writing', but this is not convincing. Nor are they obviously pictograms based on some represented object, like the broken arrows and crescents and mirrors of Pictish symbol-carvings. In a few, a part of the pattern forms a stylised bird, but that proves neither that the *tamga* began as a bird-picture which was then stylised nor that an abstract design suggested a bird-form to some later *tamga*-engraver. Either sequence could be true.

Nobody knows, in short, what *tamgas* 'mean' or what they were really for. They are first found in the Bosporan Kingdom, dated to the first century AD, inscribed on the walls of underground tombs or on ritual objects. They are evidently not Sarmatian by origin, but at the same time they seem to have something to do with Central Asian religious symbolism of this period. What is clear is that the Sarmatians adopted the *tamga* from the Bosporans, and that its function then changed. After a fairly short time, the ritual purpose becomes less important, and the *tamga* is increasingly found engraved on the personal possessions of rich and powerful men and women. It becomes a property mark, but whether this refers to individual or clan property is not clear. Almost all known *tamga* signs have been found on Bosporan territory, most of them in the Greek cities.

Tamgas also occur in the Sarmatian graves scattered across Poland, engraved on stone or inlaid in silver upon iron lance-heads. Their spread reaches from Ukraine, including the Kiev region, westwards to what is now Silesia, and the distribution and the dating of the graves makes this look very much like the track of a Sarmatian-Alan migration.

The Polish *tamgas* do not show just that Sarmatians arrived there. They can be read to suggest that the Sarmatians never went away. Long before a Polish archaeologist, the late Tadeusz Sulimirski, made this case, chroniclers and genealogists had noticed that the heraldic clan symbols used by the old Polish nobility looked like *tamgas*. In fact, the older these crests were, the more strikingly 'Sarmatian', or rather Bosporan, they looked. This is not a matter of the great Sarmatism fad which began in the sixteenth century; such crests had been used as the devices of clans like the Roch, Chamiec, Mora or Doliwa in the Middle Ages, long before Sarmatism had been invented. Where, then, had they come from?

At this point, conventional scientists get cold feet. The evidence is not abundant. Any hypothesis is flossed up out of guesswork: grounds for charges of romanticism, which is a worse academic crime than falsification of data. All the same, a circumstantial case exists. We know that a Sarmatian mounted élite, using the *tamga*, reached Poland in the third century and settled there for at least a hundred years – possibly longer. We know that Polish *szlachta* families came to think that they were the descendants of Sarmatians. Finally, we know that Polish mediaeval heraldry used a graphic language whose only known visual ancestor is the *tamga*. So the problem, it might be said, is merely a thousand-year gap between Sarmatians and *szlachta* about which we know almost nothing. It may be that these broken-off connections at either end of the gap resemble one another only by coincidence. On the other hand, it may be that a class of mounted warriors from the Black Sea steppe – or as we might call them, knights in armour – achieved such a grip over a primitive Slavonic population that they were able to spend a millennium slowly turning themselves into a mediaeval land-holding nobility.

Sulimirski charged at the problem like a lancer. In the Polish edition of his book *The Sarmatians*, he writes of the 'almost identical forms' of crests and *tamgas*, and asserts: 'It would appear that there can be no doubt about the origin of a significant proportion, if not the majority of Polish crests in Sarmatian *tamgas*.' The Antae, a component group of the Eastern Alans, were not wiped out by the Hun invasion of Poland which took place in the fifth century, and 'their descendants . . . retained their high social position.' It must therefore be assumed, says Sulimirski, that 'a significant part' of the Polish *szlachta* really does originate with the Sarmatian Alans.

He goes further. Polish aristocratic mores, Sulimirski suggests, find many of their roots in Sarmatian custom. Ancient writers record the solidarity and sense of equality among Sarmatians, much like the *szlachta* motto that 'the petty squire on his plot /Is as good as the duke'. And might not the special Polish attitude to women have its roots among those Indo-Iranian nomads too? Sarmatian noblewomen were powerful and respected, while the Polish system of aristocratic descent still shows traces of matriliny. 'Who knows', Sulimirski defiantly winds up, 'whether Polish gallantry to women, which amazes foreigners, as does the responsible role of women in family and even social life, is not a survival or echo of Sarmatian matriarchal society?'

The Sarmatians, even if their progeny are still kissing ladies' hands in Poland and helping mares foal in Lancashire, have emptied themselves into history until none of them – apart from the Ossetians – remain. Those who migrated west from the Black Sea ceased to be nomads and pastoralists. Some of the first wave, like the Iazygians, were recruited by the Roman Empire and resettled in various parts of Gaul or Britain. Others moved north-westward until they came up against the strong and firmly settled Germanic peoples. Late Roman writers, trying to describe this, fell into the habit of describing all Europe east of the Germans as 'Sarmatia', a term which was gradually applied to all the Slav peoples of the region whether or not they had a ruling class of Sarmatian origin.

The Alans, in particular, had many strange fates. One group or war-party, setting out from the Balkans in the late fourth century, rode right across the dying Roman Empire through Austria and the Rhineland, and then, with Vandal and Suevian allies, into France, Spain and Portugal, winding up in what is now Spanish Galicia. Other expeditions moved more slowly across northern France, in some cases putting down roots and forming small Alan kingdoms of their own. Over thirty French place-names, including that of the town of Alençon, allude to their presence, and there is some evidence of a long-lasting Sarmatian settlement near Orléans.

These kingdoms, replacing the shrunken remains of the Roman villa economy, seem to prefigure the mediaeval pattern of mounted knights ruling settled peasantries. For some scholars, the Sarmatians engendered 'the dawn of chivalry' in the West, not only as a new pattern of social order but in mythology, symbolism and taste. Timothy Taylor writes that 'the animal-based heraldry of mediaeval Europe . . . owes far more to this direct steppic influence than to the animal motifs – originally Persian and Thracian – mediated and transmitted by western Celtic art.'

The Eastern Alans had been the neighbours of the Huns in Central Asia, and had acquired some of their customs. One of these was skull-binding, the practice of deforming the heads of infants into an ovoid shape – flat receding forehead and long projecting cranium at the back. Partly overrun by the Hun offensive into Europe, many Eastern Alans joined their armies and travelled west with them. Some settled for a time on the Elbe, and – like their predecessors the Antae – came to mobilise and dominate the larger and less warlike Slavonic populations they found there.

One of these conquests had a powerful impact on later history. The words *Choroatus* and *Chorouatos* (Croat) occur on inscriptions found at Tanais, on the Don. It looks as if the term was originally the name of a group of Alan warriors who lived for a period in the Azov steppes and then migrated again towards the north-west. There they subjugated and then merged into Slavonic peoples living on the upper Vistula and in northern Bohemia. Byzantine and Arab chronicles in the tenth century describe a people called *Belochrobati* (White Croats) in that region, whose kings drank mares' milk and whose babies were subjected to skull-binding. Migrating southwards across the Hungarian plain towards the Adriatic, this group settled in the area which was to become modern Croatia. The name 'Serb', too, originally belonged to another Eastern Alan band which was recorded in the Volga-Don steppe in the third century and which reappeared in the fifth century on the east bank of the Elbe. In the same way as the Sarmatian 'Croats', they dominated and then melted into Slav populations around them. Some remained there, ancestors of the Slav-speaking Serb minority which still lives in Lusatia in modern Saxony. Others, like the Croats, moved south across the Danube to a permanent home in the Balkans: the future land of Serbia.

Fragments of Alan population survived in Asia for many more centuries. William of Rubruck, in the thirteenth century, was only one of several European travellers who met Christianised Alans living at the court of Tatar khans, and Marco Polo heard of similar communities in China during the Yuan/Mongol dynasty. In the fourteenth century, the missionary bishop Brother Pellegrini reported a large community of Orthodox Christian Alans, possibly mercenary soldiers, living on the south-eastern coast of China, but nothing else is known about them.

The Crimean coast between Feodosia and Alushta was still known as 'Alania' in the Middle Ages, and there were disputes about who was the rightful bishop of the Alans. These last Sarmatians on the Black Sea appear to have linked up with the Crimean Goths until 'Gothia' was overthrown by the Turks and Tatars. The final mention of the Alans, as inhabitants of Crimea in the time of the Tatar khanate, dates from the seventeenth century – only a hundred years before the Russian conquest.

Although their overlords were Moslems, the Crimean Alans remained Orthodox Christians and their faith was tolerated. By

1600, they had become a small, inoffensive community which had grown almost indistinguishable from more recent Christian settlers along the Crimean coast – indistinguishable, except for one thing. Their heads were egg-shaped. More than a thousand years since they learned the practice from the Huns, the Eastern Alans were still binding the skulls of their babies.

Chapter Ten

The law-abiding town, though small and set
On a lofty rock, outranks mad Nineveh.

Phocylides, quoted by Dio Chrysostom in
'Borysthenitica'

The old Irish term for province is *coicead*, meaning
a 'fifth', and yet, as everyone knows, there are only
four geographical provinces on this island. So where
is the fifth? The fifth province is not anywhere here
or there, north or south, east or west. It is a place
within each one of us – that place which is open to
the other, that swinging door which allows us to
venture out and others to venture in.

Mary Robinson, President of the Irish
Republic, on signing the Declaration of Office
in Dublin Castle, 3 December 1990

IN AUGUST 1992, a small, savage war broke out on the shores of
the Black Sea between Abkhazia and Georgia. It ended, just over a
year later, with the defeat of the Georgian forces led in person by
President Edward Shevardnadze and the emergence of a precariously independent Republic of Abkhazia.

Human settlement around the Black Sea has a delicate, complex
geology accumulated over three thousand years. But a geologist
would not call this process simple sedimentation, as if each new
influx of settlers neatly overlaid the previous culture. Instead, the
heat of history has melted and folded peoples into one another's
crevices, in unpredictable outcrops and striations. Every town and
village is seamed with fault-lines. Every district displays a different

veining of Greek and Turkic, Slav and Iranian, Caucasian and Kartvelian, Jewish and Armenian and Baltic and Germanic.

An ancient 'multi-ethnic' community is a rich culture to grow up in. Bosnia was once like that. So was Odessa before the Bolshevik Revolution, or Vilnius, in Lithuania, before the Second World War. The symbiosis of many nationalities, religions and languages in one place has always appealed to foreign visitors, and never more than in today's epoch of nationalist upheaval. But nostalgia makes bad history. The symbiosis has often been more apparent than real.

Living together does not mean growing together. Different ethnic groups may co-exist for centuries, practising the borrowing and visiting of good neighbours, sitting on the same school bench and serving in the same imperial regiments, without losing their underlying mutual distrust. But what held such societies together was not so much consent as necessity – the fear of external force. For one group to assail or attempt to suppress another was to invite a catastrophic intervention from above – the despatch of Turkish soldiers or Cossacks – which would pitch the whole community into disaster.

It follows that when that fear is removed, through the collapse of empires or tyrannies, the constraint is removed too. Power struggles in distant places, to which one group or another feels an allegiance, reach the village street. Democratic politics, summoning un-sophisticated people to pick up sides and to think in terms of adversarial competition, smite such communities along their concealed splitting-plane: their ethnic divisions. And, often reluctantly at first, they divide. The familiar neighbours, with their odd-smelling food and the strange language they speak at home, become part of an alien and hostile 'them'. Antique suspicions, once confined to folk-songs and the kitchen tales of grandmothers, are synthesised into the politics of paranoia.

All multi-ethnic landscapes, in other words, are fragile. Any serious tremor may disrupt them, setting off landslips, earthquakes and eruptions of blood. The peoples themselves know this, and fear it. But nationalism, when it breaks out around the Black Sea, is usually a plague which has arrived from somewhere else, and against that plague there is no known serum. This was the fate of Abkhazia.

This little region of coast and mountains, stretching from the Russian border at Sochi in the north down to the Inguri River in the south, was precisely one of those mingled Black Sea societies. The Abkhazians themselves, speaking a pre-Indo-European language, were already there when the first Greek colonists arrived in the sixth century BC. But by 1992 they had become a minority in their own land, less than 20 per cent of the population. Russians, Pontic Greeks, Armenians and migrants from the northern Caucasus had all settled in Abkhazia during the nineteenth century, while the biggest single group of inhabitants – 45 per cent – was Georgian, or rather Georgian-Mingrelian.

They were relatively recent immigrants. After 1864, when Russia annexed this part of the Caucasus, many Moslem Abkhazians fled into the Ottoman Empire. Their lands were taken by Christian Mingrelians from across the Inguri River in Georgia, a process which continued fitfully until 1949 when Mingrelians were compulsorily moved into Abkhazia to take over the farms and houses left by the deported Pontic Greeks. Here began a resentment which was soon to seem ancestral. While the Abkhazians speak a north Caucasian language, the Mingrelians belong to the Kartvelian linguistic family which also includes Georgian, Svanetian and Lazuri. To the Abkhazian villagers, the Mingrelian presence seems to convey an unspoken threat. There were only about half a million people in all Abkhazia, while Georgia had five million. After the Revolution, Abkhazia had been declared a full republic of the Soviet Union, but in 1931 Stalin – the great Georgian – had demoted the land to a mere 'autonomous republic' within Georgia.

The first shocks which began to release the landslide came with Georgia's move towards independence between 1989 and 1991. Georgian nationalists, obsessed with the danger of Russian interference, took a harsh line towards their own non-Kartvelian minorities. In South Ossetia, where descendants of the Sarmatian Alans live, there was fighting. In the summer of 1989, the Georgian government decreed that a branch of the University of Tbilisi should be set up in Sukhum, the Abkhazian capital, alongside the recently established University of Abkhazia. This provoked student riots, which soon spread into ethnic street battles in Sukhum and the southern town of Ochamchira.

Under the pressure of distant events in Tbilisi and Moscow, the whole social structure of Abkhazia began to buckle. The Soviet Union itself fell apart in 1991. Civil war broke out in Georgia. The Abkhazian leaders opened discussions with other northern

Caucasian peoples about forming a confederation and a military alliance, and declared that they wished to restore the semi-independence of the 1920s. Then, in August 1992, Georgian forces attacked and occupied Sukhum. The Georgian National Guard was called to arms throughout the territory. The Abkhazian government escaped arrest in the capital and fled north along the coast to Gudauta, where they called for resistance. Volunteers from the armed hill peoples of the northern Caucasus – Kabardians, Chechens, Adygheans, Daghestanis – arrived to support the Abkhazians. So did contingents from the big Abkhazian diaspora in Turkey. The war began.

The Abkhazians were backed not only by the volunteers but by most of the non-Kartvelian population, but it was covert Russian intervention which decided the outcome. With the apparent aim of crippling the reality of Georgian independence and reasserting Moscow's hegemony in the northern Caucasus, the Russians supplied the Abkhazian side with heavy weapons and supported their ground troops with air strikes.

The Georgians were finally driven back over the Inguri River in September 1993. In the first phase of the war, Georgian and Mingrelian militias massacred or expelled Abkhazians in the districts they controlled; later, when the counter-offensive began, the advancing Abkhazians drove before them a mass of some 150,000 desperate Kartvelian refugees. There were atrocities on both sides. The towns were wrecked and often looted. In the south, the Georgians destroyed villages as they fell back, and sowed the fields with mines. The dead – killed in battle, murdered in their homes or victims of hunger and cold as they sought to escape across the mountains – have never been reliably counted but certainly numbered many thousands.

The Abkhazians had become 'masters in their own house'. But the house was roofless, and they wandered lonely through its desolate rooms.

Nine months after the Georgian troops had been driven from the land, the Abkhazian Minister of Information sat in her tiny, shabby room and still seemed astonished to be there. Dr Natella Akaba used to be a historian; she wrote her doctoral thesis on 'Colonial Policy and British Imperialism in Qatar'. She said thoughtfully, 'In the Brezhnev days, I was one of those who listened to Radio Liberty and thought that democracy would be such a natural, simple thing. Now I realise that in real life matters are much more difficult.'

Her door was broken and splintered; the original lock had been wrenched off by marauding soldiers and replaced by a handle picked up in some nearby ruin. She was, on this point, luckier than the Minister of Education, a few streets away. His method of entering his office was to put his hand through a rent in the door-panel and pull. Once inside, he kept the door shut with a wedge of paper tied through the hole with string.

Only the Minister of Economics, who had commandeered a room in the old university building, possessed a real lock: an impressive modern thing with a number-coded button-panel. This did not mean that he kept money in his office. There was no money. Dr Akaba and her ministerial staff of fifteen boys and girls received no salaries at all. They were entitled to one free canteen meal and a loaf of bread each day. As a special privilege of office, the minister was given an expense allowance of fifteen dollars a month for her official duties.

Sukhum was once a pretty, lazy southern town. Its climate is sub-tropical; its parks and esplanades are sweetly scented by white and pink oleanders, framed in alleys of palms, shaded by banana leaves and enormous eucalyptus trees. Until the war with Georgia, its population was as much of a mixture as it had been when the Greek colony of Dioscurias stood there and – so it was said – nine different languages could be heard in its market-place. The largest group (after Stalin had expelled the Greeks) was Mingrelian or Georgian; there were Abkhazians too, of course, but they were a minority in Sukhum as they were in Gudauta, Gagra, Ochamchira and all the other towns. The Abkhazians were thought of as a village people. Their strength was not on the coast but inland, in the villages up against the first foothills of the Caucasus.

Remembering all this, I walked through the streets of Sukhum nine months after the end of the war and felt a new silence, like a sort of deafness, pressing on my ears. Where had everyone gone? Here and there a few people walked across empty streets, or stood waiting outside the offices of some international aid agency. Behind the oleanders and palms, the houses were gutted and the dead walls were stained black by smoke. The tarry smell of burned timbers, the marzipan scent of burned plaster, still hung in the air. In the park, the bronze busts of Abkhazian poets and sages were pocked with bullets, and the central lawn had become a small military cemetery.

More than half the population of Sukhum had fled, during the thirteen months between the arrival of Georgian troops in August 1992 and the town's recapture by the Abkhazians. Sukhum had been shelled and bombed, attacked by aircraft with rockets and finally taken by storm. Many of the remaining Greeks were evacuated to Greece in 'Operation Golden Fleece', when a ship brought them off from Sukhum harbour in the middle of the war. An aircraft came from Israel to rescue the Jews. Almost all the Georgian and Mingrelian inhabitants abandoned their homes and followed the retreating Georgian forces, or were chased out by the Abkhazians and their ferocious allies as they reoccupied Sukhum.

The airport was unusable; the railway to Russia, running north along the Black Sea coast to the frontier on the Psou River, had been wrecked. No merchant ships dared to put in at Sukhum until the Turks resumed an occasional ferry service from Trabzon. In June 1994 the Russian Army re-entered Abkhazia as a peace-keeping force and deployed some 3,000 men in the south to keep the Georgians and Abkhazians apart. But the Russians did little to reconstruct the country.

A year later, Abkhazia remains unrecognised. Under United Nations auspices, negotiations are dragging on between Georgia and Abkhazia to arrange the return of refugees and to settle Abkhazia's international status. The Abkhazian government would now consent to a 'confederation' with Georgia which recognised their country's right to sovereignty and independence. The Georgians, however, continue to claim that Abkhazia is an integral region of the Georgian state.

Achandara, under the foothills of the Abkhazian Caucasus range, was spared the fighting. It is a rich village, on good soil, and the sons and daughters of Achandara who have to work in Sukhum are nourished by parcels of maize-meal, fruit, honey and bread from their families. Along the road leading inland from the coast wander mares with young colts and herds of buff-coloured cattle.

Not far away is Lykhny, with its sacred tree where thousands of Abkhazians gathered in June 1989 to proclaim the 'Lykhny Declaration', demanding the restoration of full republican status within the Soviet Union. Trees matter to Abkhazians. Their two conversions to world religions, to Christianity in the sixth century and then to Islam under the Turks, have been less enduring than older ways of reverence for natural objects and for the dead. The Minister for Ecology, a young marine biologist, told me that older Abkhazians preserved a healthy 'culture of using nature', by tradition never killing more than one animal on each hunting expedition. But it goes deeper than that.

As we approached Achandara, a young woman in the back of the car asked, 'Do you see that mountain?' Behind the village rose a steep conical hill, covered with dark-green forest and capped with thunder-cloud.

'That one?'

In mild alarm, she said, 'Don't point at it. We do not point at it.'

What was its name?

'It has a name, but we must not say it.' She explained that it was forbidden to cut wood on the mountain. Once, in spite of their warnings, a tsarist general had forced an Abkhazian work-party to fell timber there, but as the first tree bowed and crashed, the general too fell paralysed to the ground.

At her parents' house, her father and his neighbours, wrapped in veils, were taking honey from the hives. The family had not been warned of our visit, but soon we were sitting down to a meal on the grass: maize bread, hard white cheese, cucumbers, little dumplings fried to celebrate the honey harvest. Then came clear red wine from grapes in the arbour, *chacha* eau-de-vie, and finally the main course: stiff maize porridge eaten with slices of cheese and spoonfuls of spicy *akhud* (bean stew with pepper paste). In front of us, women carried cloth-covered trays across the lawn as they prepared the marriage feast for one of the sons of the house.

Afterwards, we walked among orange and pear trees to see the family graves in the orchard. Here within a square of iron railings lay Grandfather. He had been arrested in 1947, for nothing more than being a prosperous peasant, and sent to a Siberian labour camp. When he felt that he could bear exile no more, he had written a letter – one page for his children, the other for his wife – and slipped it into a bottle which he hid in the grave of another Abkhazian comrade, knowing that sooner or later his friend's people would come to find his bones and bring them home. Then he cut his own wrists and died. Many years later the letter in the bottle was delivered, and in turn his own family set out for Siberia to fetch his body back to Achandara to lie beside his wife. Standing in the sun, with the unnameable hill behind her, his daughter-in-law said to me, 'You know, there was a Russian woman there who asked us why we wanted him. She said that he was just a dead body, nothing worth having. Can you believe that?'

A few yards away, there was a fresh grave. Cousin Z., a young schoolteacher, had been killed in the war against Georgia. The tomb-stone bore his portrait in relief, and beside it was a full-length oil painting showing him in camouflage fatigues, grasping his Kalashnikov. Over the grave, in the Abkhazian custom, a sun-roof had been erected so that the family could sit and keep the dead man company.

On the way back to Sukhum, a few miles down the valley, we passed a row of empty houses. The orchards round them were green, but the walls were scorched black by fire. Mingrelians had lived here since 1945, when they were resettled from western Georgia. But there had been no battles in this valley. Peaceful families had been driven from their homes by the Abkhazians simply because they belonged to the culture of the invaders.

A voice from the back of the car said, 'They shared our land, and they were our neighbours. But then they made war on us . . . '

It was more than a decade before the war began that Fazil Iskander wrote his novel *Sandro of Chegem*. It is more a series of connected tales about Abkhazian lives and fantasies, done in the manner of a volume of Isaac Babel stories, than a conventional novel. And in most of the *Sandro* tales there recur mentions of another, different people who live among the Abkhazians. Iskander called them the 'Endurskies'. In a foreword, he suggested that Enduria, their land of origin, was a 'fictitious district', and that 'the Endurskies are the mystery of ethnic prejudice'. But nobody in Abkhazia has any doubt about who is meant. What Iskander wrote about the 'Endursky'-Mingrelians, or rather about Abkhazian attitudes towards them, belongs in any manual of ethnic tensions, in any aetiology of the symptoms of group prejudice.

In 'The Tale of Old Khabug's Mule', the mule – a suitably sardonic and detached observer – remarks that

the Abkhazians have a very complicated attitude towards the Endurskies. The main thing is that no one knows exactly how they got to Abkhazia, but everyone is sure they're here to gradually destroy the Abkhazians. At first the hypothesis was developed that the Turks were sending them down ... The Chegemians [from the village of Chegem] put forward a different version of the story. Their version is that somewhere deep in the dense forest between Georgia and Abkhazia the Endurskies had been spontaneously generated from wood mould. Very likely that was possible in Tsarist times. And later they grew into a whole tribe, multiplying much faster than the Abkhazians would have liked ...

Some older Chegemians, the mule recalls, say that there was a time when Endurskies did not live in Abkhazia and only came to the village in small parties to hire themselves out for seasonal labour. Now they were a permanent, yet never fully accepted, part of the landscape.

In 'Tali, Miracle of Chegem', the narrator mocks:

The Chegemians were sure that all Abkhazians dreamed of becoming related to them. Not to mention the Endurskies, who dreamed not so much of becoming related to the Chegemians as of subjugating them, or not even subjugating but simply destroying the flourishing village, turning it into a wasteland ... so that they could go around saying that there had never been any Chegem ... None of this would prevent [the Chegemians] from maintaining quite friendly relations with their Endursky aliens in normal times.

On the Black Sea coasts, there have lived many Chegemians and many Endurskies. They inhabit Crimea under the names of Tatar and Russian Ukrainian, filling their pails at the same pump and then going home to wonder what 'they' are really plotting. They used to live in the Empire of the Grand Comnenians, when Greek, Turkish, Hebrew, Italian and Kartvelian were spoken on the streets of Trebizond, or in nineteenth-century Odessa where nobody was a native but everybody agreed that the Jews were Endurskies. They live in Moldova now, upstream from the estuary of the Dniester, where the Chegemians are the Moldovans of Romanian speech while the Endurskies are the Slav settlers of 'Transdniestria' in the east of the country. In Moldova, just as in Abkhazia and Chechnia in the northern Caucasus, the end of empire – the Soviet eclipse – meant the beginning of war between neighbours.

Independence always has an aspect of amputation. Old but still living connections are cut through. The majority celebrates, but a minority always mourns when a customs barrier shuts the familiar highway to yesterday's capital, when certain medals become impossible to wear at parades, when a much-loved newspaper in a metropolitan language is no longer delivered daily. Neighbours depart, with dignified regret or in panic. There is always loss.

The amputation of Abkhazia was brutal and untidy, and the loss was very great – not only the physical loss of human lives, burned houses, broken bridges, but also the huge cultural impoverishment inflicted by the flight of the Mingrelians and Georgians. Some of them, just possibly most of them, will find their way back. But the country will never be the same again. They were a part of Abkhazian society, and their intimacy with the other communities there – even if that intimacy was superficial and mistrustful – can never be reconstructed.

Abkhazia also lost its history. More accurately, it lost the material evidence of its own past, the relics and documents which any newly independent nation needs to re-invent and reappraise its own identity. This was not an accidental consequence of the fighting for Sukhum. It was, in part, a deliberate act of destruction.

The National Museum was not burned, but it was looted and devastated. In its dim halls, stuffed bears and spoonbills lean over torn cartons of Greek pottery shards. The huge marble relief of a woman and her children, found on the sea-bed off the site of Dioscurias, was spared because the staff (several of whom were Georgians) hid it behind boards. But the Georgian soldiers took the coin collections and even replicas of gold and silver vessels whose originals were already in the museum at Tbilisi. The cases containing Abkhazian finery, inlaid muskets and jewelled daggers and decorated wedding-dresses, were broken and emptied. Soldiers do this everywhere in occupied cities – it was no worse than the plundering of the Kerch museum in the Crimean War. But the fate of the State Archives was different.

The shell of the building stands down by the sea. Its roof has fallen in, and the interior is a heap of calcined rubble. One day in the winter of 1992, a white Lada without number-plates, containing four men from the Georgian National Guard, drew up outside. The guardsmen shot the doors open and then flung incendiary grenades into the hall and stairwell. A vagrant boy, one of many children who by then were living rough on the streets, was rounded up and made to help spread the flames, while a group of Sukhum citizens tried vainly to break through the cordon and enter the building to rescue burning books and papers. In those archives was most of the scanty, precious written evidence of Abkhazia's past, as well as the recent records of government and administration. The Ministry of Education, for example, lost all its files on school pupils. The archives also contained the entire documentation of the Greek community, including a library, a collection of historical research material from all the Greek villages of Abkhazia and complete files of the Greek-language newspapers going back to the first years after the Revolution. As a report compiled later in Athens remarked: 'the history of the region became ashes'.

The young official in Sukhum explained to me the national symbols of his country. Here was the state flag: the white hand on a red background stood for the ancient Abkhazian kingdom; the star for the Absilian ancestors; the seven green-and-white stripes for the traditional tolerance of the Caucasian peoples among whom Islam and Christianity existed together in peace. Here was the national coat of arms, devised from an Abkhazian epic legend. A horseman riding the winged steed Arash shoots his arrow at the stars: at a large one representing the sun, and at two smaller ones which are tokens of 'the union of the cultural worlds of East and West' . . .

All this is the normal kitsch of nationalism, with an element of modern high-mindedness: the allusions to 'traditional tolerance' (not always so traditional in the northern Caucasus), or to 'the union of cultural worlds'. But the ethnic mythology of the Abkhazian minority dominates both flag and crest. Every nationalism has to answer the question 'Who belongs? Who is an Abkhazian – or a Scot or a German?' These national symbols seemed to suggest a narrow, ominous definition.

When I came to Abkhazia, it seemed to me natural territory for 'Pol-Pottery'. A small, village people, regarding itself as the original and native population of the land, had conquered the towns and put most of their non-Abkhazian inhabitants to flight. It seemed likely that a dramatic ideology of ruralism would be imposed, insisting that the 'true' Abkhazian identity was to be found in the country-side while the towns were dangerous, cosmopolitan places in which that identity would always be dissolved. In the same way, I expected that the new government would reassemble loyalty to the new state around the Abkhaz language, forcing it on all its subjects as a condition of citizenship. There were enough melancholy precedents in the history of modern nationalism.

But, surprisingly enough, no such mood is to be found in the new Abkhazian government or among its supporters. They recognise the diversity of Abkhazia, and have no intention of forcing a single culture on its peoples. There is a coherent effort to rescue and reorganise the teaching and practice of Abkhazian culture, above all in music and dance. But members of the government in Sukhum insist that Greek, Armenian 'and even Georgian' culture would be developed as well: 'we do not blame the whole Georgian people, and we appreciate their traditions.' No special primacy will be given to the Abkhaz language. It will be one of the two official languages, with Russian (spoken in practice by everyone in the country) as the other. But the pre-war balance of languages used in schools as the medium of instruction is to be restored as far as possible, assuming that the refugees and exiles return (there used to be a hundred schools teaching in Abkhazian, seventy in Russian and a hundred and fifty in Georgian). All non-Abkhazian schools will continue to study the language, as they did before the war, but there is to be no pressure to give it more prominence in the curriculum.

This moderation has several sources. One is common sense. Abkhazia's wealth has depended upon beach tourism from Russia and Georgia and upon the insatiable Russian and Ukrainian demand for Abkhazian fruit and vegetables. Even if a combination of state terror and isolationism was used to 'Abkhazianise' the land, it would end in ruin. But nationalism can be immune to common sense, and a more important reason for tolerance is the personal origins of the new leadership.

They are sophisticated, professional men and women, often educated in Moscow or Leningrad. Several were senior officials in the old Communist Party. A good many of them speak little or no Abkhaz, which they regret but do not regard as disabling. After all, they reassure themselves, even Fazil Iskander writes in Russian.

They are not villagers, though most of them have village relations. Neither are they plebeians who have risen to power as officers in an insurrectionary army – that element which has so often overturned the first, more worldly generation of liberators (men like Ben Bella in Algeria, for example) and diverted a country towards peasant-worship and religious fundamentalism. Such people exist, angry and disoriented, in Abkhazia during this aftermath of war. But for the moment they have not found their way to challenge the urban intellectuals who are in charge. For the latter, with their mixed cultural inheritance, an Abkhazian is simply somebody who lives in Abkhazia and is committed to Abkhazia: nothing more ethnic or exclusive than that. It is a Black Sea solution, worthy of the Spartocids who ruled the Bosporan Kingdom and all its peoples two thousand years ago.

Natella Akaba said to me, 'We must not become a conservative rural community. There has to be a balance between past and future, country and town. Some Georgian scholars wanted the Abkhazians to become like aboriginals living in a native reserve, and that must not be allowed to happen.

'We can survive for some time like this. Perhaps the world will alter its view of us, if we can hang on. And a change must take place at the beginning of the twenty-first century, a change in political mentality, or everyone will perish in these little local wars. I don't think the aim of the Ossetians or the Abkhazians or the people of Karabagh is to isolate themselves from the world. We want to enter it, while keeping our own identity. Maybe, one day, that will be understood.'

Chapter Eleven

' . . . But tell me – why is he kicking his heels around here? What is he after?'

'He's studying marine life.'

'No, no, that's not it, old man,' sighed Layevsky. 'From what I gathered from a passenger on the steamer, a scientist, the Black Sea's poor in fauna, and organic life can't exist in its depths owing to the excess of hydrogen sulphide. All serious students of the subject work in the biological stations of Naples or Villefranche. But Von Koren's independent and stubborn. He works on the Black Sea because no one else does.'

Anton Chekhov, 'The Duel'

It is a happy world, after all. The air, the earth, the water, teem with delighted existence.

William Paley, *Natural Theology*

THEY SAY: 'the Black Sea is dying.' I open an American newspaper and read: 'The Black Sea, the dirtiest in the world, is dying an agonising death.' I am told, on the authority of a UN document, that the Black Sea constitutes 'the marine ecological catastrophe of the century' because '90 per cent of the basin is now anoxic.'

Here are treasures in the museum of self-accusation, the international gallery of eco-doom. It is entirely true that the Black Sea is nine-tenths dead, and that its waters below the 200-metre oxycline are poisoned with hydrogen sulphide gas. But they always were.

When the *Argo* fled back from Colchis to the Danube delta, with the navy of King Aeetes in pursuit, she was flying over a lifeless gulf nearly half a mile deep. Had she sunk on the journey, her timbers and the Argonauts themselves would still be sitting intact on the blue-grey bottom mud, for there is no oxygen in the water which would allow them to rot. Down there, only metal is consumed. Their bronze swords and helmets, the studs on their belts and the rings on their fingers, would have been dissolved away to nothing. As for the Golden Fleece, it would have lost all the bullion glare that made it worth the voyage from the Pagasaean Gulf in Greece to Colchis. It would lie there to this day, across the laps of dead Jason and Medea, but now returned to its old innocence, whiteness and sheepishness.

This death or near-death of a sea was not caused by the human race. It apparently annoys some fanatics that an ecological catastrophe can be achieved by ecology itself, without any need to call on expert human assistance. All the same, it was the natural action of natural forces which brought about this huge act of pollution: the decay of billions of tons of up-country mud and leaves and living ooze and dead micro-organisms, poured onto the sea floor since the last Ice Age by the five great rivers of the Black Sea.

It was not our fault. That is a fact, but a fact which might excuse the human race many other sins if it were too widely known. In consequence, journalism and propaganda about the condition of the Black Sea seldom mention hydrogen sulphide. If they do (as in the case of that UN document), they slip in a hint that the anoxia is in some way connected with human crimes against the environment.

What is dying, or rather being murdered, is not the Sea but its creatures. What is being polluted by human agency is not the main body of water (apart from the tipping of drums of toxic waste by Italian ships), but the surface layer whose abundance has shaped the whole prehistory and history of the Black Sea littoral. These are not small distinctions. Something terrible and perhaps final really is taking place. But there is no way to appreciate the scale of this threat without drawing back and surveying the precariousness of the entire Black Sea system: a surface film of life stretched over an abyss of lifelessness.

Out of twenty-six species of Black Sea fish being landed in commercial quantities in the 1960s, only six now survive in numbers worth netting. The *hamsi* anchovy provided 320,000 tons of fish as recently as 1984; within five years it has fallen to a mere 15,000 tons. The fish catch from all species is less than one seventh of what it was ten years ago, and some species are now almost certainly extinct. In the Sea of Azov, where all the Black Sea problems are multiplied, landings of sturgeon which averaged 7,300 tons a year in the 1930s had been reduced to 500 tons by 1961; almost all Azov sturgeon are now bred on fish farms. As for the mammals of the Sea, the monk seal is now extinct, reputedly because a Bulgarian hotel-builder dynamited its last cave-refuge, while the three species of dolphin or porpoise have been reduced from almost a million in the 1950s to anything between a third and a tenth of that number today.

Monstrous plankton blooms have begun to appear on the shallow north-western shelf of the Black Sea, where the bottom is above the anoxic level and where many of the important fish species spawn. 'Red tides' formed from dying phytoplankton began to occur with regularity in the early 1970s. The worst of these, in the Bay of Odessa in 1989, reached the horrifying concentration of one kilogram of plankton for every cubic metre of sea-water. Hydrogen sulphide, generated in the shallows rather than rising from the depths, began to reach the surface so that the stench spread through the city streets and the bay was covered with dead fish; much the same happened that season off Burgas, in Romania. The penetration of light in these increasingly turbid coastal waters has dropped by anything between 40 and 90 per cent, killing off bottom-living creatures like flatfish, molluscs and crustaceans and destroying almost the entire pasture of sea-grass. At the other end of the Black Sea, in the Bosporus, bottom marine life has declined so steeply in the last few decades that one of the main food sources – molluscs, urchins, marine worms – needed by the migrating fish shoals on their way to breed in the Sea of Marmara is disappearing.

The meaning of these facts and figures is that, for the first time, mankind is about to extinguish life in an entire sea. Some forms will survive: sterile algae or jelly-like drifting creatures. But the living creatures with whom the human race grew up here – the billions of silvery fish migrating round the same track since the last glaciation, the grinning dolphins whom the Greeks appointed the patrons of Trebizond – these are about to leave us.

The causes are known. All of them, with a few consciously criminal exceptions like the dumping of toxic waste, derive from human immaturity. At least 160 million people now live in the Black Sea basin – that is to say, in the area drained by rivers which run into the Sea – and among them are farmers, industrial workers, fishermen and seamen. But in the last fifteen or twenty years, their trades have all been overwhelmed with technical innovations, with modern fertilisers, supertankers, industrial processes based on hydrocarbons, dioxin or CFCs, electronic fish-location gear and modern drift-nets. Learning to operate these technologies takes all the mental concentration of Black Sea people, and for the wider questions of what these novelties do to the Sea and its life-systems and even to its human inhabitants they can spare almost no attention. When boats were made of wood, when peasants strewed their own dung on the fields and the worst industrial effluent was chlorine or sulphuric acid, there was at least more time to reflect; more opportunity for estate owners, iron-masters or ships' captains to take a broader and more inclusive view of the consequence of what they were doing. But now the toy has grown so big that it plays with the child.

The biochemical disaster is about 'eutrophication', an excess of organic and chemical nutrients. These are mostly nitrates and phosphates from agriculture and the residues of detergents. The phosphate concentration on the north-western shelf, for example, multiplied by nearly thirty times in the ten years between 1966 and 1976. The Danube's own phosphate discharge is 21 times greater than it was fifteen years ago, and the river also carries down 50,000 tons of spilled oil a year (worth $7.2 million at current prices, which would be enough to finance an ecological rescue programme for the entire Black Sea). It is this impossible surfeit of nutrients which causes 'red tides', plankton blooms and the loss of light and dissolved oxygen which is devastating the only area of the Sea's floor where life can exist.

There is also heavy-metal pollution, radio-active contamination since the Chernobyl accident in 1986 and the damage done by reckless use of sophisticated pesticides. The insecticide Lindane, dangerous to human health, is present in the Dniester River at ten times the permitted maximum concentration. In the headwaters of the same river, far up in the Carpathian foothills, an industrial reservoir at Stebniki burst its dam in 1983 and released 400 tons of potassium compounds downstream, traces of which were still fouling water supplies ten years later. And then there is simple, traditional human filth: domestic rubbish and sewage.

The Turkish novelist Yashar Kemal described the Golden Horn at Istanbul: 'that deep well surrounded by huge ugly buildings and sooty factories, spewing rust from their chimneys and roofs and walls, staining the water with sulphur-yellow liquid, a filthy sewer filled with empty cans and rubbish and horse carcases, dead dogs and gulls and wild boars and thousands of cats, stinking . . . A viscous, turbid mass, teeming with maggots.' The sewage of a city of ten million people (increasing at the rate of one a minute) gushes almost untreated into the Golden Horn and the Bosporus. Few towns on the Black Sea are any cleaner. Swimming off the north Turkish coast, far from the nearest village, I have often had to dive under floating islands of ordure.

The river waters are far worse than the Sea, even though they are still the direct source of water for most Black Sea households. Everyone I met in Odessa boiled their water, or even ran home-made distilling plants in their apartments, to protect themselves against water piped directly from the Dniester. Sometimes it is chlorinated, but so crudely that strange compounds form and make it undrinkable, and these days every summer brings an outbreak of cholera along the arc of coast between the Dnieper and Danube estuaries.

The rivers themselves have been tamed and castrated. The building of colossal dams to control water flow, to irrigate and to generate electricity, has diminished the natural rise and fall of the estuaries, doing fatal damage to the life-patterns of anadromous fish which run upstream to breed. The reservoir at Tsimlyansk on the middle Don has practically abolished the annual flooding of the river's delta, while the barrage on the Kuban River ended the run-up of sturgeon, shad and salmon. The construction of Stalin's monumental dam on the Dnieper submerged under an inland sea the seven cataracts first listed by the Byzantine emperor Constantine Porphyrogenitus, over which the Norsemen used to pull their boats on their way from Kiev to Constantinople.

The Danube delta still survives. Claudio Magris in his book *Danube* describes it as 'an exuberance of plants and animals, reeds and herons, sturgeon, wild boar and cormorants, ash-trees and cane-brakes, a hundred and ten species of fish and three hundred species of bird – a laboratory of life and the forms of life'. Yet its escape has been narrow. The late Romanian dictator Nicolae Ceauşescu planned to drain the delta, fell all its vegetation and replace it with rice-paddies.

It was in the early 1980s that Soviet marine biologists trawled up a creature unknown to them. It was an unimpressive little being, a bell-shaped thing of transparent jelly found swimming in the shallow waters of the north-western shelf. The scientists recognised that this was a species of ctenophore, an organism not unlike a jellyfish, and within a few months they identified it as *Mnemiopsis leidyi*, a native of the shallow estuaries on the Eastern Seaboard of the United States. Pretty clearly, it had been brought to the Black Sea in the water-ballast of freighters.

As Black Sea people know only too well, a weakened polity attracts invaders who can settle without meeting resistance. They find a niche, and flourish. Much the same applies to ecologies. *Mnemiopsis* was not the first alien settler in waters whose natural defences – the biological diversity of other species – were in steep decline. The big marine snail *Rapana*, probably brought from its home in the seas off Japan in the same way, had already decimated the Sea's oyster stocks before itself becoming the target of a profitable fishery. But nobody was prepared for the consequences of *Mnemiopsis*.

In the late 1980s, mostly between 1987 and 1988, there took place one of the most devastating biological explosions ever recorded by science. *Mnemiopsis*, an animal with no known predators to control it, spread suddenly and incontinently through the Black Sea. It fed voraciously on zooplankton, the food of young fish, and on fish larvae. In the Sea of Azov, *Mnemiopsis* consumed almost the entire zooplankton population, which in 1989 and 1991 collapsed to one-six-hundredth of its normal average. Its total biomass in the Black Sea and the Sea of Azov reached 700 million tons of translucent jelly, and its impact was entirely catastrophic. No recorded destruction by human pestilence or locust swarm compares with this damage to fish and their resources, and that was only the most obvious part of the disaster. Zooplankton feed upon phytoplankton which, liberated from their normal predators, multiply uncontrollably into the vast 'blooms' which consume dissolved oxygen and destroy life in shallow waters.

The *Mnemiopsis* disaster, more than anything else, finally convinced the governments of the Black Sea states that they must take action. A series of international conferences, guided by United Nations agencies, is now trying to draw up detailed rescue programmes to cut back pollution discharges and face the consequences of overfishing. But *Mnemiopsis* itself, with no known natural enemies, is also immune to governments. Nobody knows what to do about it. One radical school of thought holds that the breakdown of the old Black Sea ecosystem has to be accepted as irreversible, and that the only hope now is to introduce other alien species selected to prey on these invaders – fish, jellyfish, ctenophores and molluscs – and eventually construct a new but stable ecological balance. Other scientists regard this as reckless, and prefer to concentrate on slow but predictable measures like the reduction of nutrients coming down-river.

Meanwhile, unexpectedly, a change has come over the *Mnemiopsis* hordes. Like some of the nomad invaders of the Pontic Steppe who ran out of grass for their horses and set off for fresh pastures, *Mnemiopsis* appears to have eaten the Black Sea bare. The total biomass is thought to be falling. In some areas, the creature is descending to greater depths, closer to the oxycline, and attacking the tiny organisms which until now have survived as the main food of Black Sea sprats. More ominously, outlying raiding parties have begun to turn up in the Sea of Marmara and even off the Aegean coast of Turkey. *Mnemiopsis* is heading west. The spectre arises of an annihilating plague breaking out in vulnerable parts of the Mediterranean: the Nile delta, the Tunisian coast, even the Gulf of Lyon off Marseille.

Appalling difficulties confront any programme for saving the marine life of the Black Sea. One of them – the most pathetic – is the bankruptcy of science in the countries of the former Soviet Union. All round the coasts of Ukraine and southern Russia, from Odessa and Sevastopol to Kerch, there once stood a chain of magnificent institutes of marine biology and oceanography. Their standards of research, not only in the Black Sea but in the oceans, were as high as any in the world, and their equipment – above all their fleet of specially fitted ships – was the envy of their Western colleagues. As far as knowledge of the Black Sea went, no other country could match the expertise built up through more than a century's work by Russian and then Soviet scientists.

At exactly the moment when awareness of the desperate situation in the Sea began to dawn on the world, this magnificent and indispensable resource was paralysed by financial collapse. In Russia, money for almost all public scientific bodies – for scientific salaries as well as for research – dried up to a mere trickle at the end of 1991. In Ukraine, the research institutes funded by the old Soviet Academy of Sciences in Moscow were transferred to the Ukrainian government, which had no budget to carry their programmes forward.

In Odessa, I visited the Scientific Centre for Marine Ecology, which used to specialise in research on the open oceans. Its concrete tower near Langeron Point had become a place of ill-concealed despair. The centre's six ocean-going ships and the two smaller vessels for Black Sea exploration swung uselessly at their moorings, unable to sail for lack of fuel. Two of its laboratories had already closed. In the others, little work was going on. The assistants sat watching football on black-and-white television or making tea in kettles plugged into the adaptors of Finnish-made computers; a cat lay yawning on a cupboard which proved to contain old cardboard portraits of Brezhnev and Andropov.

In the midst of this desolation, scientists with dazzling records and qualifications were shuffling through the data of their past expeditions and experiments. They were concentrating on the last area for which there was any kind of official support: studies of the ecology of the Black Sea coastal shelf. Their devalued salaries now barely kept their families alive. Their foreign contacts which had kept them abreast of work abroad had been severed. Their careers seemed to be over, unless they had the luck to be headhunted by some laboratory in America or Western Europe.

Some showed that soldierly devotion to science, that monkish indifference to physical hardship and official abandonment, which I had met among archaeologists in Russia and Ukraine. Others appeared close to nervous breakdown. Later, I heard that the ships had been leased out for shopping voyages, hired by private 'suitcase businessmen' heading for Turkey to buy clothing, blankets and food which they could resell in street markets at home. In June 1994, according to the *Washington Post*, 27 out of the 40 ships which once formed the Black Sea research fleet of the Soviet Union were docked at Istanbul. It is not science, but at least it is income.

A second obstacle to the rescue of the Black Sea's ecology is the attitude of Turkey. Among all the causes of the Black Sea crisis, the most direct and obvious is overfishing. Species after species is being wiped out, or reduced to a few insignificant survivors, by genocidal and shortsighted greed which pays no attention to warnings about fish stocks until catch numbers and average weight have fallen below the point of no return. Most of the overfishing is done by Turks. This is a demonstrable fact, but a fact which Turkish fishermen, politicians and even scientists find almost impossible to admit. Ignorance, and the crude spoils-system of Turkish regional politics, contribute to this reluctance. But the most powerful motive is patriotic resentment. Once again, the outside world is perceived to be picking on Turkey and meddling in Turkish internal affairs.

Professor Mehmet Salih Çelikkale, a bouncy, fair-haired figure, is Turkey's most prominent expert on fish stocks. One unbearably hot afternoon in summer, I made my way up the hill above Trabzon to see him at the Black Sea Technical University. He does not deny that overfishing is in some degree to blame for the collapse of species, especially for the disappearance of the *hamsi* and bonito. But he is unwilling to make the Turkish fishing industry the main culprit. For Professor Çelikkale, pollution on the north-western shelf where the fish breed is the real problem, and here he accuses the Western European states above all – the European Union, which Turkey so desperately longs to join – of neglecting their responsibilities to clean up the Danube. Turkey, he protests, has taken steps to limit fish catches off the Anatolian coast, but the 'international community' is unwilling to invest in a fund to compensate the fishing villages for their losses –money which a poor country like Turkey cannot afford.

The professor also claims that there are too many dolphins in the Black Sea. In the 1950s, when Turkey began intensive dolphin fishing, there were about a million of them: common dolphins, bottle-nosed dolphins and harbour porpoises. By 1983, when the anguish of foreign environmentalists persuaded Turkey to ban the fishery, they had been reduced by anything between two-thirds and a half. Professor Çelikkale believes that there were about half a million dolphins left by 1987, which other scientists consider a large over-estimate (the Russians, who did a survey in the same year, put the figure at between 60,000 and 100,000). He claims that they eat no less than a million tons of fish a year and are increasing at the rate of 40,000 annually: two more figures regarded with scepticism by other marine biologists, who would divide this figure for fish consumption by about four. The Çelikkale appeal for a 20 per cent cull of dolphins, to restore the sprat and *hamsi* stocks, is not taken very seriously outside Turkey.

The Turkish fishermen are not just predators. They and their families are victims too. When I went to the fish-market at Trabzon, it was almost deserted, its slabs bare except for a few mullet, a spiny turbot (once common, now rare) and boxes of farmed rainbow trout. East of Trabzon, where the dark-green mountains come steeply down to the sea, the fishing-boats are pulled up along the shore and men sit all day in the tea-houses. They are paying the penalty for crude and short-sighted planning which has achieved exactly what it set out to prevent: the ruin of their livelihood.

As population increased along the coast, and the subdivision of peasant farms by inheritance led to growing land hunger, the Turkish government decided to make fishing more profitable. A programme of generous loans and grants – financed with the help of foreign investors, including the World Bank – made it possible for villagers to buy or build larger boats, equipped with new fishing and fish-locating technology. At first, all went well. The catch rose amazingly. Fortunes were made, especially by the fish-meal companies set up to take advantage of the new finance.

Then, in the 1980s, the whole project began to slew off course. Fish numbers fell away, and the average size of fish declined sharply. As the *hamsi* and bonito became scarcer, so ever more expensive and sophisticated electronic gear was required to find them. The cost of an effective boat began to soar out of reach of most Black Sea fishermen, while the interest charges on loans ruined family after family. Politicians tried to keep their grip on the Black Sea vote by promising higher levels of grant, even by encouraging boat owners to fish illegally and out of season. But the disaster continued to deepen, as society in the little ports and fishing-harbours divided in a desperate struggle between the precariously rich and the chronically poor. The big-boat owners fell back on the most reckless and destructive fishing methods to meet their debts. The small-boat people, many of whom had owned larger vessels during the boom but had been driven bankrupt, saw their last chance of a living, the remnants of the fish stocks, being plundered away by crews with more powerful engines and larger nets.

There was hatred, and even violence. But this is a trap from which there is no escape. The big boats have to go on fishing, even though the stocks are so near extinction that few ever make a profit: it is that or ruin and emigration. The owners of the small boats now set nets all winter for a few whiting or mullet a day; it is that or hunger. The Turkish government, with some justice, asks why bodies like the World Bank are not ready to pay to repair the damage which they helped to create a few years ago.

But this, for once, is not a story special to the Black Sea. It is a tragedy as familiar to fishing communities in Norway or Peru as it is in Turkey, and the heavy word 'over-capitalisation' conceals the crudity of its plot. A government encourages the murder of fish species merely to win a respite from social pressures. A state, anxious to be popular, pays a whole deluded human community to set out on a journey which starts from one sort of poverty and must end in another. In the Black Sea region of Turkey, this journey lasted some thirty years. Now the people are back more or less where they started, but the fish have gone.

Behind all predictions of what will happen to the Black Sea, there creeps a nightmare. It is a possibility so terrible that most scientists prefer not to discuss it. Many of them – to be fair – have brought forward good reasons to argue that it need not be taken seriously. It is a Black Sea apocalypse.

This nightmare is known by the harmless word 'turnover', a phenomenon which has been observed and studied in lakes whose depths are anoxic and charged with hydrogen sulphide. 'Turnover' means a sudden rolling-over of water layers, as if the whole balance of pressures and densities which had kept the heavier mass below the lighter, fresher mass were reversed and overthrown. With 'turnover', in some lakes an annual event which takes place in autumn, the deep and poisoned waters burst through to the surface, annihilating all life.

It is possible to define the Black Sea as merely the biggest of all anoxic lakes. If 'turnover' were to take place in the Black Sea, it would be the worst natural cataclysm to strike the earth since the last Ice Age, more devastating in its human consequences than the eruption on Thera in about 1500 BC which destroyed the Minoan cultures, or than the Krakatoa eruption in Indonesia in 1883.

A first warning sign would be a rise of the anoxic water-level. A few years ago, American researchers on a study voyage in the Black Sea claimed that the oxycline, the upward limit of the poisonous undermass, had risen by thirty metres in only twenty years. Pollution and the effect of reduced river flows on the Sea's water-density, they concluded, were beginning to create the conditions for the ultimate disaster.

They were probably wrong. Russian oceanologists at once pointed out that they had been measuring the oxycline level for far longer than the Americans, and had registered variations of up to thirty metres upwards and downwards since they began surveys some seventy years before. The British marine environmentalist Laurence Mee, who runs the Global Environment Facility task force for the Black Sea at Istanbul, calculates that the rivers would have to run at half their present flow for more than a century before the density balance of the Sea could be seriously affected. All this is reassuring; the weight of scientific evidence suggests that the Black Sea is not about to capsize. But, as Mee allows, 'the debate continues'. An edge of fear, a shadow of apocalypse, has entered all discussions on the rescue of the Black Sea, and it will never quite go away.

Change cannot be avoided, but man-made disaster sometimes can. As I came to know better some of the scientists and politicians concerned with the Black Sea, I noticed that those with most experience were also those least ready to issue melodramatic forecasts of doom. To be truly familiar with the Sea is to appreciate the resilience – sometimes almost inexplicable – of its ecological system. The crisis is real enough; the damage done in the last few decades by pollution, overfishing and the reduction of river flows is so great that much of it cannot be reversed. But it was always wrong to think of 'restoring' the Sea to its previous status quo. A natural ecosystem is not eternal and static, but a process of continuous change and adaptation. Currents alter their direction; fish vary their migration routes. New and intrusive species do not need transport by ships' water-ballast but in the past were brought in by freak winds or by birds, to exterminate existing life-forms and upset an older ecological balance. Until now, the Black Sea and its marine life have been able to absorb these impacts and arrange them into a new and different equilibrium.

The Black Sea has not yet lost this power. There have been a few seasons in recent years when the Don River was allowed to flow with its old freedom through the Tsimlyansk dam; sturgeon and shad ran up the Don again to breed, and there were astonishing revivals of fish stocks in the Sea of Azov. Some new surveys suggest that damage by *Mnemiopsis* to the zooplankton mass on the north-western shelf is much less in some areas than scientific projections suggested. This cannot easily be explained, but the Bulgarian biologist Violeta Vasileva said to me in Odessa, 'We were astonished at the way in which the ecosystem had rebalanced itself. I now feel that the Black Sea has far more fight-back capacity than I used to think.' Fishing restrictions in Turkey are beginning to produce a rapid climb in *hamsi* numbers, rather to the alarm of conservationists who worry that the boats will put to sea again before the recovery is complete and once more push the species to the verge of extinction.

Even the economic slump which ran round the Black Sea after the collapse of the Communist systems has brought unexpected relief. The closing of factories and the new, prohibitive costs of imported fertilisers and chemicals have made the big rivers temporarily cleaner, and slowed down the eutrophication of coastal waters. In Abkhazia, the sewage treatment plants at Sukhum were blown up during the 1993 war with Georgia, but so many of the inhabitants have fled that the sea off Sukhum's beaches is purer than it has been for twenty years.

Best of all, there is a display of human will to 'save' the Black Sea. In Odessa, a long and desperate battle was fought by the independent ecologist Alla Shevchuk and her friends to stave off the Ukrainian oil-terminal project, an ostentatious scheme forced ahead in the early 1990s by President Leonid Kravchuk; when elections deposed Kravchuk in 1994, his successor promised at once that the project would be reduced or even cancelled. And in the same city, in 1993, I watched Ministers for the Environment from Bulgaria, Romania, Ukraine, Russia, Georgia and Turkey sitting down with experts from several different United Nations agencies and the World Bank to draft a declaration on the protection of the Black Sea, as part of a continuous action plan. I heard the Turkish delegate and the Bulgarian delegate warmly welcoming each other's ideas – something inconceivable at normal international conferences, where proceedings have often been held up for days while Turkey and Bulgaria wrangle about history and minorities. And all the ministers happily let themselves be steered by discreet UN advice from offstage – something which could never happen at a conference on the North Sea, where governments, especially those of Britain or France, are neurotically touchy about maintaining the appearance of sovereignty. There is a good spirit stirring here. The international campaign for the Black Sea has become popular. All hopes are still fragile, of course. Much depends on persuading polluter states far upstream in the Danube basin – Germany, Austria, Slovakia, Hungary – to collaborate and to contribute their money and wisdom. But it may be that the cause of the Black Sea itself, of its waters and its creatures, is at last beginning to achieve what so many millennia of human activity have failed to achieve: the union of the peoples who live around it.

Epilogue

THE NAVAL MUSEUM at Istanbul, a seaside palace in the Beşiktaş district, stands next to one of the busy ferry terminals for commuters travelling to work across the Bosporus. The museum has few visitors. Often there is nobody there at all, apart from the man at the ticket desk. But the thump of engines from freighters passing through the Narrows and the whistles of the ferries make its silence companionable.

Huge state galleys are preserved here, with benches for a hundred and forty oarsmen. There is an imperial harem boat, its thirteen banks of oars manned by black-whiskered male dummies in fez, sash and baggy trousers; the kiosk aft for the women of the seraglio is thickly curtained, furnished with upholstered seats piled with cushions. Around the walls of the museum are models of ironclads in glass cabinets, and the garden outside is a park of antique naval guns.

Near the entrance, overshadowed by the galleys and their carved prow-spikes, lies the Chain. Only a few links survive. They are made of black, rough-forged iron, each link a metre long and beaten into a figure-of-eight shape which was then crudely welded together at the waist. This is what is left of the great chain made in the eighth century to the order of the Byzantine emperor Leo III, 'the Isaurian'.

Supported on a string of timber rafts or buoys, the Chain was stretched across the mouth of the Golden Horn in times of danger. It kept out the Arabs in the time of Leo III, and a hundred years later blocked the attacking ships of Thomas the Slav, a pretender to the imperial throne. In the eleventh century, the Viking warrior Harald Hardrade, commander of the Empire's 'Varangian Guard', ran his galleys against the Chain during his escape from Byzantine service to claim a kingdom in Norway.

Harald had been forbidden to leave the city by the Empress Zoe, co-ruler with the emperor Michael Kalafates, who ordered his arrest. In revenge, Harald and his men attacked and blinded the emperor and kidnapped Maria, niece of the empress, as a hostage. Then, according to the *Heimskringla* sagas, Harald and his followers

> went to the Varangians' galleys, of which they took two, and rowed to Saevidarsund [the Golden Horn]. And when they came to the iron chain that lay across the sound, Harald said that the men should fall to their oars on both galleys and that the men who were not rowing should run aft and each should have his sack with him. Thus they ran the galleys onto the iron chain, and as soon as the ships were fast and their movement stopped, he bade all his men run forward again. Then the galley Harald was on plunged forward, and after swinging on the chain slipped off, but the other galley stuck fast to the iron chain and broke its back, and many were drowned, though some were picked up from the water. In this way Harald came out from Micklegarth [Constantinople] and thus went into the Black Sea. But before he sailed away from land he put the girl ashore and gave her a good escort back to Micklegarth . . .*

The Chain was used again in a vain attempt to hold off the attacking Crusaders in 1203, and it was run out for the last time during the final siege of Constantinople by the Ottoman Turks in 1453. The navy of Mehmet II, 'the Conqueror', failed to break through it by direct assault, and the Sultan, taking over command from his humiliated admiral Baltaoglu, prepared his own plan to outflank the Chain altogether. If the fleet could not enter the Golden Horn by sea, then it would enter it by land. A two-mile track of log

---

* Harald Hardrade (the Ruthless) belonged to the Scandinavian-'Varangian' military elite whose raiding voyages for a time connected the Black and Baltic Seas. They were the founders of the 'Kievan Rus' kingdom on the Dnieper, which was the precursor of the Russian state. Born in Norway, at the age of fifteen he fought on the losing side in the battle of Stiklestad (1030) against the Danes, and fled to the court of Jaroslav the Wise at Kiev. Later he enlisted in the Byzantine service under the emperor Michael IV, and commanded the Empire's Varangian mercenaries in wars from Sicily to Palestine.

After his flight from Constantinople, Harald returned to Kiev, married Jaroslav's daughter Elisabeth ('the gold-decked maid'), and went on northwards to seize the Norwegian throne. He ruled until 1066, when he was killed at the battle of Stamford Bridge during an attempt to conquer England.

rollers laid on brushwood was constructed uphill from the Bosporus at Beşiktaş, and a few days later the Greek defenders of the city saw from the battlements the appalling sight of topmasts slowly appearing over the ridge to the east of the Golden Horn. With sails up and drums beating, more than seventy Turkish warships were dragged up the slope and down the other side until they reached the water of the Golden Horn and moored under the walls of Byzantium. From that moment the fall of Constantinople, the extinction of the Byzantine Empire and the triumph of Islam and the Ottomans were only a matter of time.

Are these dark links really the same Chain which Leo the Isaurian commanded to be forged thirteen hundred years ago, the very metal rammed by Harald's ships on his way back to Norway? It seems unlikely. Chains break, iron rusts, and links require replacement every so often. And yet the thought leads to a familiar philosophical riddle: even though every link may have been renewed over the centuries, yet this is in essence still the Chain itself.

All around the Black Sea, reading its history or climbing through its ruins or talking to its people, I have remembered the old saying: 'This is my grandfather's axe. My father gave it a new helve, and I gave it a new head.' That is the truth about the Chain of Constantinople. But it is also the truth about ethnic identities; the only wise comment on all the claims to 'be' a Pontic Greek, a true Scythian, a Cossack, a Romanian, an Abkhazian, a Ukrainian.

Those who cherish and revive their 'native' language usually have ancestors who spoke a different one. Those who claim 'pure' lineage, in the genetic sense, are all to some degree mongrels. Even a secluded hill people like the Abkhazians might find in their pedigrees – if they could rescue and study the ramifications of each family tree over the centuries – a Greek waitress, a Jewish pedlar, a Mingrelian cattle-dealer, a Russian officer's widow, an Armenian tinker, a Circassian slave-girl, an Eastern Alan bandit, a Persian refugee, an Arab magistrate. Those who claim always to have dwelled in 'our' land can often be shown to have lived somewhere else in the not too distant past, like the Lazi or the Tatars or almost the entire population of the Lower Don.

Even the portrait of a common cultural tradition, as evidence of ethnic identity, all too often dissolves away at the first application of rigorous fact. The sense among the Pontic Greeks that 'home is

Hellas' could logically be challenged by pointing out that many of them cannot speak Greek, that their education was Russian, that their biological mingling with Turkic, Iranian, Kartvelian and Slav peoples has been marginal but continuous for more than three thousand years, that most of them were born and brought up not among olive-trees and sea-winds but in Soviet Central Asia.

You could, if you were unwise, walk up to Crimean Tatars as they built their houses on waste lots outside Simferopol and suggest that their burning conviction of homeland and ethnic identity was false. And you could support that with some evidence. You might remind them that the Tatars of the Golden Horde had exchanged their own Mongolian language for the Turkic spoken by the local Kipchaks, that they abandoned shamanism for Islam, that they have interbred continuously with Turks and Russians and that – like the Greeks, and for the same tragic reason of deportation – the 'land of their birth' is usually not Crimea but Kazakhstan or Uzbekistan. But, in both the Greek and the Tatar case, you would have missed the point.

To demonstrate that tradition is wrong or invented does not put an end to this story. A claim to national independence does not fall simply because its legitimising version of national history is partly or wholly untrue – as it often is. The sense of belonging to a distinct cultural tradition, of 'ethnic identity', can be subjectively real to the point at which it becomes an objective social-political fact, no matter what fibs are used for its decoration. Grandfather's axe still lies on the table, gleaming, sharp and very solid.

This is a book about identities, and about the use of mirrors to magnify or to distort identity – the disguises of nationalism. Eric Hobsbawm has warned, most insistently in the years since the 1989 revolutions, that it is the duty of the historian always to denounce the element of myth in the construction of nations or ethnicities, and his hero in that particular struggle – one of mine, too – is T. G. Masaryk. This pedantic, authoritarian, invincibly honest man was the father and first President of independent Czechoslovakia. But Masaryk, facing down a tempest of abuse, was not afraid to proclaim that the 'Libuše Manuscripts', the epic poems which seemed to authenticate an antique and distinct Czech culture, were forgeries.

Hobsbawm fears above all the voice which proclaims: 'We are different from the others – and better.' On the Black Sea, that voice has often been heard in recent years, speaking Russian or Turkish or sometimes Romanian or Georgian. But it is a thought from inland, whose second point about 'superiority' has seldom carried much weight on the coast itself. There, the differences were blatant and numerous, and ethnic tensions were never absent. But it was elsewhere that sweeping moral conclusions were drawn. It was not the Ionian colonists at Olbia or Chersonesus who invented the polarity between 'our civilisation' and 'their barbarism', but wartime intellectuals far away in Athens.

When Adam Mickiewicz came to the Black Sea, once in his youth and the second time to die, he came as a Polish patriot whose supreme purpose was the restoration of Poland's independence and nationhood. But his nationalism, old-fashioned and 'pre-modern', did not assume that Poles were better than others and did not accept that a free Poland required false identity papers to re-enter history.

The human imagination, endlessly boastful and inventive, extends itself over landscapes and seas until its fabric conceals them completely. But at precisely that moment of intellectual conquest the fabric begins to fray, to develop widening holes, to disintegrate until nothing is left of it but hanks of brittle thread blown about by the wind. There reappears a coast inhabited by people who are not the sons and daughters whom their ancestors expected, a Sea whose fish change themselves and alter their paths a little in every season.

In *El Hacedor*, a collection of short pieces published in 1960, Jorge Luis Borges included a fragment attributed to 'Suarez Miranda: *Viajes de Varones Prudentes*; Lérida 1658'. Whatever the truth of that attribution, the passage is Borgesian, and – as far as this account of the Black Sea is concerned – leaves no more to be said.

OF RIGOUR IN SCIENCE

. . . In that Empire, the art of Cartography reached such Perfection, that the map of one single Province covered a whole Town. With time, these excessive Maps ceased to give satisfaction, and the Colleges of Cartography drew up a Map of the Empire which was done to the same scale as the Empire itself, and which coincided with it at every Point. Less absorbed in the Study of Cartography, the following Generations came to conclude that this vast Map was useless and, not without Impiety, abandoned it to the Inclemencies of the Sun and of the Winters. In the deserts of the West, there survive shattered Ruins of the Map, inhabited by Beasts and by Beggars; in all the Land, no other relic of the Cartographic Disciplines remains.

Chronology

c. 850–800 BC   Early Scythians appear in Black Sea steppes.

c. 750–700 BC   First Ionian Greek colonists found trading posts on Black Sea shores.

c. 700 BC   Foundation of Greek colony at Olbia.

512 BC   First Persian invasion of Europe. Darius crosses the Bosporus and Danube, and (according to Herodotus) pursues the Scythians into the Don steppes.

490 BC   Persian Army defeated at Marathon.

480 BC   Second major Persian expedition, under Xerxes, defeated by Athens at naval battle of Salamis.

c. 480 BC   Greek colonies in Crimea and Taman region combine into Bosporan state.

472 BC   First production at Athens of *Persae*, by Aeschylus.

c. 450 BC   Herodotus visits Olbia and subsequently begins publication of *Histories*.

440–37 BC (?)   Pericles sends naval expedition to acquire Greek colonies on the northern Black Sea coast for Athens.

438 BC   Spartocid dynasty installed over the Bosporan Kingdom, at Panticapaeum.

432 BC   Completion of the Parthenon at Athens.

431 BC   First production of *Medea*, by Euripides.

431–404 BC   Peloponnesian War.

356 BC   Birth of Alexander (the Great) of Macedon.

334 BC   Alexander defeats Persia, at battle of Issus.

323 BC   Death of Alexander.

Third century BC   Sarmatian peoples enter the Black Sea steppes and push the Scythians westwards.

107 BC   Death of Peirisades the Last; Mithridates Eupator, King of Pontus, becomes ruler of the Bosporan Kingdom.

63 BC   Death of Mithridates at Panticapaeum, after defeat by Roman armies under the command of Pompey. Bosporan Kingdom becomes Roman dependency. Sack of Olbia by Dacian-Getic Army.

55 and 54 BC   Julius Caesar takes Roman expeditionary force to Britain.

49 BC   Roman conquest of Gaul completed.

44 BC   Julius Caesar appointed Roman dictator for life.

27 BC   Collapse of Roman Republic; beginning of Roman Empire.

c. 8 AD   Ovid exiled from Rome to Tomi (Constanţa), by the emperor Augustus.

43 AD   Roman invasion of Britain.

70 AD   Romans destroy the Temple at Jerusalem.

c. 95 AD   Dio Chrysostom visits Olbia.

c. 240 AD   Goths arrive on Black Sea, invading Roman possessions there.

313   Christianity granted toleration in Roman Empire.

330   Capital of Roman Empire transferred to Constantinople.

370   Huns enter Black Sea steppe and attack Roman Empire. Destruction of Tanais and Olbia.

378   Combined Vizigoth-Sarmatian Army defeats Romans at Adrianople in Thrace.

410   Vizigoths sack Rome. Withdrawal of Roman troops from Britain.

527   Justinian crowned emperor at Constantinople.

610   Accession of Emperor Heraclius; Empire now known as 'Byzantine'.

632   Death of the Prophet Mohammed.

641   Arabs conquer Egypt and invade Maghreb.

Eighth century   Khazars establish empire in Black Sea steppe and ally with Byzantine Empire.

800   Coronation of Charlemagne in Rome, as ruler of new Western (later Holy Roman) Empire.

862   Rurik from Scandinavia founds Novgorod, in Russia.

882   Capital of Russian-Viking state moved to Kiev.

960   Mieszko I founds Polish Kingdom, under the Piast dynasty.

991   Vladimir of Kiev allegedly baptised at Chersonesus, in Crimea.

1055   Seljuk Turks, arriving from east, take Bagdad.

1071   Seljuk Turks defeat Byzantine Army at Manzikert, in eastern Anatolia.

1096   First Crusade.

Twelfth century   Arrival of Karaite Jewish sect in Crimea.

1204   Fourth Crusade; Byzantium conquered and looted by Frankish Crusaders. Alexius Comnenus founds Grand Comnenian Empire of Trebizond.

c. 1204   Venetians establish colony at Soldaia (Sudak) in Crimea.

1206   Mongols led by Chingiz (Genghis) Khan begin conquest of Asia.

1234   Mongol conquest of China; Chin dynasty overthrown.

1236   Mongol conquest of Russia.

c. 1240   Batu Khan settles the Golden Horde on the lower Volga.

1241   Tatar-Mongol invasion of Europe.

1253   Friar William de Rubruquis (Rubruck) travels to meet Batu Khan.

1261   Byzantine Empire restored at Constantinople.

1264   Kublai Khan founds Yuan (Mongol) dynasty in China.

1275   Marco Polo of Venice arrives in China.

c. 1280   Foundation of Genoese colony at Kaffa, Crimea.

1296   Venetian fleet attacks Genoese at Kaffa.

1347   Black Death reaches Kaffa, then spreads to Europe.

1380   Timur (Tamberlane) begins campaign of conquest.

1398   Timur sacks Tana, on river Don, and invades India.

1440–4   Establishment of Crimean Tatar Khanate, independent of the Golden Horde, under the Giray dynasty.

1453   Ottoman Turks (Mehmet the Conqueror) capture Constantinople.

1461   Trebizond surrenders to Turks.

1475   Fall of Mangup-Theodoros, Kaffa, Tana, etc. to Turks and Tatars.

1478   Tsar Ivan III defeats the Mongol-Tatars.

1569   Union of Lublin completes Polish-Lithuanian Commonwealth.

1637   Cossacks capture Azov from Turks, but lose it again.

1693   Peter the Great constructs a Russian navy at Taganrog, on Sea of Azov.

1696   Peter captures Azov.

1772   First Partition of Poland.

1774   Treaty of Kuchuk-Kainarji: Russia expels Ottoman Turks from part of Black Sea coast.

1783   Empress Catherine II (the Great) of Russia annexes Crimea; end of the independent Tatar Khanate.

1789   French Revolution.

1790   Russia storms Ismail, Turkish-held city at Danube mouth.

1792   Treaty of Jassy between Turkey and Russia: advances Russian frontier on the Black Sea to the Dniester.

1793   Second Partition of Poland.

1794   Foundation of Odessa.

1795   Third (and final) Partition of Poland between Russia, Prussia and Austria.

1815   Congress of Vienna.

1821   Greek War of Independence.

1825   Exile of Adam Mickiewicz in Odessa and Crimea. Death of Tsar Alexander I; accession of Nicholas I; Decembrist Conspiracy in St Petersburg.

1828–9   Russo-Turkish War.

1830   November rising in Poland.

1841   Death of Lermontov in a duel at Pyatigorsk.

1848   Foundation of Polonezköy (Polish settlement) in Turkey by Prince Adam Czartoryski.

1854–6   Crimean War.

1855   Death of Adam Mickiewicz at Constantinople.

1863   January rising in Poland.

1864   Russian annexation of northern Caucasus.

1877–8   Russo-Turkish War.

1905   Revolution in Russia.

1914   Outbreak of First World War.

1917   Fall of tsardom; Bolshevik Revolution.

1918   Collapse of German and Habsburg empires; end of First World War. Poland regains independence. Allied intervention in Russian civil war begins.

1919–20 Polish-Soviet War. Brief period of Ukrainian independence.

1920 Evacuation of Denikin's White armies from Novorossisk. Mustafa Kemal heads Turkish nationalist rebellion against partition of Turkey.

1922 Greek invasion of Turkey repelled.

1923 Republic proclaimed in Turkey. The 'Exchange' of populations between Greece and Turkey.

1928 Stalin assumes supreme power in the Soviet Union.

1933 Adolf Hitler becomes Chancellor of Germany.

1939 Outbreak of Second World War.

1941 Nazi Germany invades Soviet Union: **1941–5** Great Patriotic War.

1944 Soviet forces recapture Crimea. Deportation of Crimean Tatars, Chechens and Ingush.

1945 Collapse of Nazi Germany. Yalta and Potsdam conferences.

1949 Deportation of the Greeks in the southern regions of USSR.

1953 Death of Stalin.

1954 Crimea ceded to Ukraine from Russia by Nikita Khrushchev.

1985 Mikhail Gorbachev becomes general secretary of the Communist Party of the Soviet Union (CPSU).

1986 Explosion in nuclear power station at Chernobyl, in Ukraine.

1988 Catastrophic spread of ctenophore *Mnemiopsis leidyi* in Black Sea.

1989 Collapse of Communist regimes in Poland, Hungary, East Germany and Czechoslovakia. Revolution in Romania; death of President Nicolae Ceausescu.

1990 Lithuania declares independence. Gorbachev becomes President of the USSR.

1991 (June)   Boris Yeltsin elected President of Russia.

1991 (August)   Failed putsch against Gorbachev, led by Gennadi Yanayev and others. CPSU suspended and later dissolved.

1991 (December)   Dissolution of the Soviet Union. Independence of Ukraine, Belarus, Moldova, Georgia, Armenia, Azerbaijan, etc.

1992   Abkhazian-Georgian war. Convention for the Protection of the Black Sea signed by six riparian states.

1993   Russian parliament refuses presidential order to dissolve. Troops loyal to President Yeltsin bombard parliament into surrender.

1994–5   Russian Army suppresses self-proclaimed independence of Chechnya, in northern Caucasus.

Select Bibliography

'Aër' (pseudonym of Adam Rzązewski). *Mickiewicz w Odessie*. Warsaw, 1898.

Aeschylus. *Persae*. Tr. P. Vellacott. London and New York, 1991.

Alliés contre la Russie, Les. Various authors. Paris, 1926.

Apollonius Rhodius. *The Argonautica*. Tr. T. C. Seaton. London, 1912.

Archeion Pontou (vol. 35). Athens, 1979.

Barbaro, Josafa [Giosafat], and Contarini, Ambrogio. *Travels to Tana and Persia*. Tr. William Thomas. London, 1873.

Blanch, Lesley. *The Sabres of Paradise*. London and New York, 1960.

Blondal, Sigfus. *The Varangians of Byzantium*. Cambridge, England, 1978.

Bogucka, Maria. *W Kręgu Sarmatyzmu*. Warsaw, 1974.

—— *Świat Sarmatów*. Warsaw, 1991.

—— 'Gesture, Ritual & Social Order in 16th and 17th-century Poland'. In *A Cultural History of Gesture*, eds. J. Bremmer and H. Roodenburg, London, 1991.

Borges, Jorge Luis. *Obras Completas*. Buenos Aires, 1974.

Borja-Villel, Manuel (ed). *Krzystof Wodiczko*. Barcelona, 1992.

Bremner, Robert. *Excursions in the Interior of Russia*. London, 1840. 2 vols.

Broniowski (Broniewski), Marcin. 'Collections . . . contayning a Description of Tartaria'. In: *Purchas, his Pilgrims*. London, edn. 1906, vol. 13.

Bryer, A. A. M. 'Greeks and Turkmens: the Pontic Exception', Dumbarton Oaks Papers No. 29. Washington, DC, 1975.

—— *The Empire of Trebizond and the Pontos*. London, 1980.

Chadwick, H. M. *The Heroic Age*. Cambridge, England, 1912.

Chapman, Malcolm. *The Celts: The Construction of a Myth*. London, 1992.

Chekhov, Anton P. *The Russian Master & Other Stories*. Tr. Ronald Hingley. Oxford, 1990.

—— *The Steppe & Other Stories*. Tr. Ronald Hingley. Oxford, 1991.

—— *The Witch & Other Stories*. Tr. C. Garnett. London and New York, 1918.

Clot, André. *Mehmet II le conquérant de Byzance*. Paris, 1990.

Czapska, Maria. *Szkice Mickiewiczowskie*. London, 1963.

Davidson, Allan. *A Kipper with My Tea*. London and New York, 1988.

Deacon, Margaret. *Scientists and the Sea: 1650–1900*. Academic Press, 1971.

Deleuze, G. and Guattari, F. 'Traité de Nomadologie'. In *Mille Plateaux*. Paris, 1980.

Denikin, General A. *The White Army*. London, 1930.

Dio Chrysostom. 'Borysthenitica'. In *Works*, tr. Cahoon and Lamar Crosby. London, 1940.

Duker, Abraham. 'Mickiewicz and the Jewish Problem'. In Kridl, q.v.

Euripides. *Medea*. Tr. Philip Vellacott. London and New York, 1963.

Feschbach, Murray, and Friendly, Arthur. *Ecocide in the USSR*. London, 1992.

Feurstein, Wolfgang. ' "Völker der Kolchis". Aspekte Ihrer Mythologie.' In *Caucasologie et mythologie comparée*, ed. Cathérine Paris. Paris, 1992.

—— 'Lazische Ortsnamen'. In: *Studia Caucasologica I*. Oslo, 1988.

Fisher, Alan. *The Crimean Tatars*. Palo Alto, California, 1978.

Franklin, Simon. 'Literacy and Documentation in Early Mediaeval Russia'. *Speculum* (Cambridge, Mass.), vol. 60, January 1985.

Gimbutas, Marija. *The Goddesses and Gods of Old Europe*. London and New York, 1992.

Greeks in the Black Sea, The. Ed. Marianna Koromila. Athens, 1991.

Hall, Edith. *Inventing the Barbarian*. Oxford, 1989.

Hartog, François. *The Mirror of Herodotus*. Tr. Janet Lloyd. Berkeley, California, 1988.

Herlihy, Patricia. *Odessa, a History: 1794–1914.* Cambridge, Mass. 1986.

Herodotus. *Histories.* Tr. A. D. Godley. Cambridge, Mass. and London, 1990.

Herrin, Judith. *The Formation of Christendom.* Princeton, 1987.

Herzen, Alexander. *From the Other Shore.* Tr. Moura Budberg. London and New York, 1956.

Hippocrates (pseudo-). *Airs, Waters, Places.* Tr. W. H. Jones and E. T. Withington. London, 1922–31.

History of Poland. By Aleksander Gieysztor et al. Warsaw, 1979.

Iskander, Fazil. *Sandro of Chegem.* Tr. Susan Brownsberger. London and New York, 1993.

Istoricheskaya Geografia Dona i Severnogo Kavkaza. Eds Maximenko & Korolev. Rostov, 1992.

Jastruń, Mieczystaw. *Mickiewicz.* Tr. into German by C. Poralla. Berlin, 1953.

Journal of Refugee Studies. Special Issue: The Odyssey of the Pontic Greeks. Vol. 4, No. 4, 1991. Oxford.

Kemal, Yashar. *The Sea-Crossed Fisherman.* Tr. T. Kemal. London and New York, 1985

Kleiner, Juliusz. *Mickiewicz.* Tom I – *Dzieje Gustawa.* Lublin, 1948.

Krasnov, Piotr N. *From Two-Headed Eagle to Red Flag.* Vol. 4. London, 1923.

—— *Kostia the Cossack.* London, 1931.

Kridl, Manfred (ed.). *Adam Mickiewicz, Poet of Poland.* London and New York, 1951.

Lermontov, M. Yu. *Stichotvorenya 1828–41.* Moscow, 1961.

—— *Major Poetical Works.* Tr. Anatoly Liberman. London, 1983.

—— *A Hero of Our Time.* Tr. Vladimir and Dmitri Nabokov. London and New York, 1992.

Magris, Claudio. *Inferences from a Sabre.* Edinburgh, 1990.

—— *Danube.* London and New York, 1990.

Mallory, J.P. *In Search of the Indo-Europeans.* London and New York, 1989.

Mandelstam, Osip. *Selected Poems.* Tr. Clarence Brown and W. S. Merwin. Oxford, 1973.

Mankowski, Tadeusz. *Genealogia Sarmatyzmu.* Warsaw, 1946.

Mickiewicz, Adam. *Dzieła Poetyckie* (4 vols.). Warsaw, 1973.
—— *Drames Polonais*. Paris, 1867.
Miller, A. A. *Kratkiy otchet o rabotach Severo-Kavkazskoy Ekspeditsii*. GAIMK, 1926.
—— *Arkhaeologicheskiye raboty Severo-Kavkazskoy Ekspeditsii*. GAIMK, 1929.
Miller, Mikhail. *Archaeology in the USSR*. London, 1956.
Milner, Rev. T. *The Crimea*. London, 1855.
Mitchison, Naomi. *The Corn King and the Spring Queen* (1931). Reprint: Edinburgh, 1990.
Mongait, A. L. *Archaeology in the USSR*. Tr. M. W. Thompson. London, 1961.
Morgan, David. *The Mongols*. Oxford, 1986.
Ocherki Istorii Azova. Various writers. Azovskii Krayevedcheskii Muzei, 1992.
Oliphant, Laurence. *The Russian Shores of the Black Sea in the Autumn of 1853*. London, 1853.
Ovid (P. Ovidius Naso). 'Tristia ex Ponto'. *Works* (Vol. 6). Tr. A. L. Wheeler. Cambridge, Mass. and London, 1988.
Pagden, Anthony. *European Encounters with the New World*. New Haven, Conn., 1993.
Paustovsky, Konstantin. *Story of a Life* (5 vols.). Tr. Manya Harari and Andrew Thomson. London and New York, 1967–8.
Pruszyński, Ksawery. *Opowieść o Mickiewiczu*. Warsaw, 1956.
Randsborg, K. 'Barbarians, Classical Antiquity and the Rise of Western Europe'. *Past & Present*, Oxford, No. 137, November, 1992.
Ratchnevsky, Paul. *Genghis Khan*. Oxford, 1991.
Rawson, Claude. 'Agamemnon, Smith and Thomson'. Review in *London Review of Books*, 9 April 1992.
Robb, Graham. *Balzac*. London and New York, 1994.
Rolle, Renate. *The World of the Scythians*. London and New York, 1989.
Rostovtzeff, M. *Iranians and Greeks in South Russia*. Oxford, 1922.
Rubruck (Rubruqis), Friar William de. 'Journal'. In: *Travels of Sir John Mandeville*. Reprint: New York, 1964.
Salway, Peter. *Roman Britain*. Oxford, 1985.
Science of the Sea, The. Ed. C. P. Idyll. London, 1970.
Słowacki, Juliusz. *Briefe an die Mutter*. Tr. Roswitha Matwin-Buschmann. Berlin, 1984.

Strabo. *Geography* (vol. 3). Cambridge, Mass. and London, 1983.

Struve, Joseph C. von (Anon.). *Travels in the Crimea, a History of the Embassy from Petersburg to Constantinople in 1793.* London, 1802.

Sturluson, Snorri. *Heimskringla.* Reprint: New York, 1991.

Sulimirski, Tadeusz. *The Sarmatians.* Thames & Hudson 1970.

—— 'Sarmaci'. Warsaw, 1979.

Symeon the New Theologian. 'Hymnes'. *Sources Chrétiennes* Nos. 156; 174; 196. Paris, 1969–73.

Taylor, Timothy (and T. Sulimirski). 'The Scythians'. Chapter in *Cambridge Ancient History* (2nd ed.) 1991.

—— 'The Gundestrup Cauldron'. Article in *Scientific American*, March 1992.

—— 'Thracians, Scythians and Dacians'. Chapter in *Oxford Illustrated Prehistory of Europe*, 1994.

—— 'Scythian and Sarmatian Art'. Chapter in forthcoming *Dictionary of Art.* Macmillan, due 1996.

Trigger, Bruce G. *A History of Archaeological Thought.* Cambridge, England, 1989.

Troyat, Henri. *Pouchkine.* Paris, 1953.

Ulewicz, Tadeusz. *Sarmacja: studium z problematyki słowiańskiej xv i xvi wieku.* Craków, 1950.

Vigny, Alfred de. *Servitude et grandeur militaires.* Oeuvres complètes. Paris, 1948.

Wrangel, Baron P.N. *Memoirs.* London, 1929.

Zamoyski, Adam. *The Last King of Poland.* London, 1992.

Index

Gaymanova, 222; Chertomlyk, 222; Tsarski Kurgan, 225–6
Kursk, battle of, 90

Lacroix, Jules, 165, 166
Lacroix, Paul, 165
Lancashire, 236–7, 241
Langeron, A., 137, 143
Latvia, 42
Lausanne, Treaty of (1923), 177, 187
Lazi, the, 11, 196–209, 273
Lazuri (language), 199–201, 204
Learmouth, 84, 87
Leipzig, 109
Lejbowicz, Jamkiel (see Frank, J.)
Lenin, V.I., 12
Leningrad (see also St Petersburg), 13, 41, 255
Leo III, the Isaurian, Byzantine Emperor, 271
Lepier, archaeologist, 27
Lermontov, M., 10, 84–8
Leuco, King, 220, 226–7
Lévy, Armand, 173
Libuše Manuscripts, 274
Lindane, 260
Lithuania, 22, 42, 147, 152, 159, 161; union with Poland, 148
Lloyd, Janet, ix
Lloyd George, 187
Lombardy, 92
London, 175
Lord Jim (Conrad), 206
Louvre, the, 131
Loyalists (Ulster), 100–1
Lusatia, 242
Lwów (Lvov, Lemberg), 167
Lykhny, 249

Maeotian Lake (see Sea of Azov)
Maeotians, 80, 118, 120, 220, 227
Margis, Claudio, Inferences from a Sabre, 36; Danube, 261–2
Maisons, Comte de, 137
Malaya Zemlya, 213
Malchenko, Zhenya, x

Malewski, Franciszek, 145; sister Zosia, 156
Mamelukes, 95
Manchuria, 96
Mandelstam, Osip, 10, 67, 111
Mangup, 22–7
Manstein, General von, 30, 32
Maraslis, George, 185
Marathon, battle of, 53, 186
Marco Polo, 242
Marcus Aurelius, Emperor, 236
Mariupol, 187
Marius (Consul), 28
Marmara, Sea of, 2, 259, 263
Marr, N.Y., 75
Marrism, 75
Marseille, 263
Masaryk, T.G., 274
Medea (Euripides), 63, 83, 200, 258
Mediterranean Sea, 4, 19, 51, 226, 263; slave-trade around, 96
Mee, Laurence, ix, 268
Meganom, Cape, 9
Megara, 63
Mehmet II, The Conqueror, 272–3
Mesopotamia, 37
mesotes (measuredness), 63
Messianism (Polish), 160–1
metal-detectors, 133
Michael Kalafates, Byzantine Emperor, 272
Mickiewicz, Adam, x, 10, 145–66, 169, 171–5, 229; early works, 147; Polishness of, 147–8; lovers in Odessa, 151; and Sobańska, 151–3; Crimean Sonnets, 159; Messianism of, 160–1; and Jews, 161–2, 172–5; wife Celina, 172; in Turkey (1855), 171–5; death, 174; nationalism of, 275
Micklegard/Micklegarth (Byzantium), 182, 272
migration theory, 43–5, 54–6, 76
Miletus, 68
Miller, Alexander, 44, 129
Miller, Mikhail, Archaeology in the USSR, 44, 75, 130

Shchegolov, Ensign, 139
Shevardnadze, Edward, 244
Shevchuk, Alla, 269
Sholokhov, M., 111
Shulz, D.G., 131
Siberia, 129–30, 153, 160, 165, 188, 189, 235, 250–1
Signoria (Venice), 95
Sikorski, General W., 167; Museum, London, 175
Silesia, 239
Silk Routes, 18, 92–6, 180, 199
Simferopol, 14, 15, 27, 32, 33, 158, 274
Sindi, 80, 118, 220
Sinop, 6, 98
Sivash, 17
skull-binding, 241–3
slavery, 9, 33, 62; slave trade, 95–6, 226
Slavs, 232, 240–2, 252
Slovakia, 270
Słowacki, Juliusz, 170, 175
Smyrna (Izmir), 171
Śniadecka, Ludwika, 169–72, 174, 175
Sobańska, Karolina, 149–59, 162–6, 235–6
Sobański, Hieronym, 149, 157
Sobieski, King John III, 168, 233
Sochi, 245
Solovetsky Islands, 134
Soltys, Inna, x
Solzhenitsyn, A., 213
Sophocles, 51, 63
Sophronios, monk, 184
Sorbs, 242
Soviet Union, 12, 13, 15, 32, 218, 246, 249, 263; collapse of, 42; Academy of Sciences, 52, 94, 102, 264; Greeks in, 186–90, 192–6
Spain, 81, 241
Sparta, 211
Spartocid dynasty, 220, 224–5, 256
Sphaeros, 211
sprats, 263, 266
SS, 31, 36, 109

Stalin, J.V., 10, 12, 29, 31–2, 43, 44, 45, 102, 103, 105, 188, 192, 193, 246, 248, 261
Stamford Bridge, battle of, 272(n)
Stanisław August Poniatowski, King, 150, 234
Stebniki, 261
Steelyard, The (London), 80
steppe, the, 59, 60
Stiklestad, battle of, 272(n)
Stoicism, 72, 73, 211
Strabo, 6, 115, 215
sturgeon, 5, 51, 215, 259, 261, 269
submarine, Cossack version of, 98
Suchtelev, General, 69
Sudak (Soldaia), 9, 21, 94
Suevians, 241
Suez Canal, 185
Sukhum (Sukhumi), 8, 193, 246, 247–9, 251, 253–4, 269
Sulimirski, Tadeusz, x, 239–40
Sulkiewicz, General, 30
Sumela, monastery, 182–4, 195
Suvorov Street (Rostov), 99, 104–5
Svanetia, Svan language, 200, 208
Sweden, 231
Symeon the New Theologian, 47–8, 72
Syria, 199
Szekelyi, 191
Szemiotowa, E., 151
szlachta (Polish nobility), 231, 232, 234, 238, 240

Tabiti, 116
Tabriz, 180
Taganrog, 60, 156, 157, 164, 217
Talbot-Rice, D., 179
Tallinn, 42
Taman, 88, 130, 215, 216, 220
Taman Division, 34
tamgas, 238–40
Tana, 10, 18, 77, 93–6, 128–9
Tanais, x, 10, 79, 89–93, 106, 122, 124, 130, 220, 227–8, 242
tanks (battle), 55
Targitaus, 118